# CLAMP

11



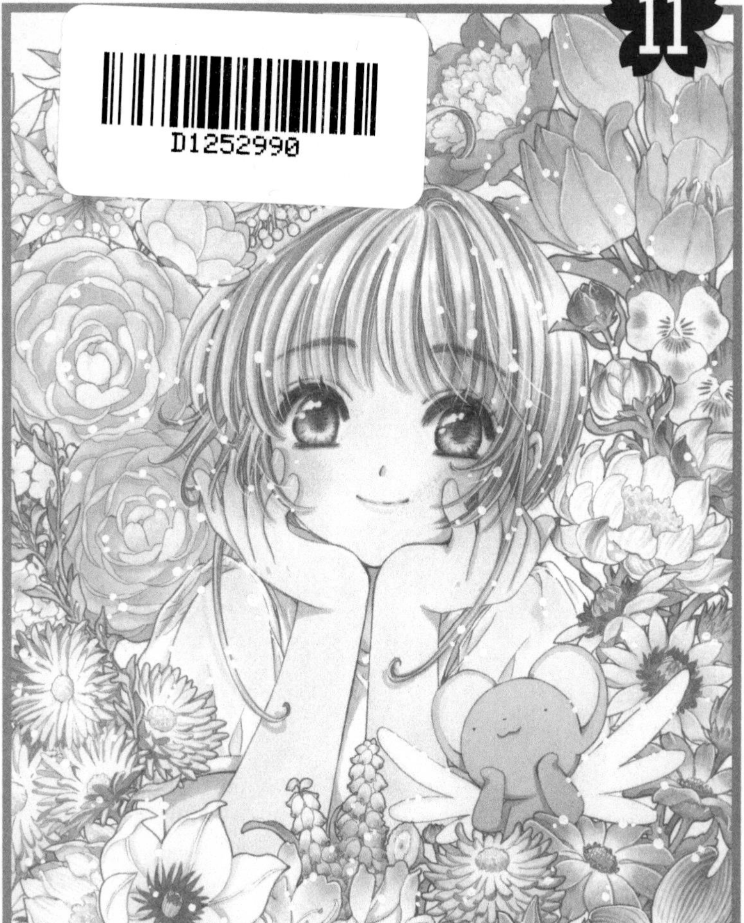

# Cardcaptor Sakura

CLEAR CARD

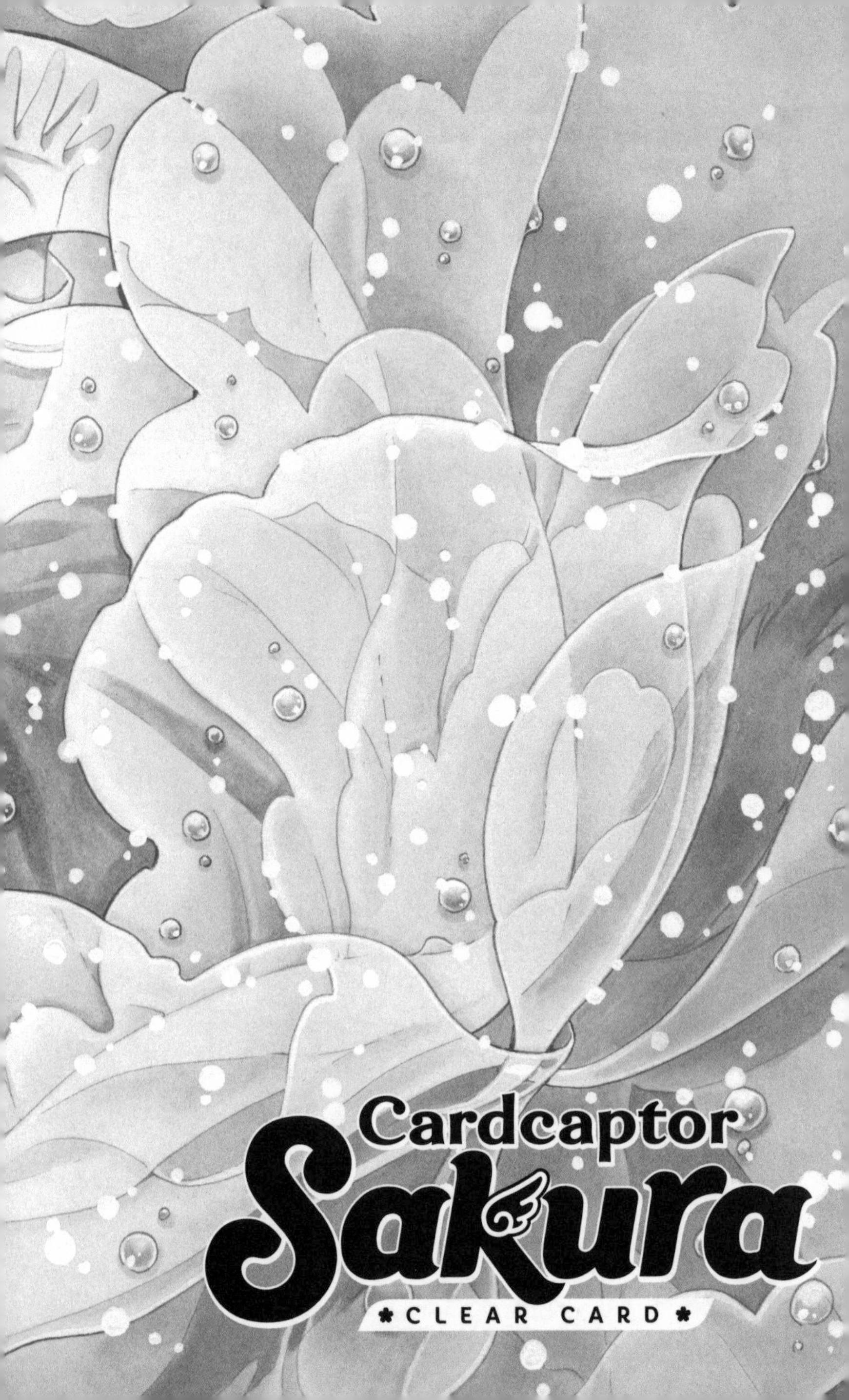
Cardcaptor
Sakura
CLEAR CARD

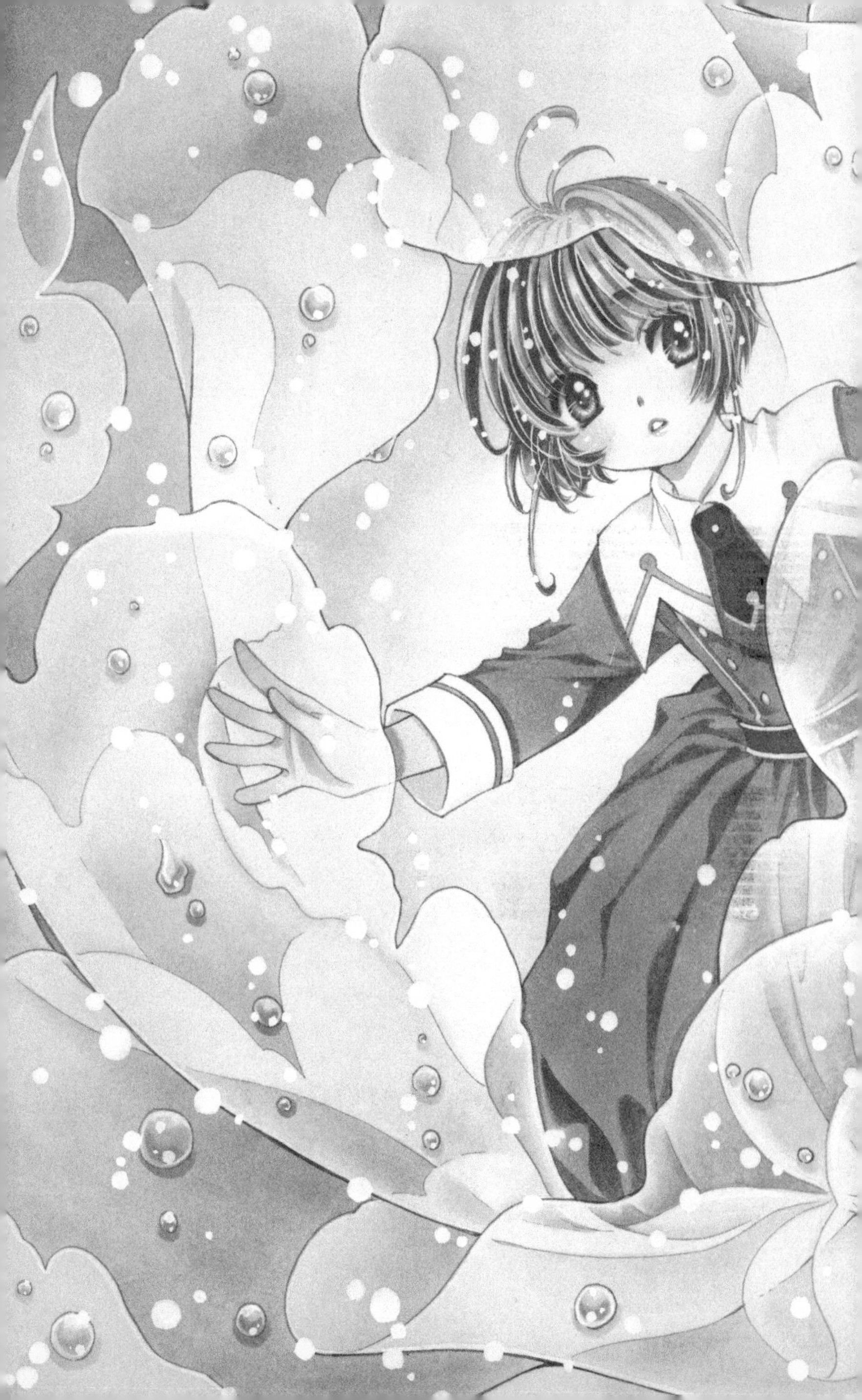

Cardcaptor
Sakura
CLEAR CARD

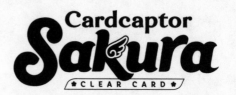

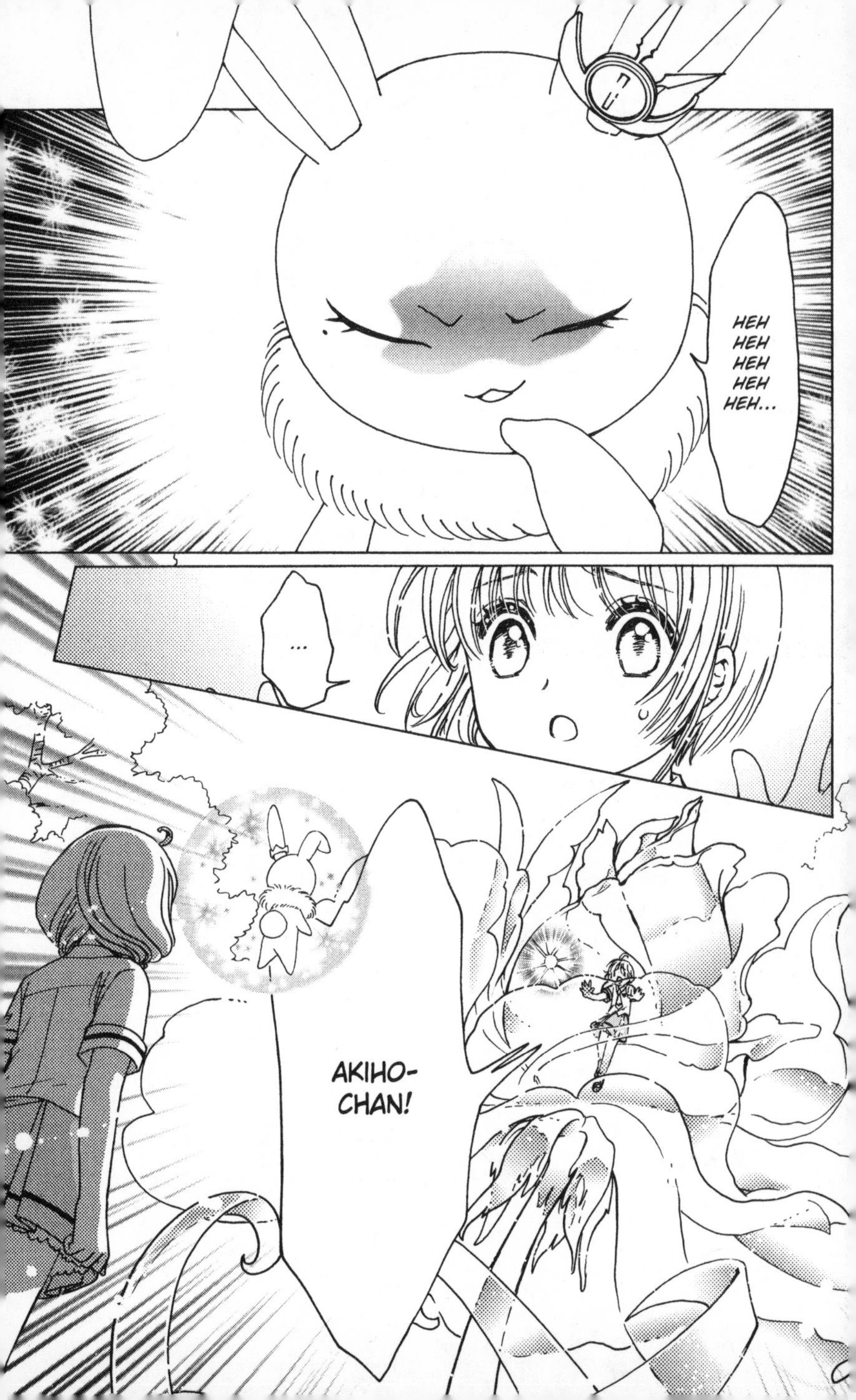
HEH HEH HEH HEH HEH...
...
AKIHO-CHAN!

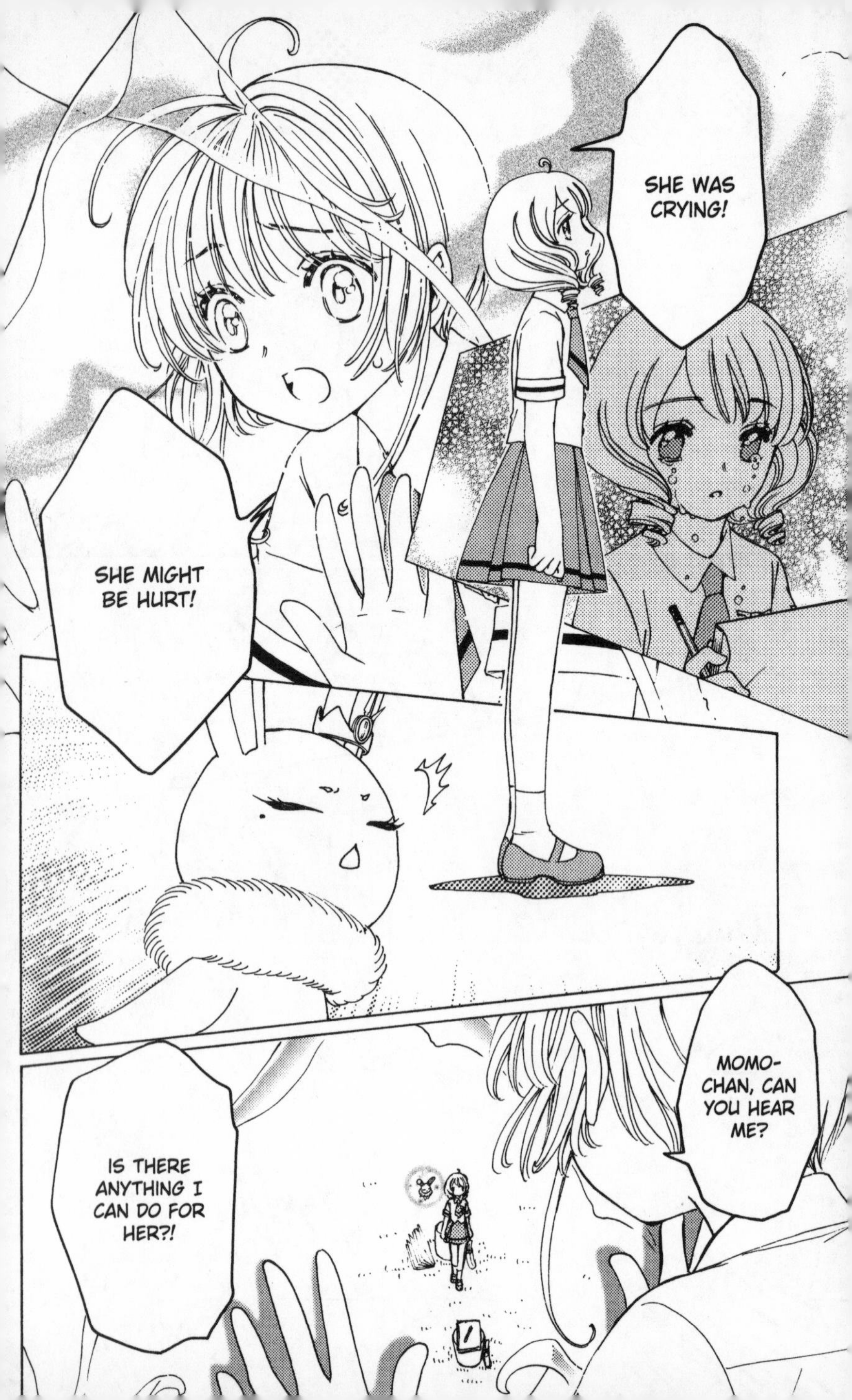
SHE WAS CRYING!
SHE MIGHT BE HURT!
MOMO-CHAN, CAN YOU HEAR ME?
IS THERE ANYTHING I CAN DO FOR HER?!

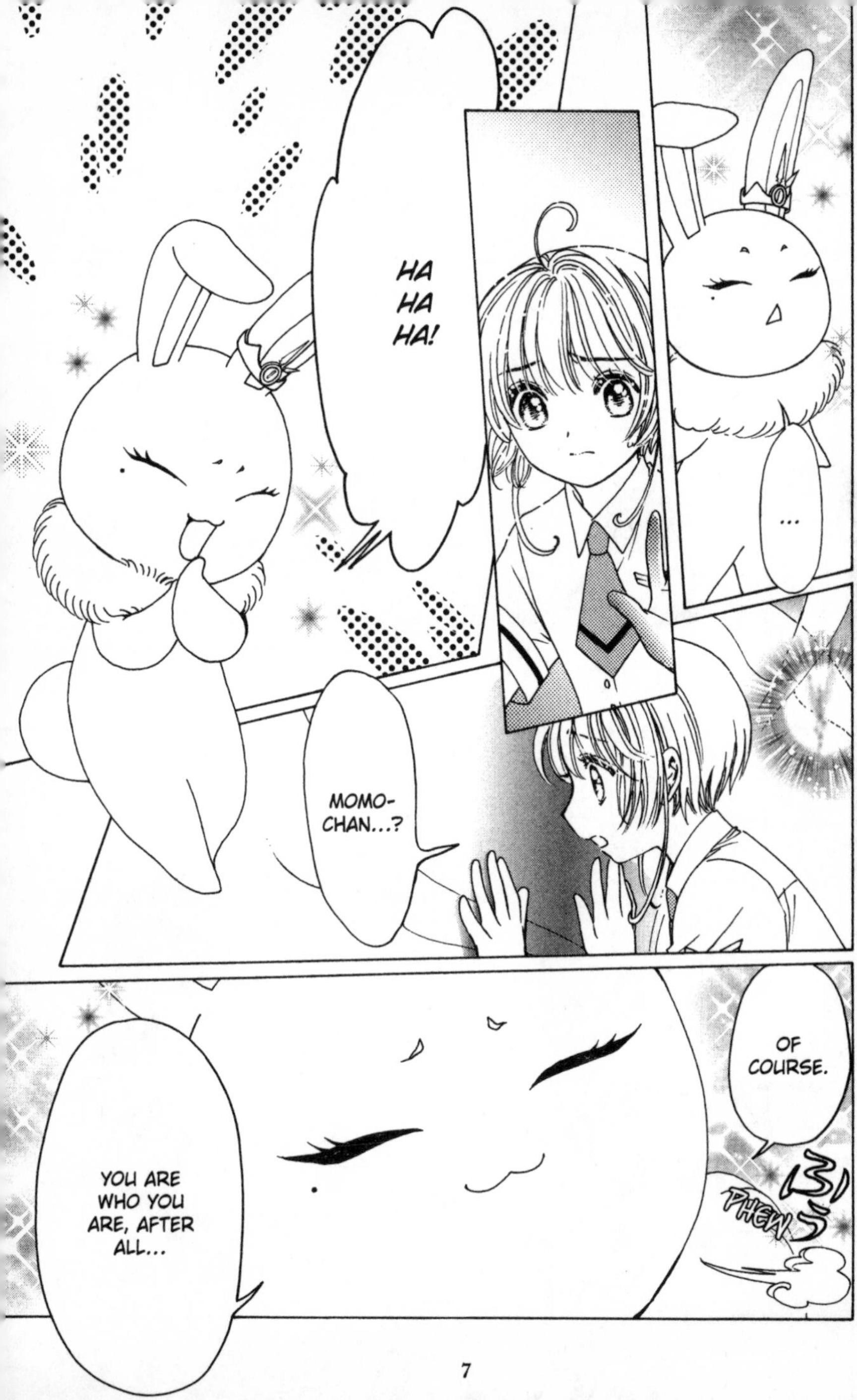
...
MOMO-CHAN...?
HA HA HA!
OF COURSE.
PHEW
YOU ARE WHO YOU ARE, AFTER ALL...

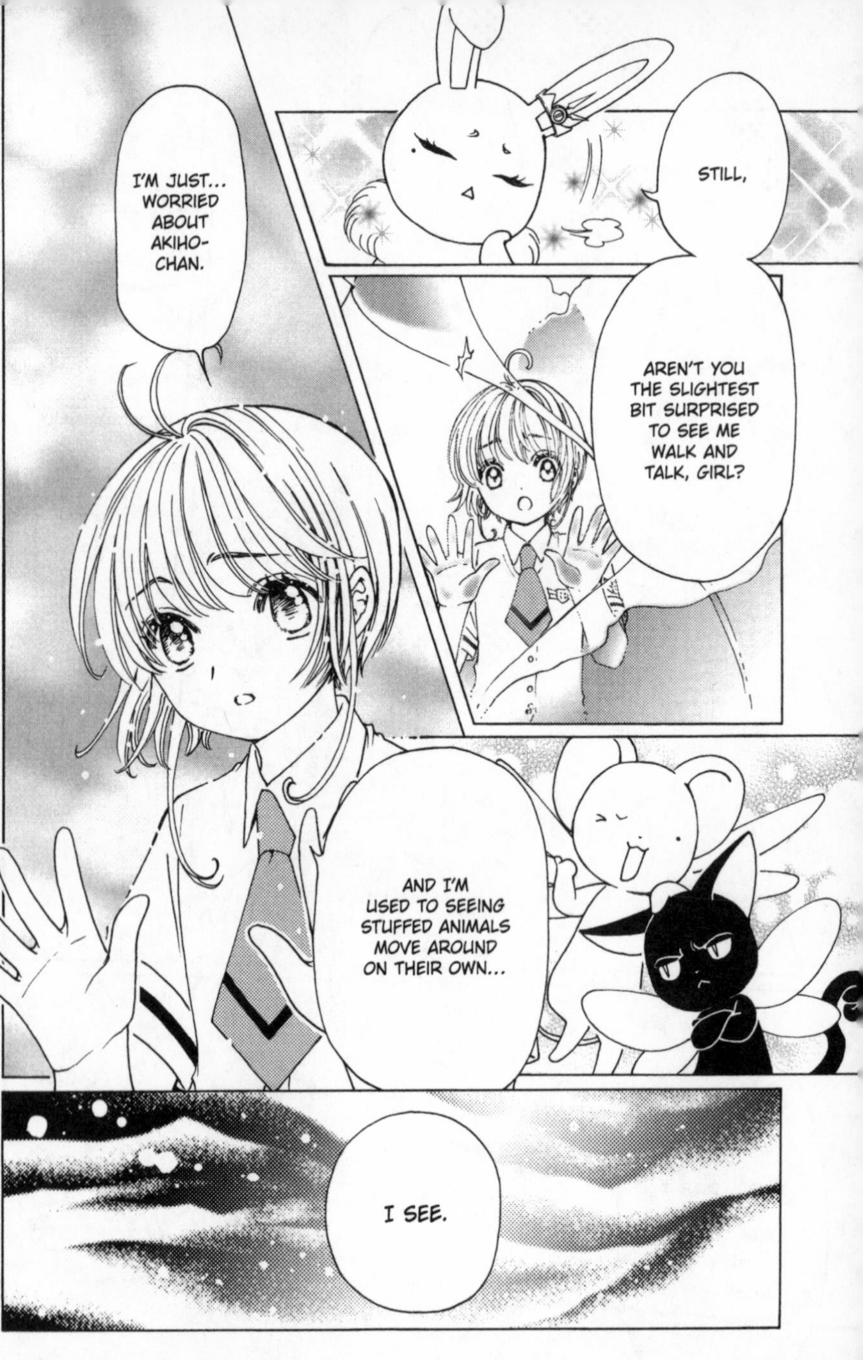
STILL,
AREN'T YOU THE SLIGHTEST BIT SURPRISED TO SEE ME WALK AND TALK, GIRL?
I'M JUST... WORRIED ABOUT AKIHO-CHAN.
AND I'M USED TO SEEING STUFFED ANIMALS MOVE AROUND ON THEIR OWN...
I SEE.

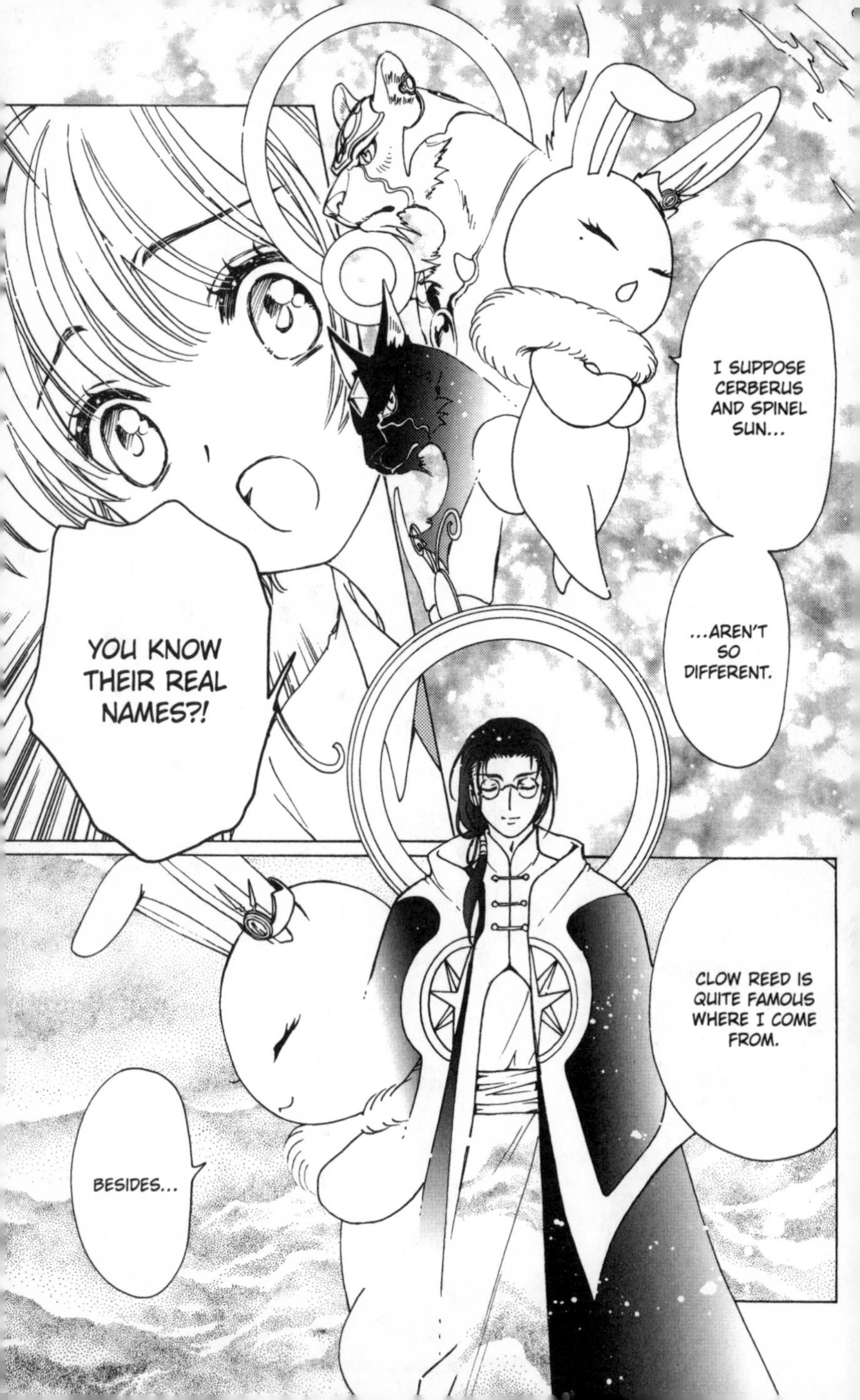
I SUPPOSE CERBERUS AND SPINEL SUN...
...AREN'T SO DIFFERENT.
YOU KNOW THEIR REAL NAMES?!
CLOW REED IS QUITE FAMOUS WHERE I COME FROM.
BESIDES...

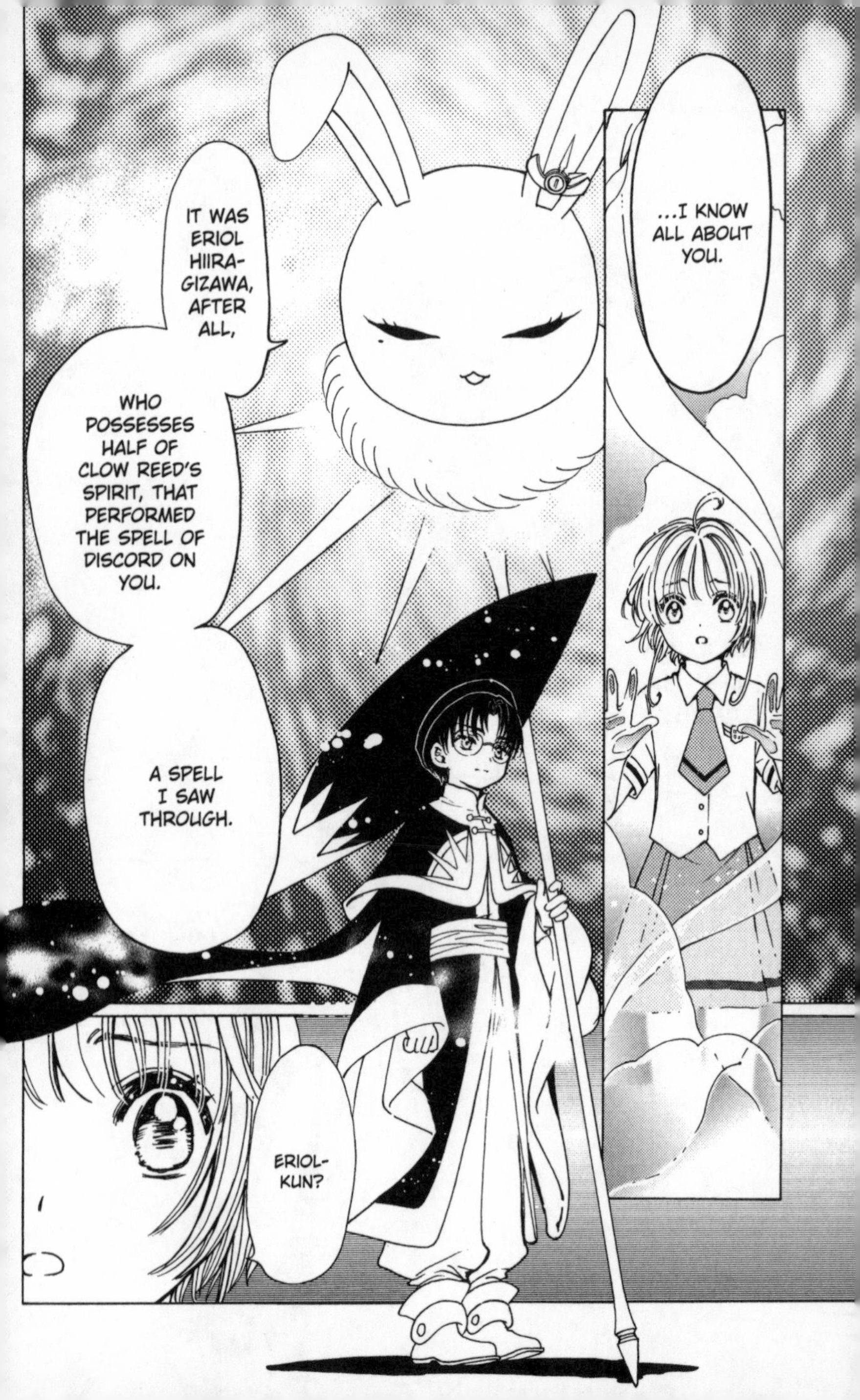
...I KNOW ALL ABOUT YOU.
IT WAS ERIOL HIIRA-GIZAWA, AFTER ALL,
WHO POSSESSES HALF OF CLOW REED'S SPIRIT, THAT PERFORMED THE SPELL OF DISCORD ON YOU.
A SPELL I SAW THROUGH.
ERIOL-KUN?

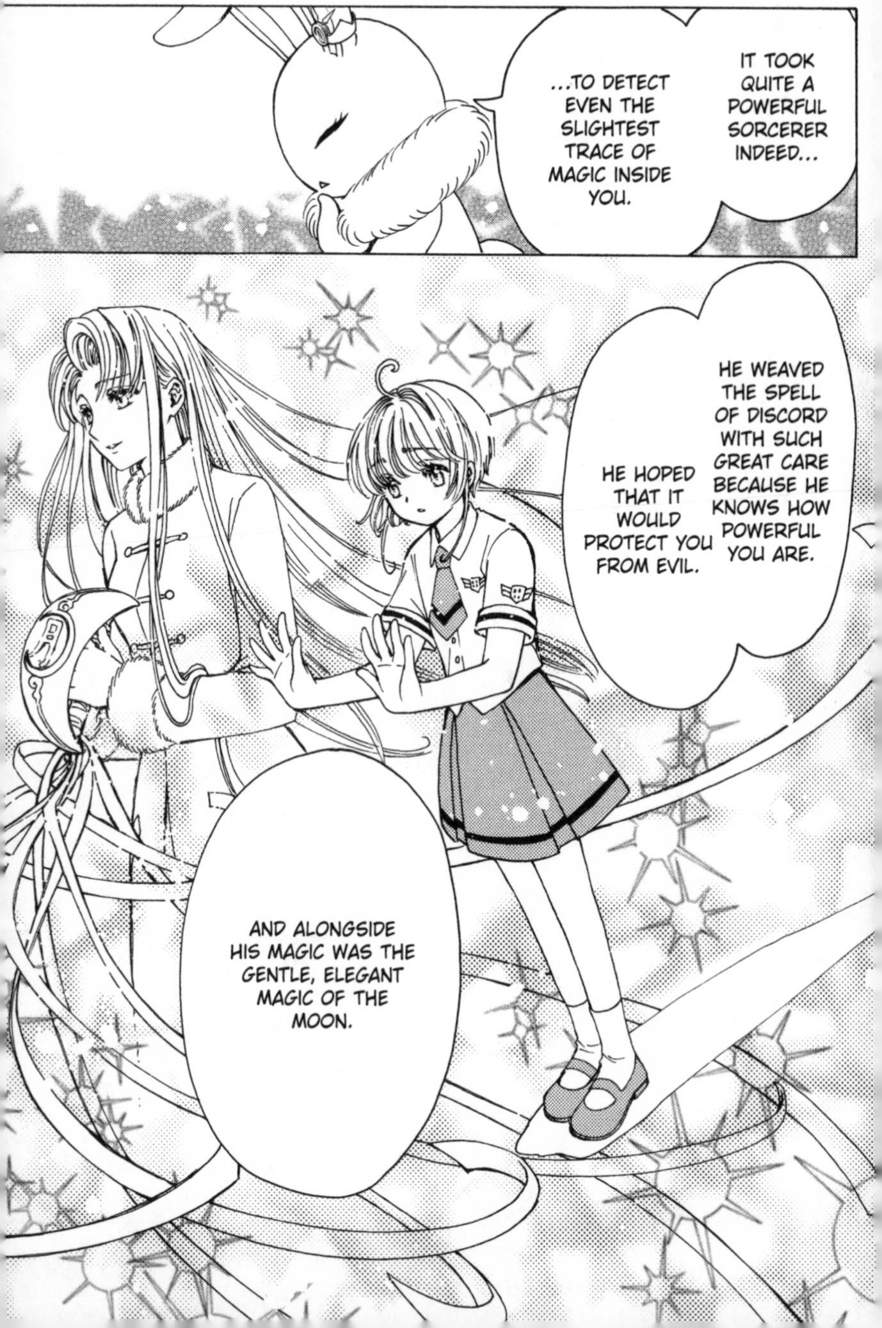
IT TOOK QUITE A POWERFUL SORCERER INDEED...
...TO DETECT EVEN THE SLIGHTEST TRACE OF MAGIC INSIDE YOU.
HE WEAVED THE SPELL OF DISCORD WITH SUCH GREAT CARE BECAUSE HE KNOWS HOW POWERFUL YOU ARE.
HE HOPED THAT IT WOULD PROTECT YOU FROM EVIL.
AND ALONGSIDE HIS MAGIC WAS THE GENTLE, ELEGANT MAGIC OF THE MOON.

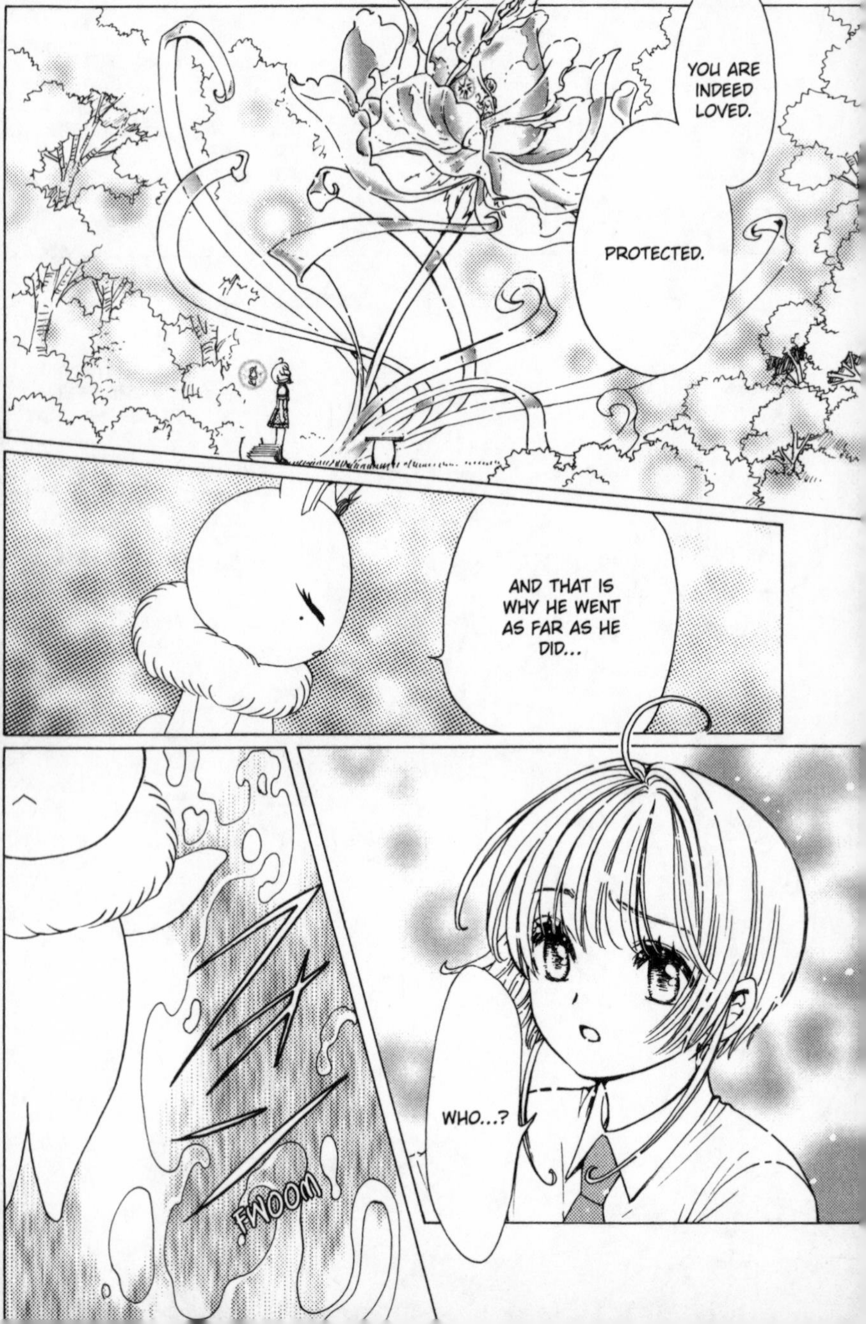
YOU ARE INDEED LOVED.
PROTECTED.
AND THAT IS WHY HE WENT AS FAR AS HE DID...
WHO...?
FWOOM

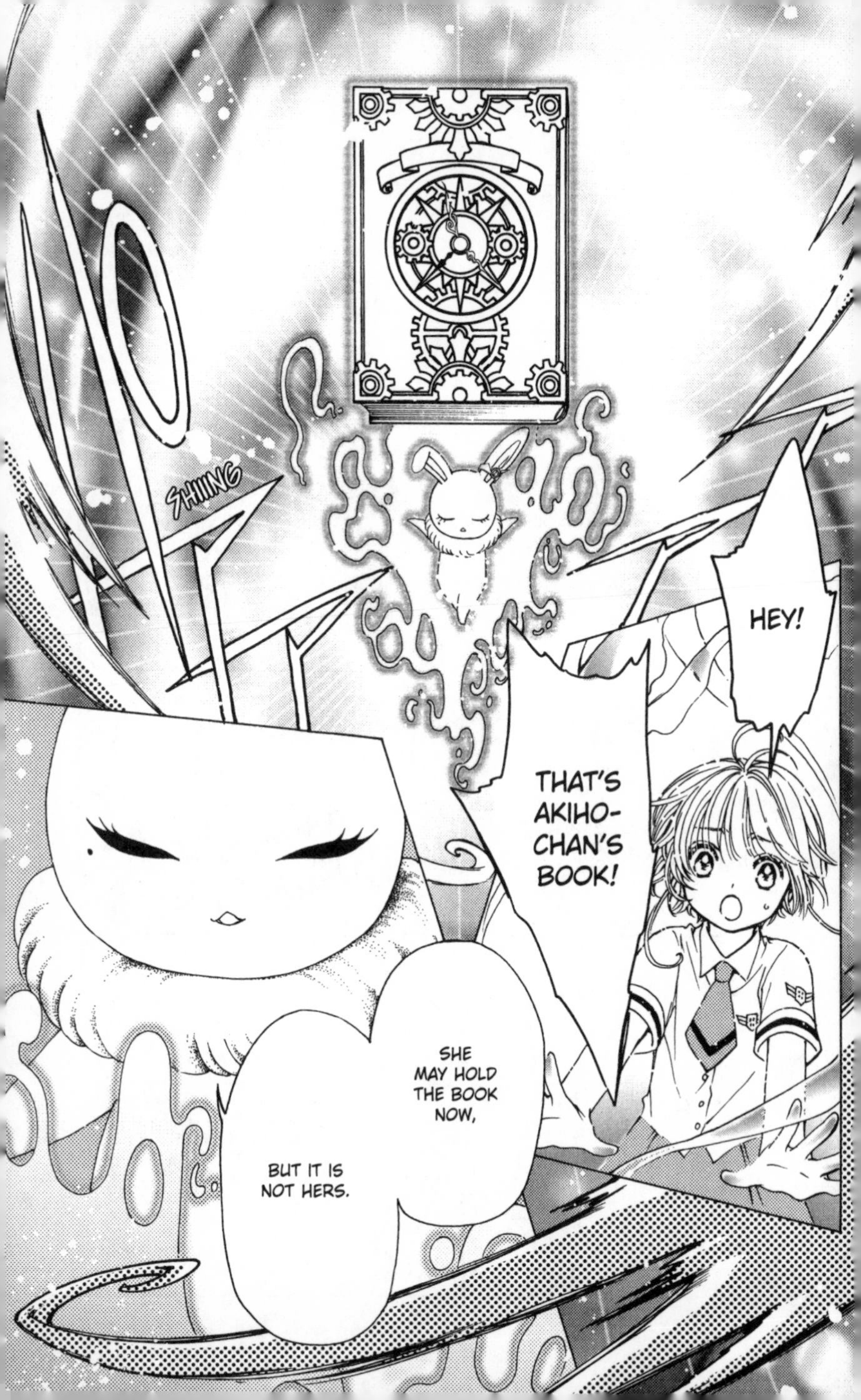
SHIIING
HEY!
THAT'S AKIHO-CHAN'S BOOK!
SHE MAY HOLD THE BOOK NOW,
BUT IT IS NOT HERS.

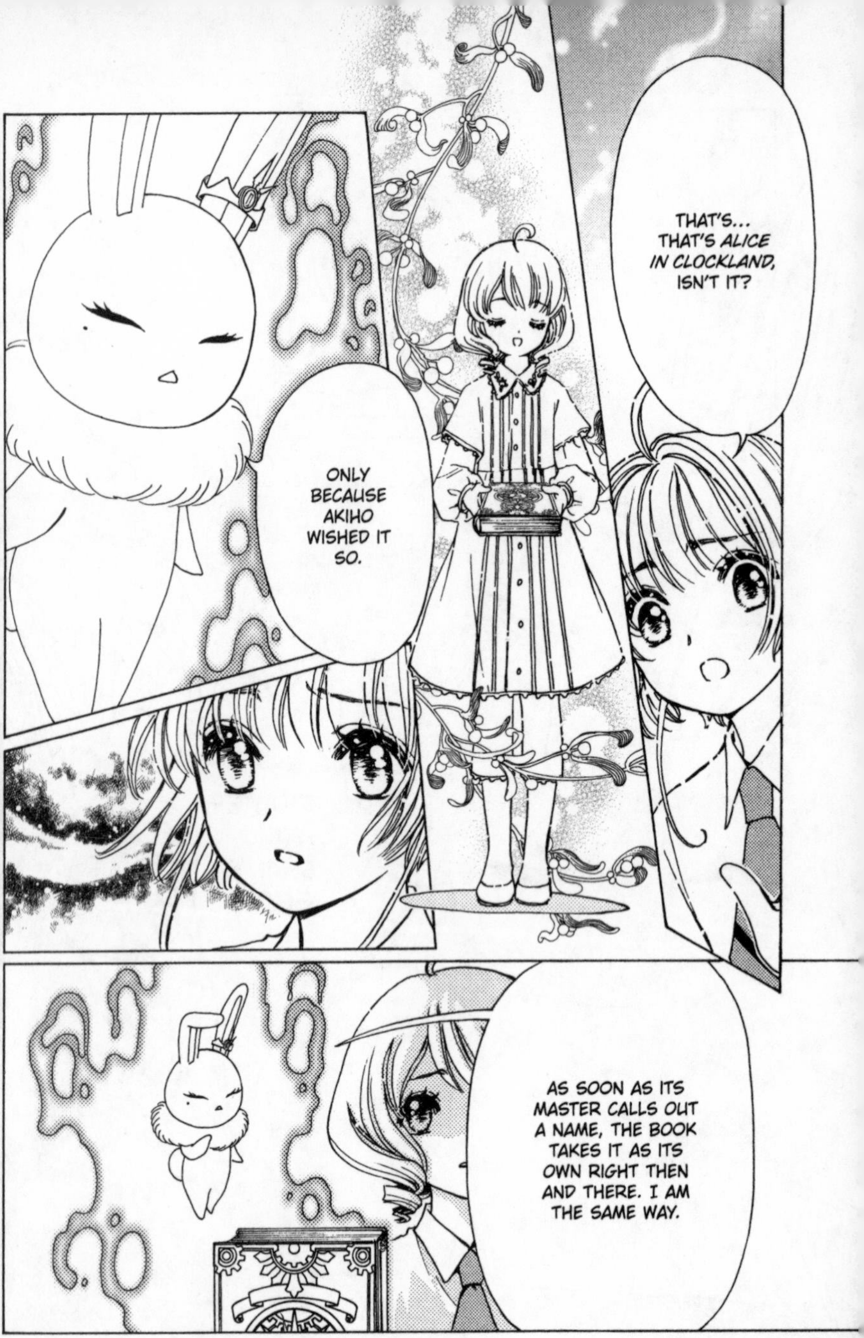
THAT'S... THAT'S *ALICE IN CLOCKLAND*, ISN'T IT?
ONLY BECAUSE AKIHO WISHED IT SO.
AS SOON AS ITS MASTER CALLS OUT A NAME, THE BOOK TAKES IT AS ITS OWN RIGHT THEN AND THERE. I AM THE SAME WAY.

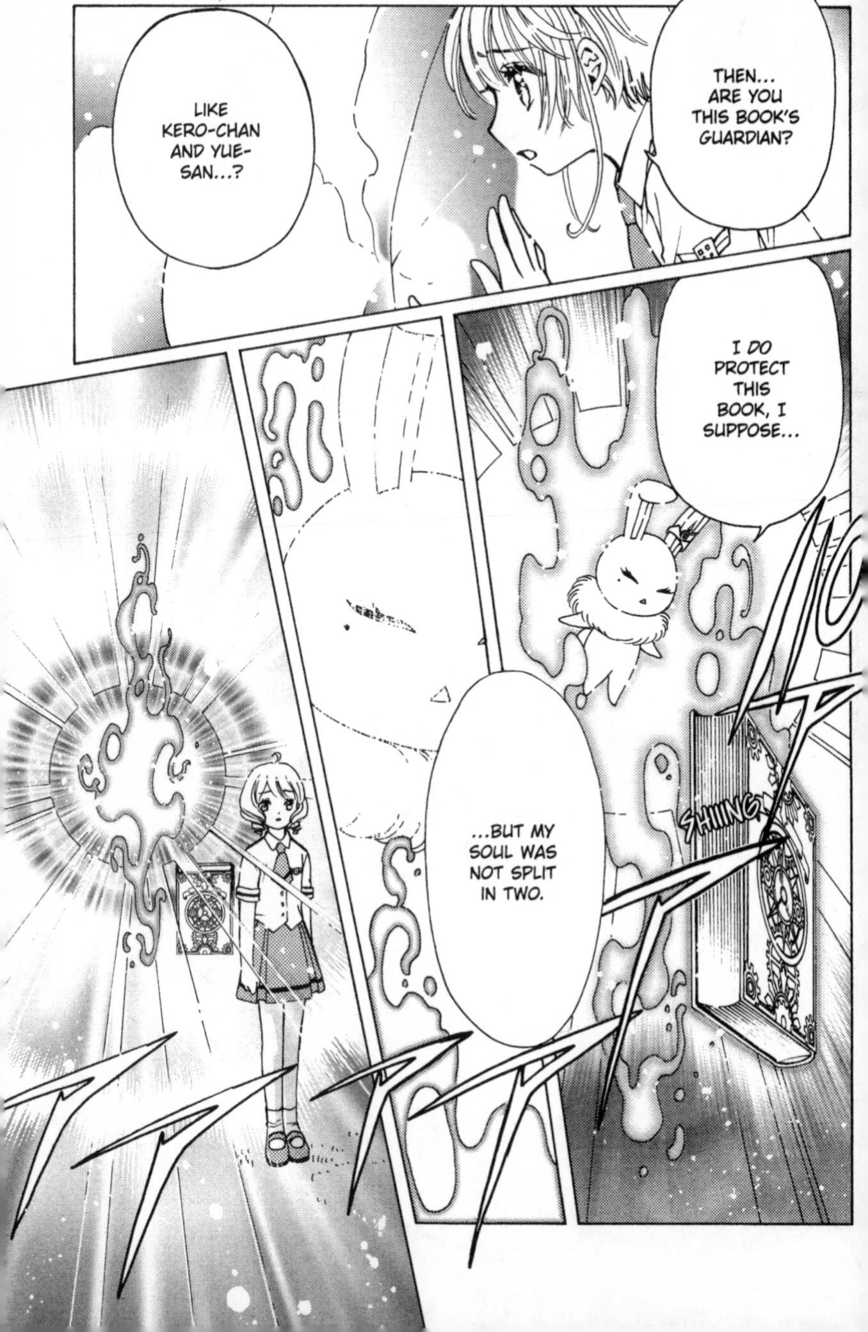
THEN... ARE YOU THIS BOOK'S GUARDIAN?
LIKE KERO-CHAN AND YUE-SAN...?
I DO PROTECT THIS BOOK, I SUPPOSE...
SHIIING
...BUT MY SOUL WAS NOT SPLIT IN TWO.

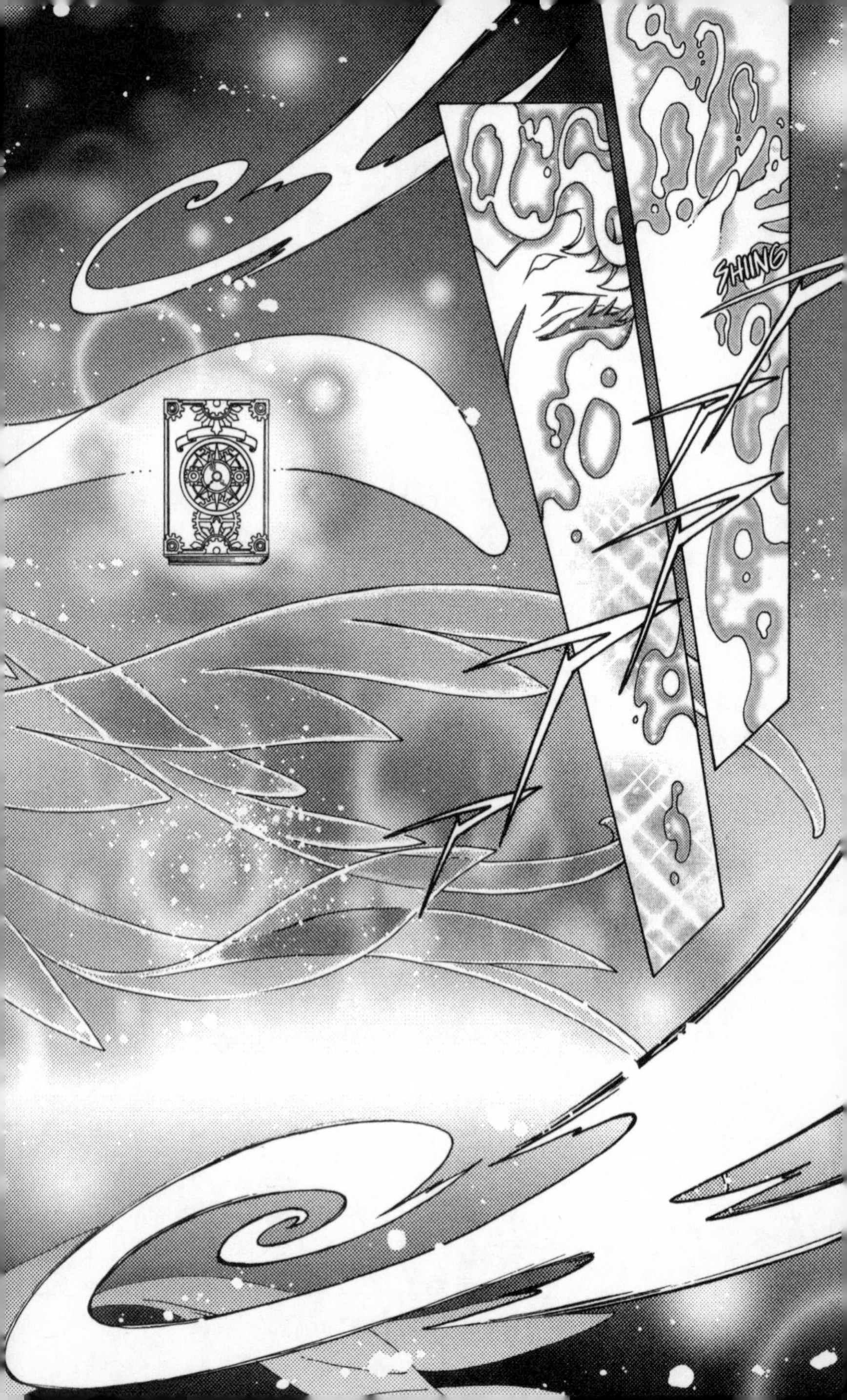
SHIING

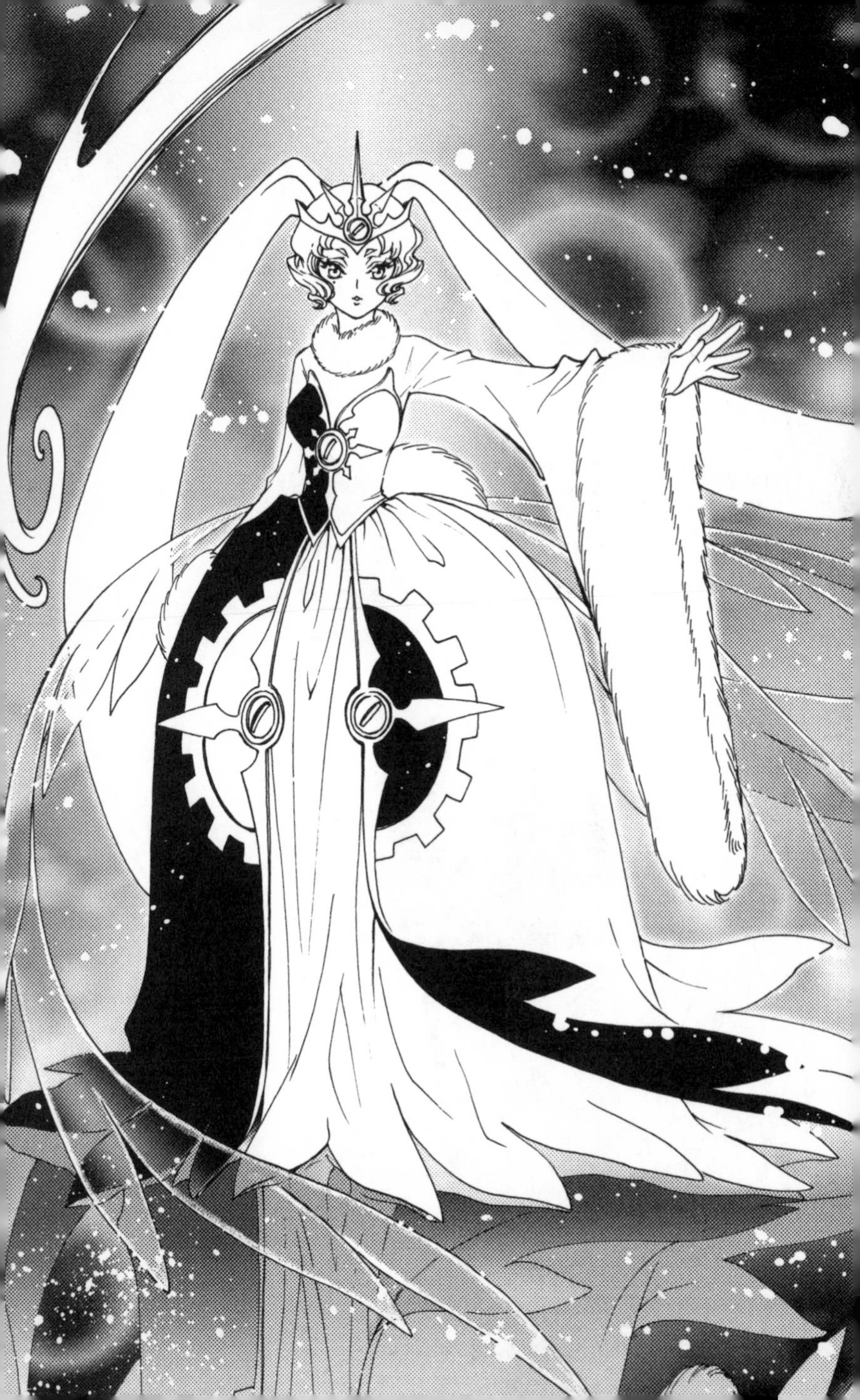

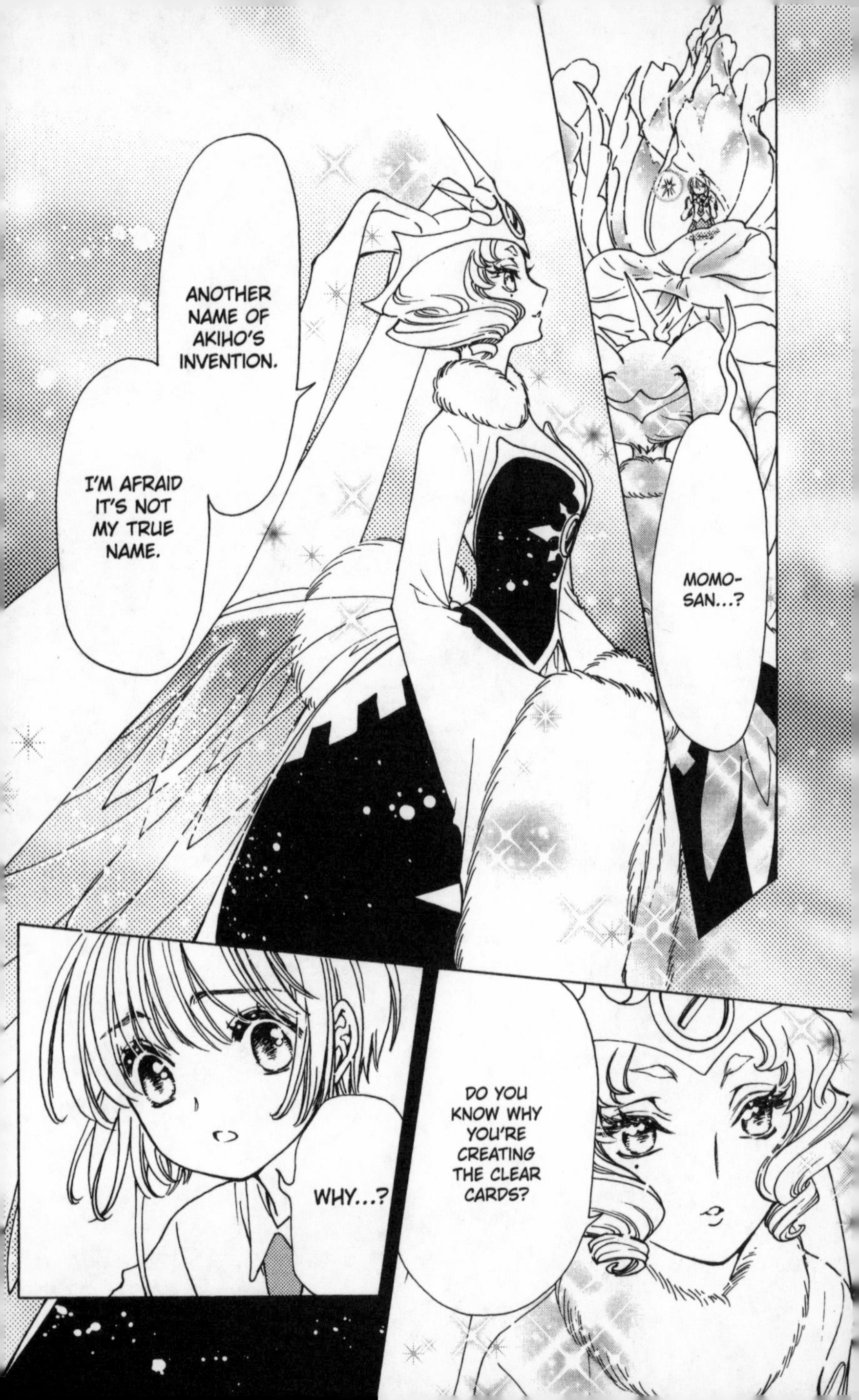
MOMO-SAN...?
ANOTHER NAME OF AKIHO'S INVENTION.
I'M AFRAID IT'S NOT MY TRUE NAME.
DO YOU KNOW WHY YOU'RE CREATING THE CLEAR CARDS?
WHY...?

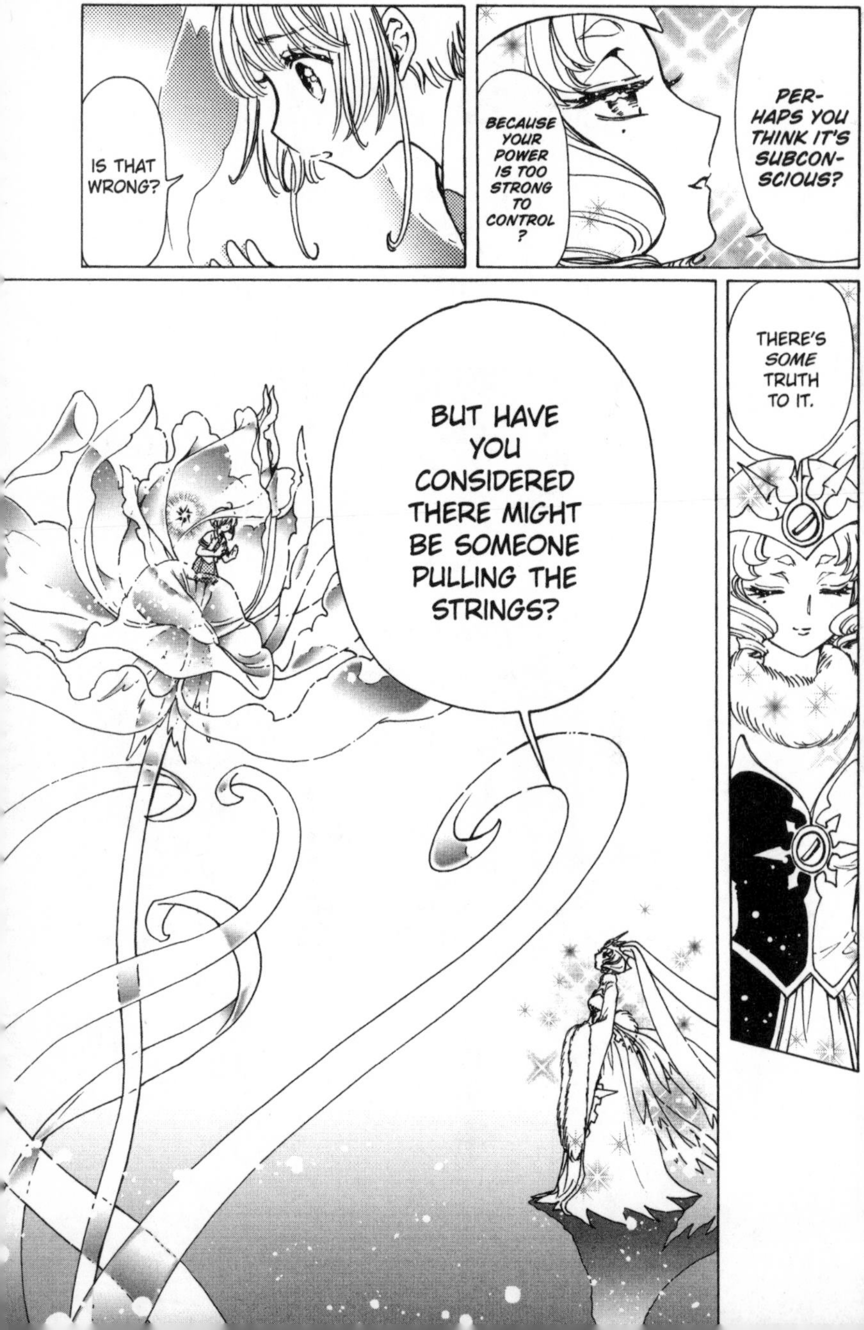
PER-HAPS YOU THINK IT'S SUBCON-SCIOUS?
BECAUSE YOUR POWER IS TOO STRONG TO CONTROL?
IS THAT WRONG?
THERE'S SOME TRUTH TO IT.
BUT HAVE YOU CONSIDERED THERE MIGHT BE SOMEONE PULLING THE STRINGS?

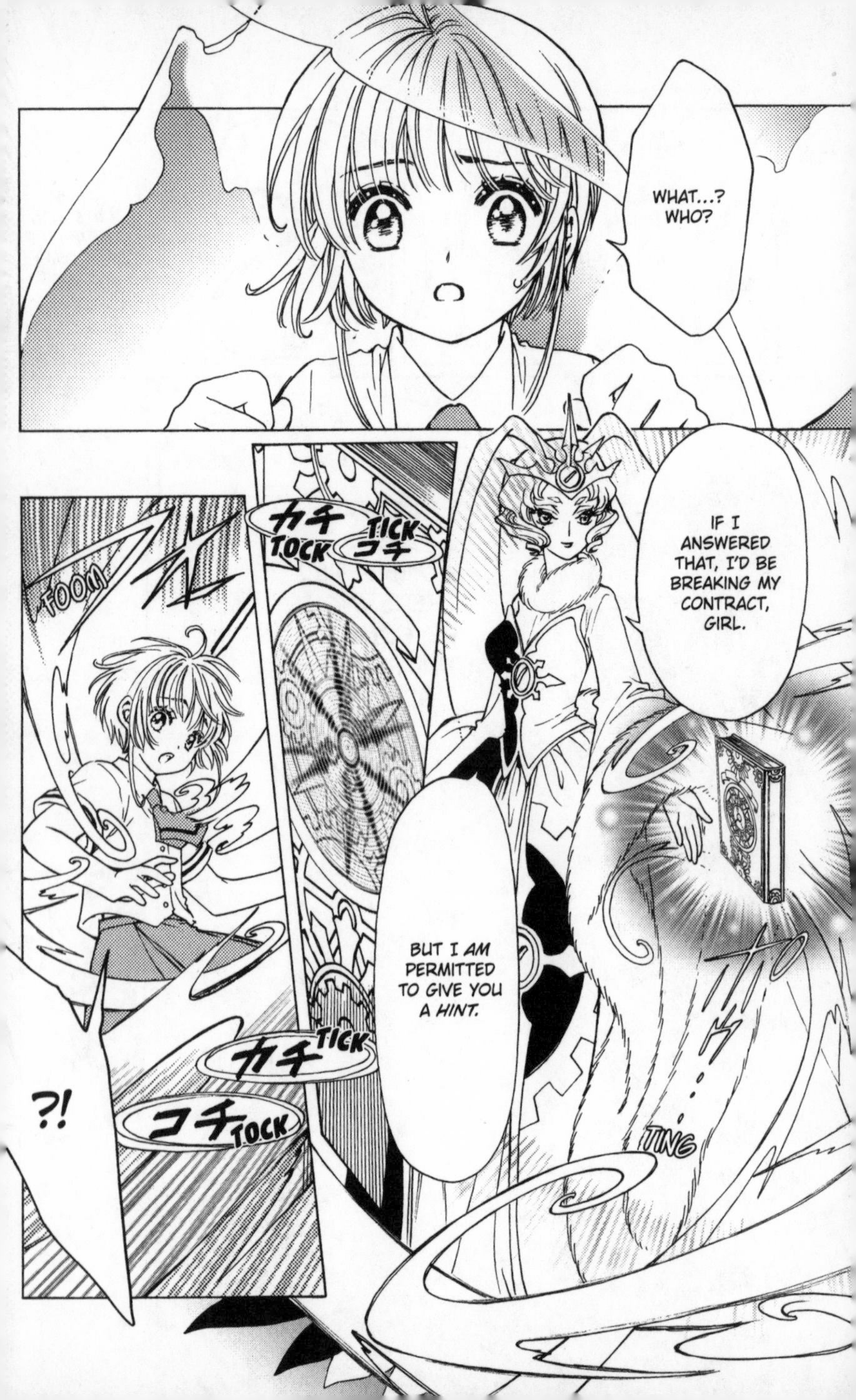
WHAT...? WHO?
IF I ANSWERED THAT, I'D BE BREAKING MY CONTRACT, GIRL.
BUT I AM PERMITTED TO GIVE YOU A HINT.
TING
カチ TOCK
TICK コチ
FOOM
?!
カチ TICK
コチ TOCK

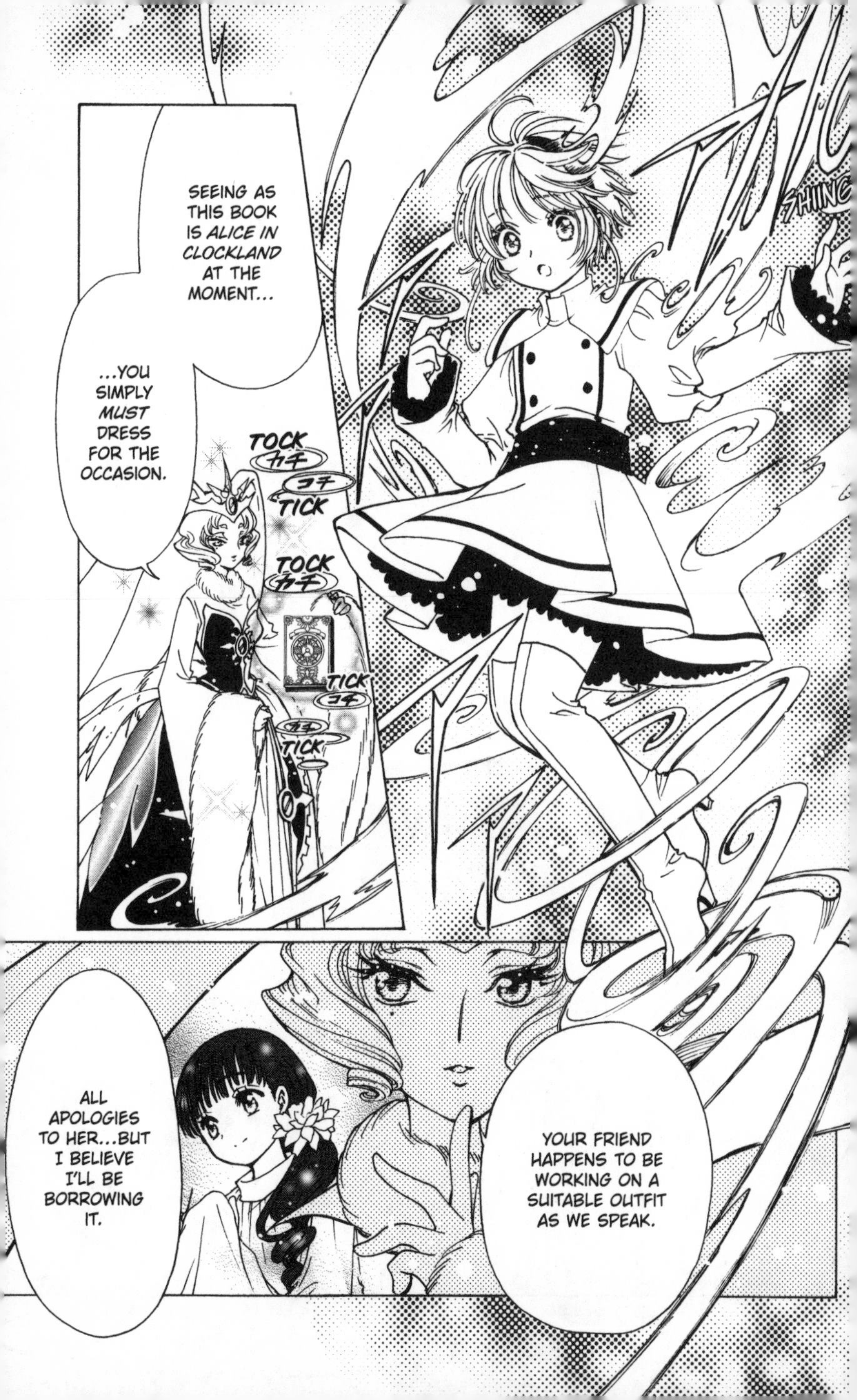
SHIING
SEEING AS THIS BOOK IS *ALICE IN CLOCKLAND* AT THE MOMENT...
...YOU SIMPLY *MUST* DRESS FOR THE OCCASION.
TOCK カチ
コチ TICK
TOCK カチ
TICK コチ
カチ TICK
YOUR FRIEND HAPPENS TO BE WORKING ON A SUITABLE OUTFIT AS WE SPEAK.
ALL APOLOGIES TO HER...BUT I BELIEVE I'LL BE BORROWING IT.

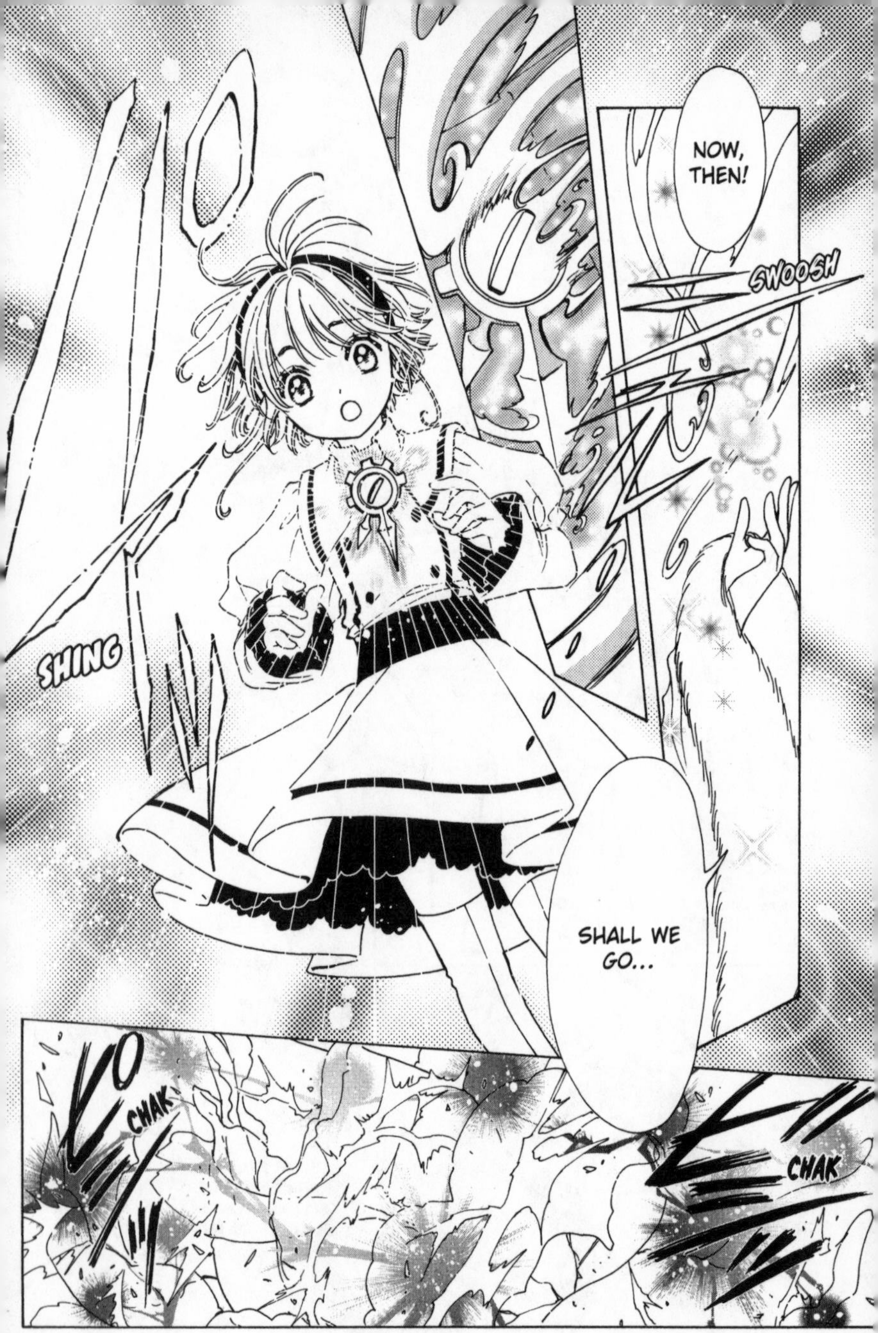
NOW, THEN!
SWOOSH
SHALL WE GO...
SHING
CHAK
CHAK

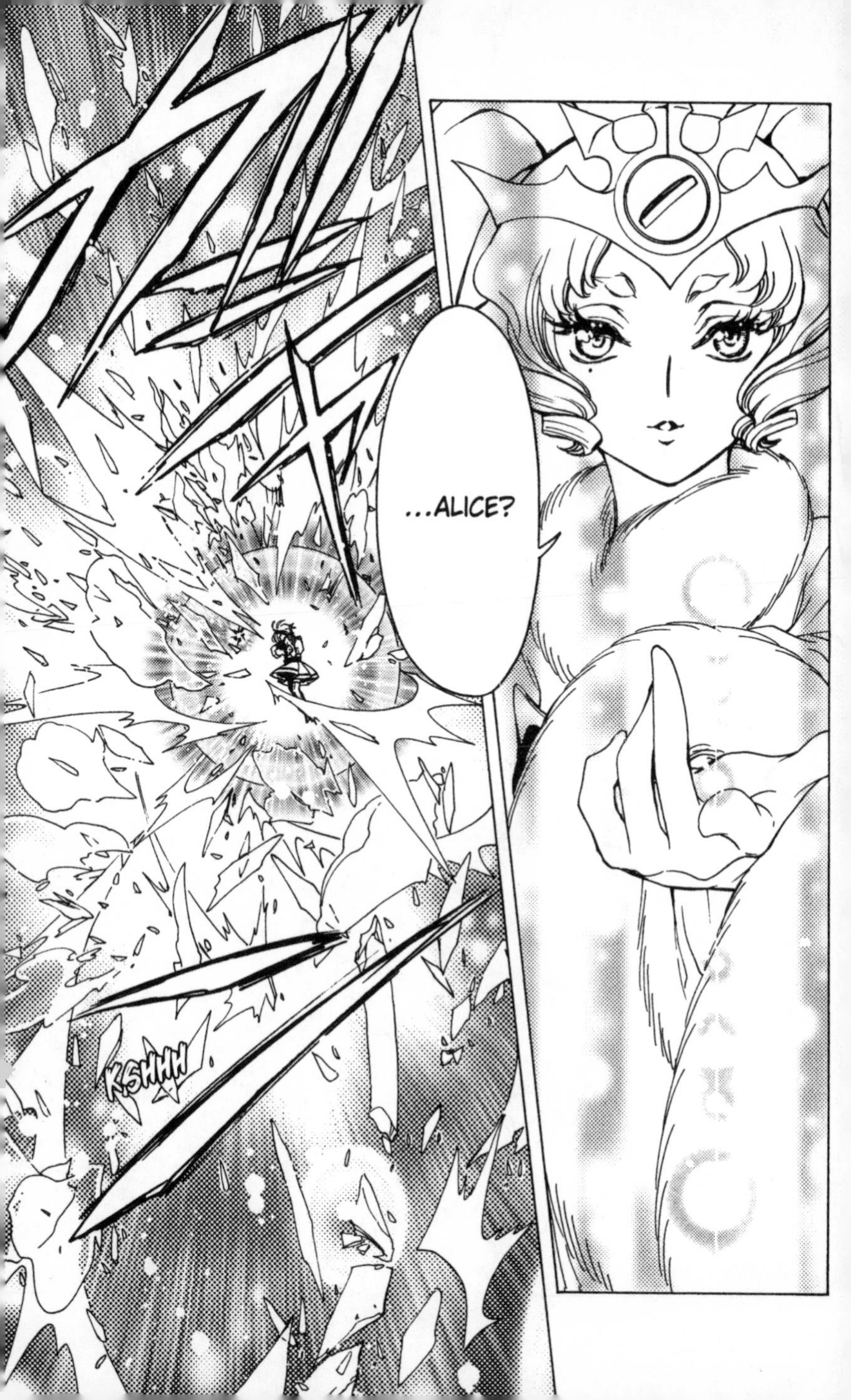
...ALICE?
KSHHH

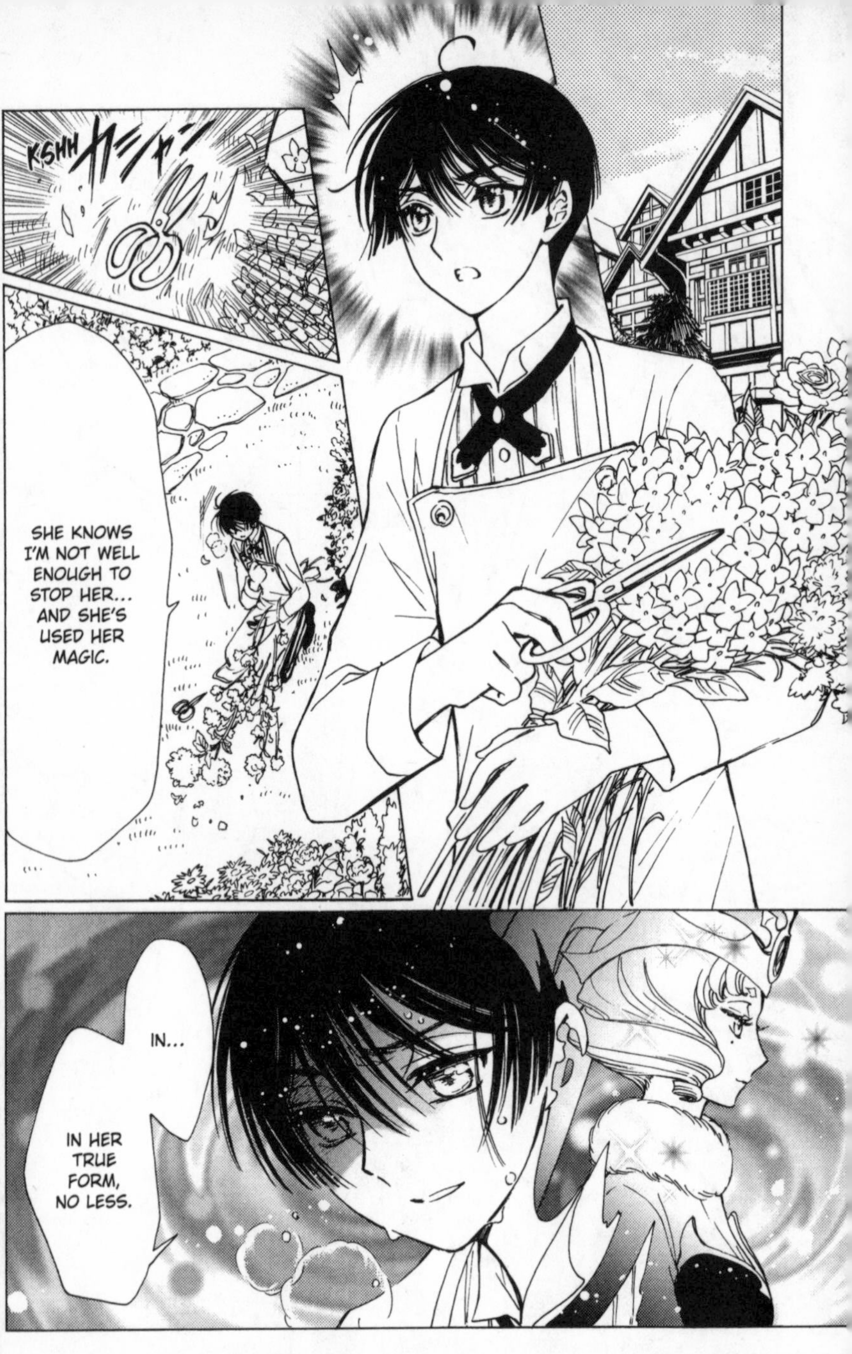
KSHH
カシャーン
SHE KNOWS I'M NOT WELL ENOUGH TO STOP HER... AND SHE'S USED HER MAGIC.
IN...
IN HER TRUE FORM, NO LESS.

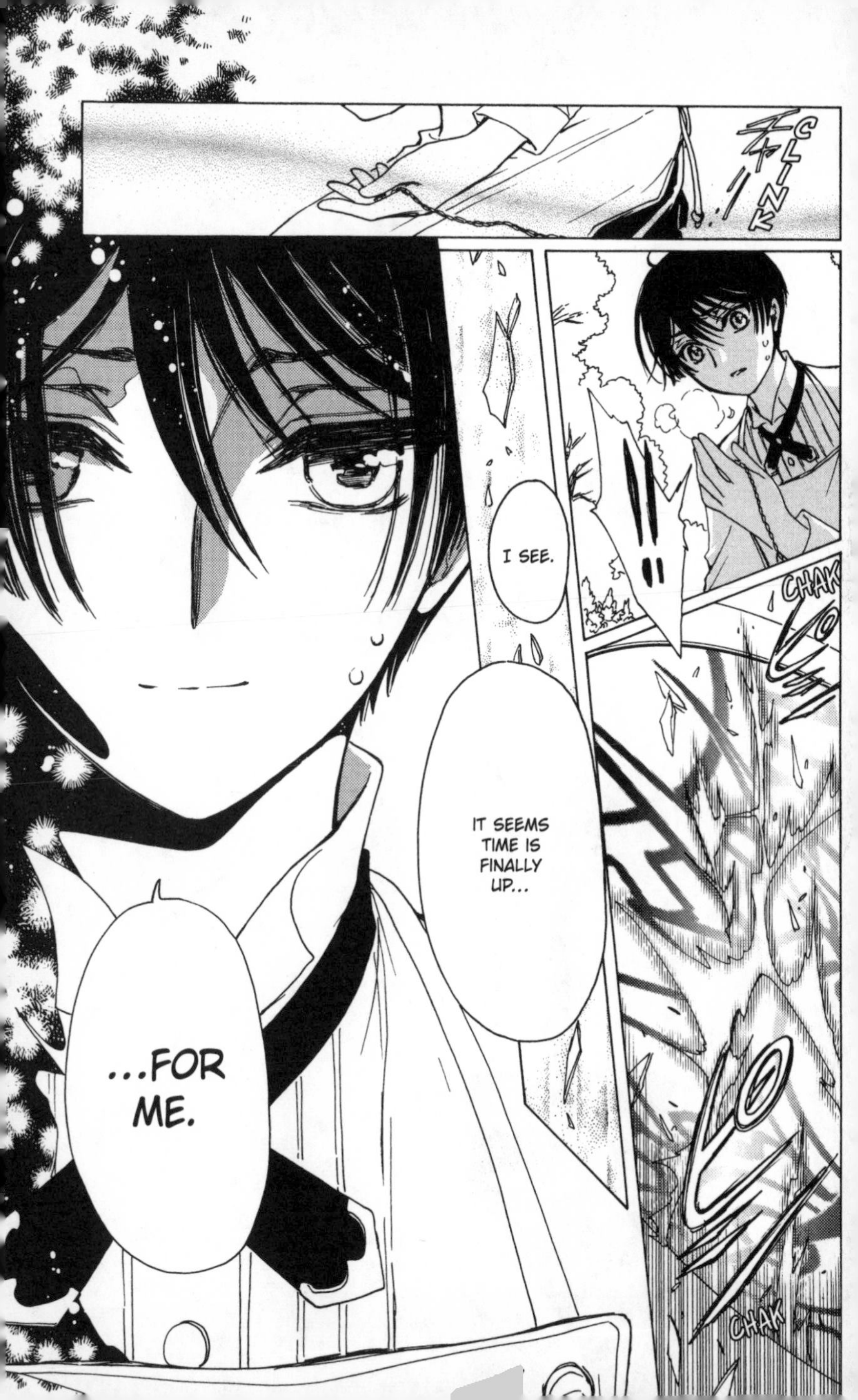

CLINK
!!
I SEE.
CHAK
IT SEEMS TIME IS FINALLY UP...
...FOR ME.
CHAK

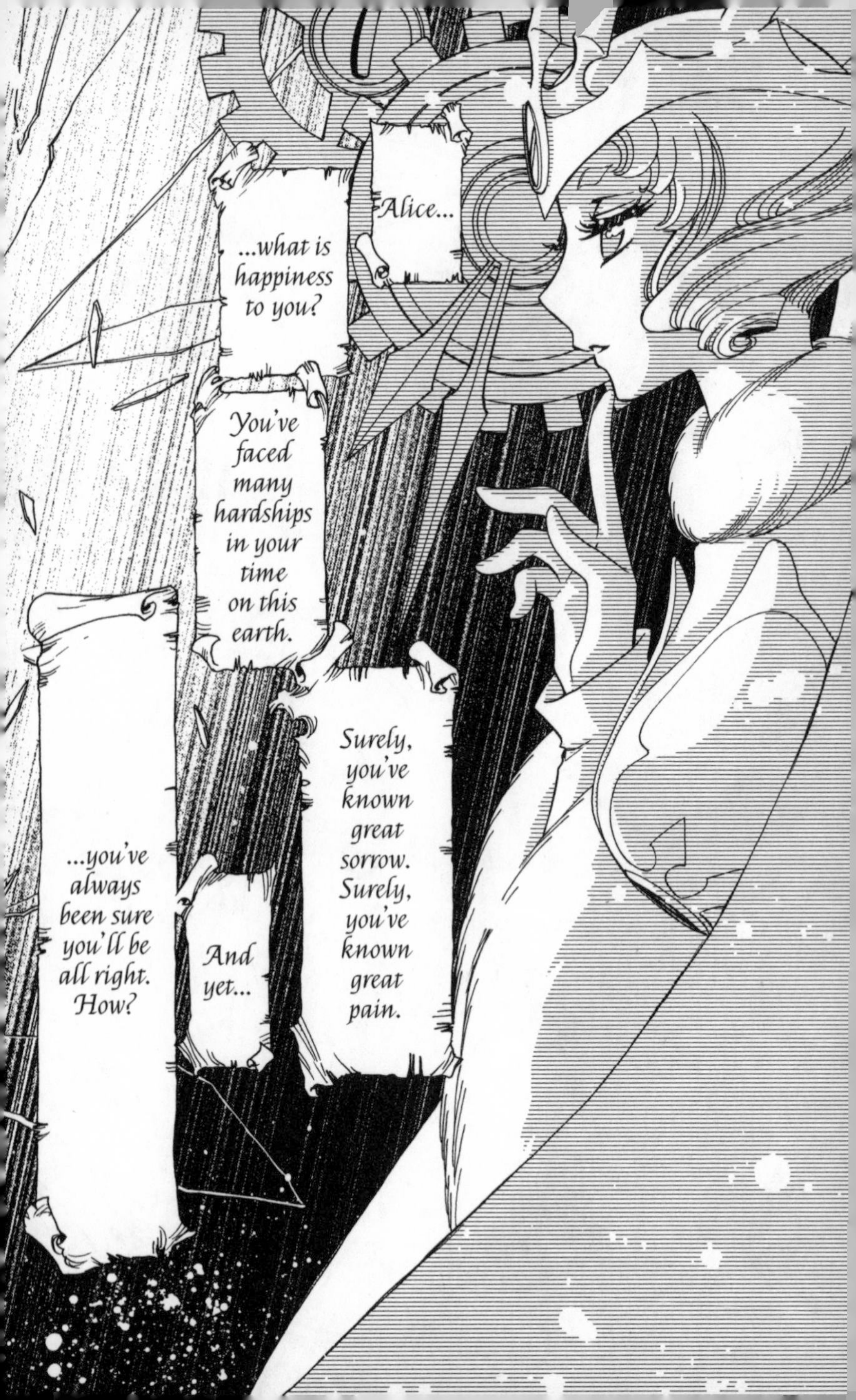
Alice...
...what is happiness to you?
You've faced many hardships in your time on this earth.
Surely, you've known great sorrow. Surely, you've known great pain.
And yet...
...you've always been sure you'll be all right. How?

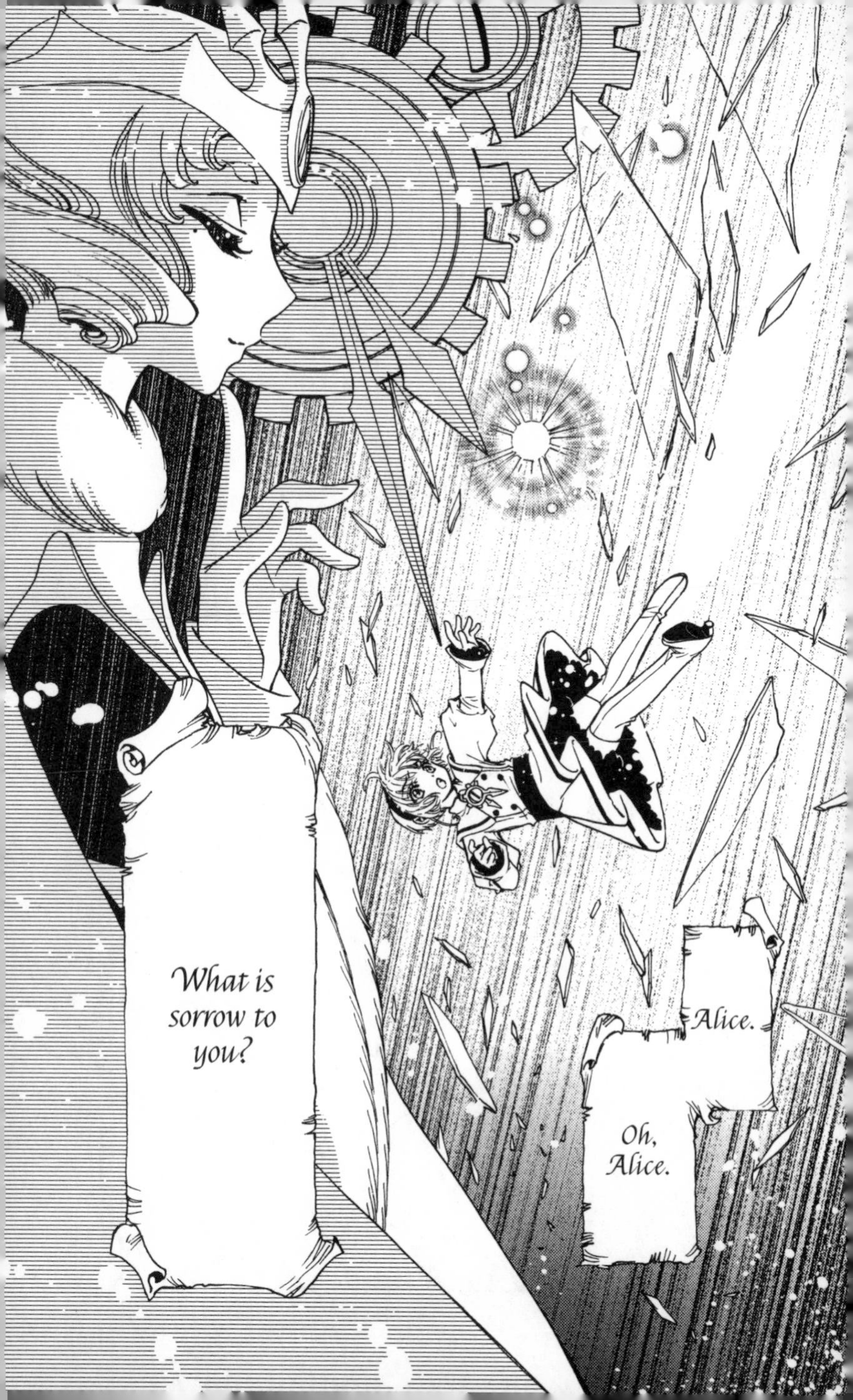
Alice.
Oh, Alice.
What is sorrow to you?

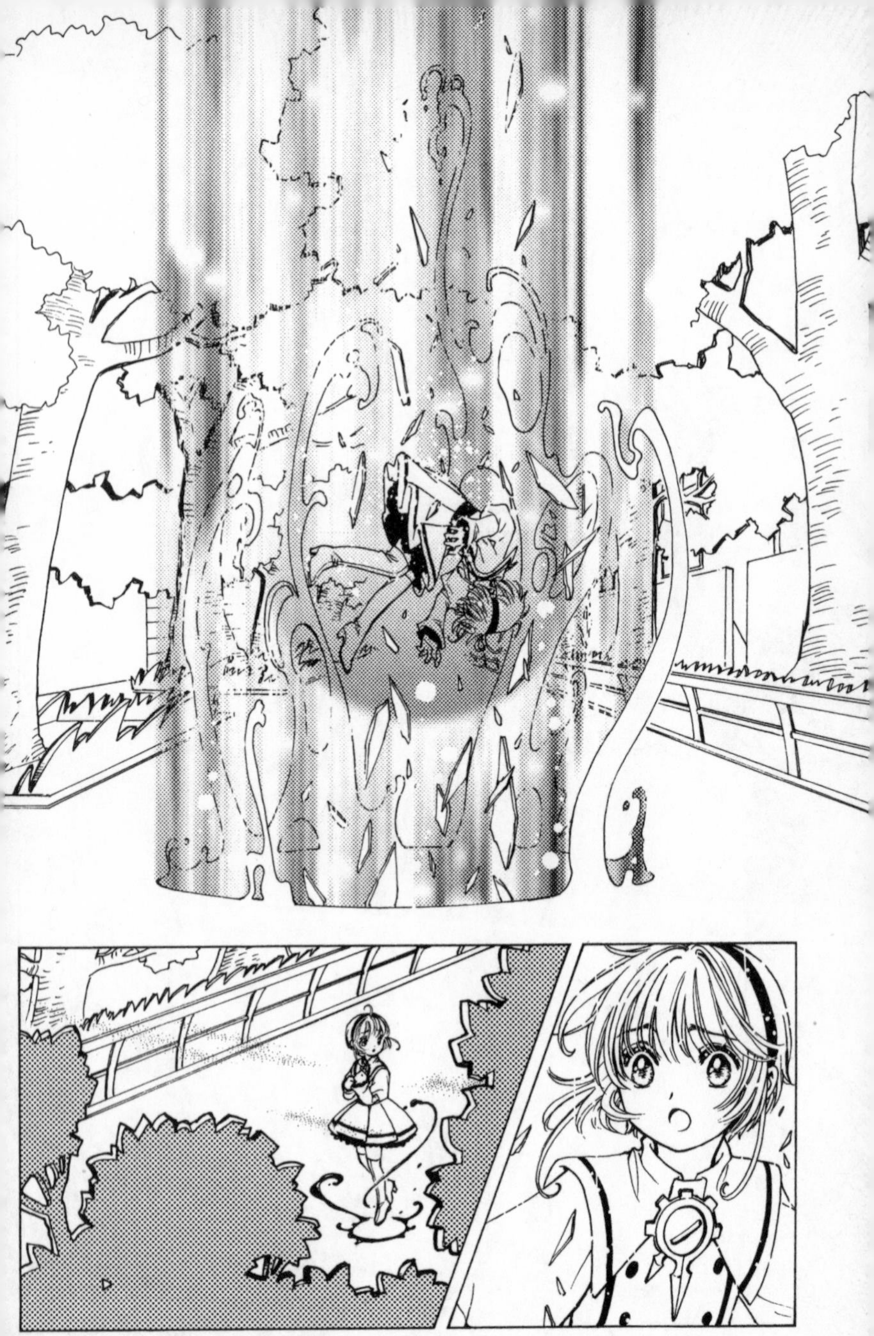

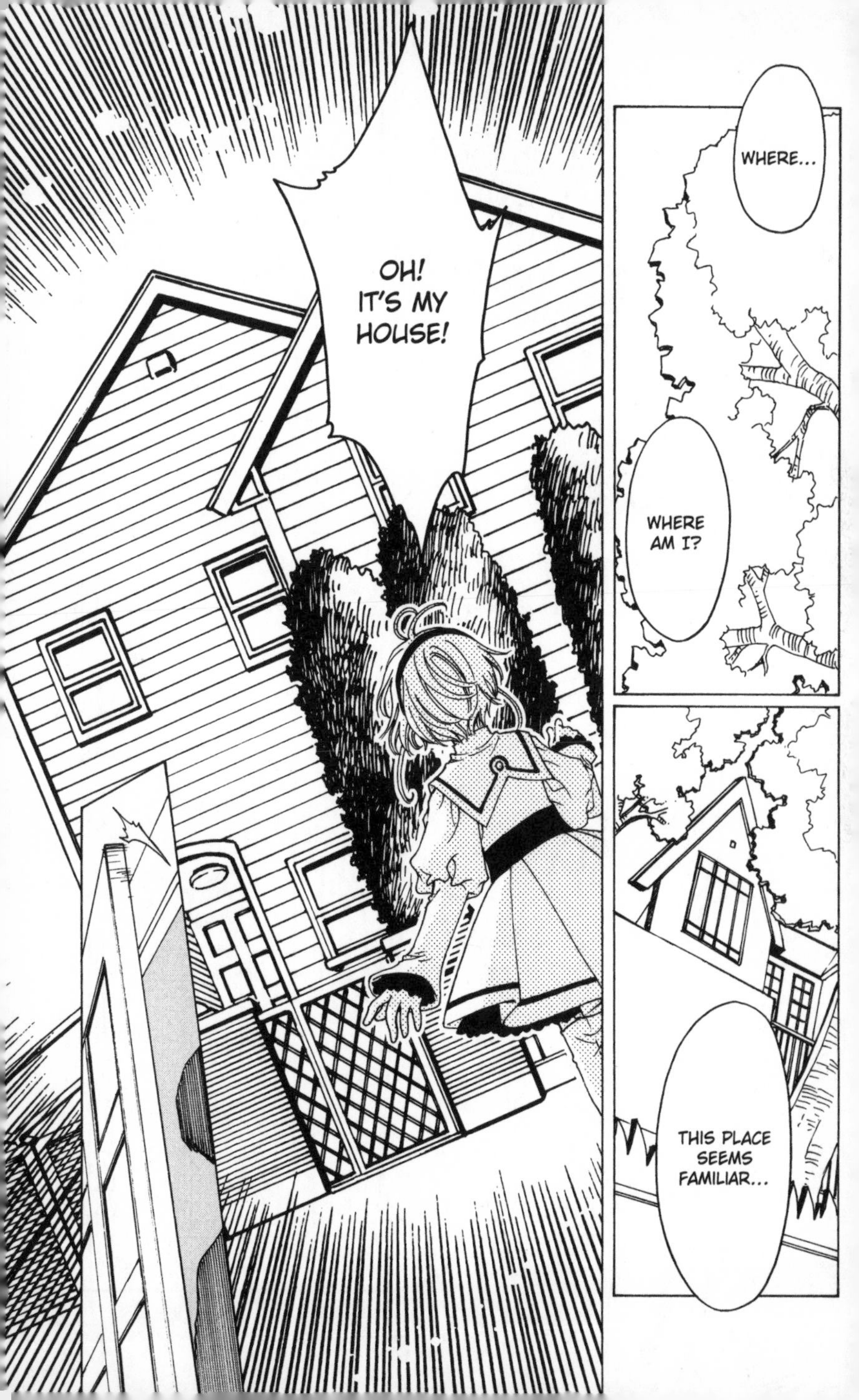
WHERE...
WHERE AM I?
THIS PLACE SEEMS FAMILIAR...
OH! IT'S MY HOUSE!

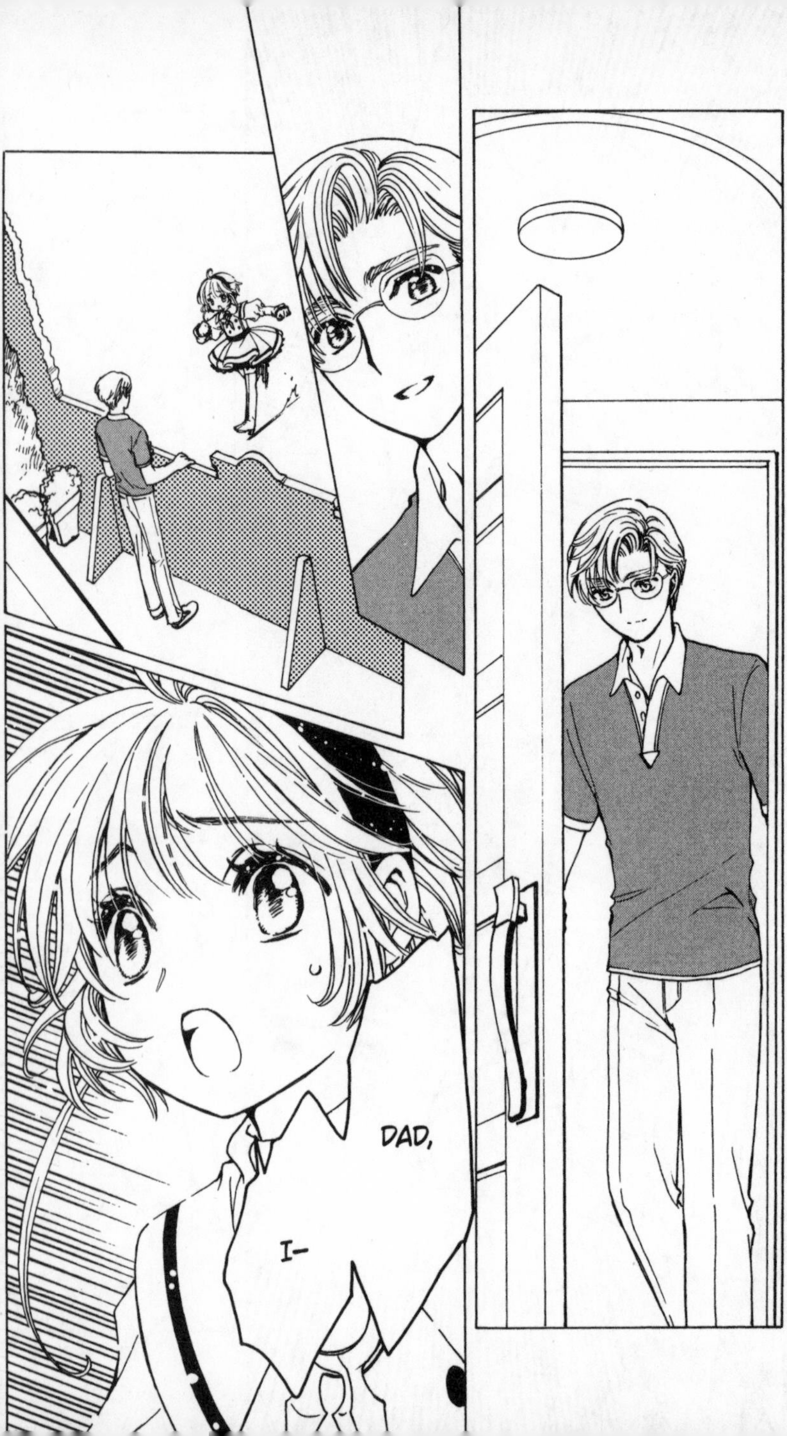
DAD,
I–

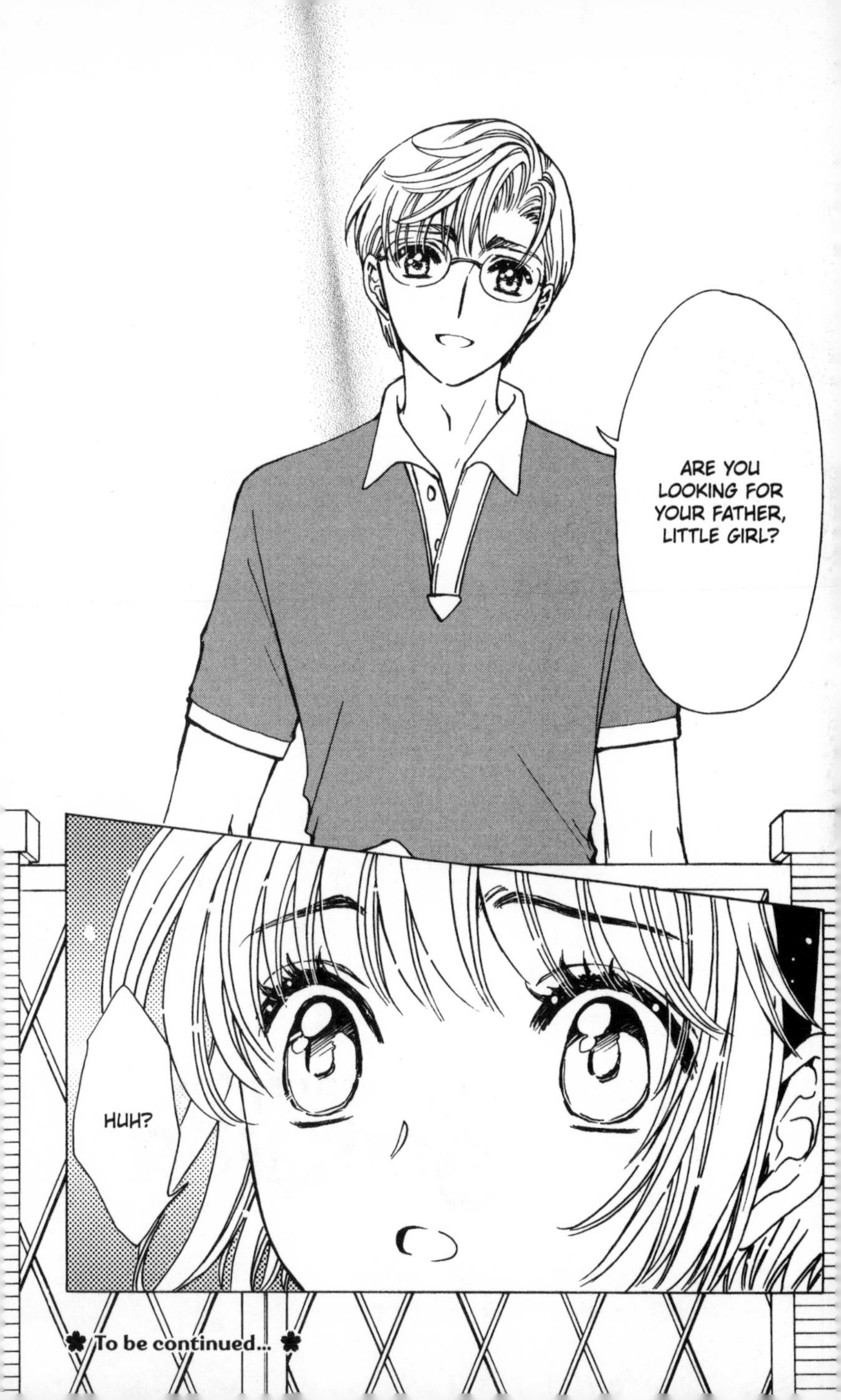
ARE YOU LOOKING FOR YOUR FATHER, LITTLE GIRL?
HUH?
To be continued...

Cardcaptor Sakura

CLEAR CARD

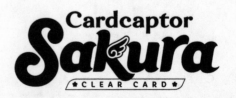

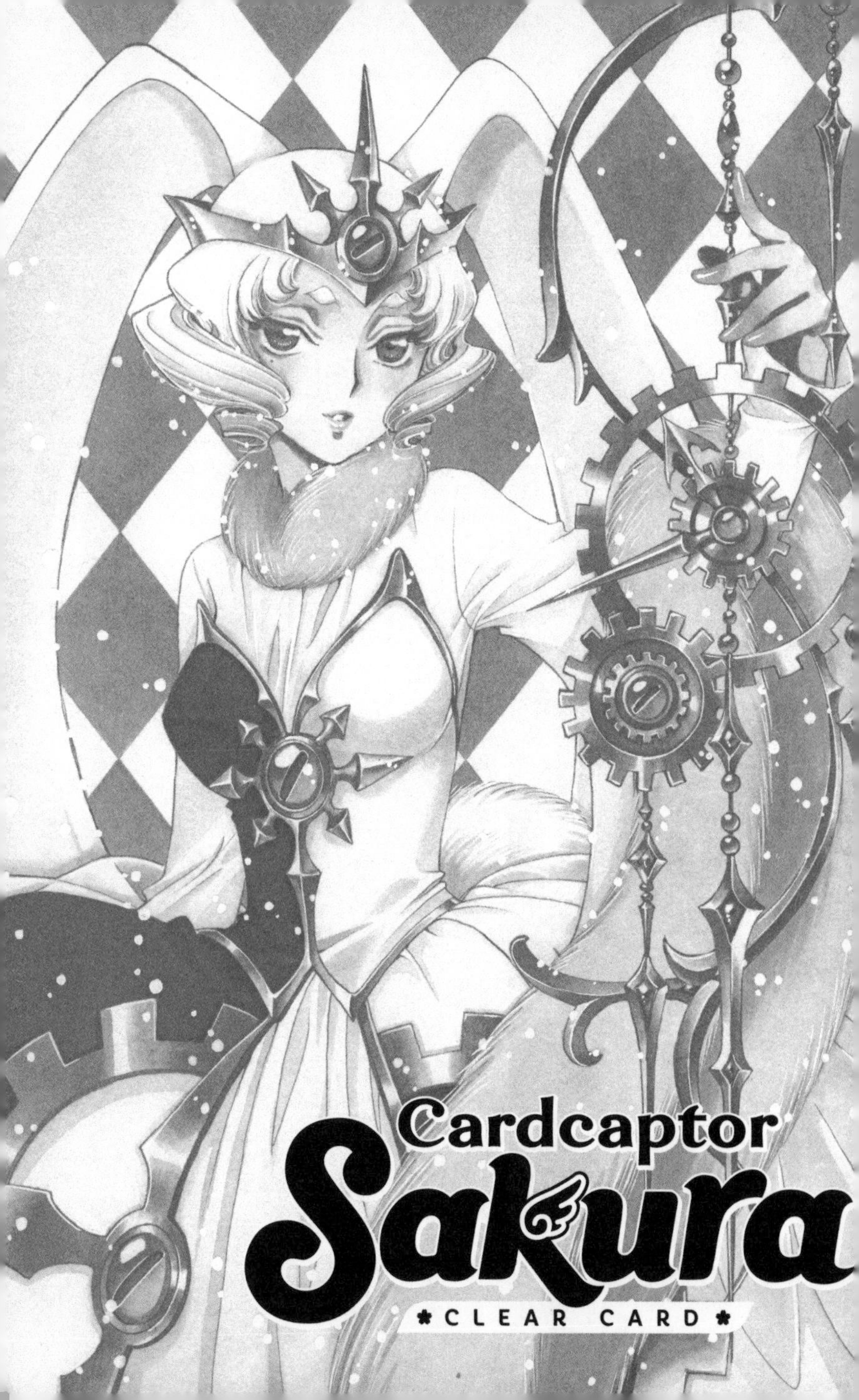
Cardcaptor
Sakura
CLEAR CARD

Cardcaptor Sakura

CLEAR CARD

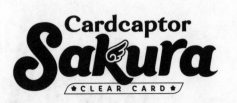

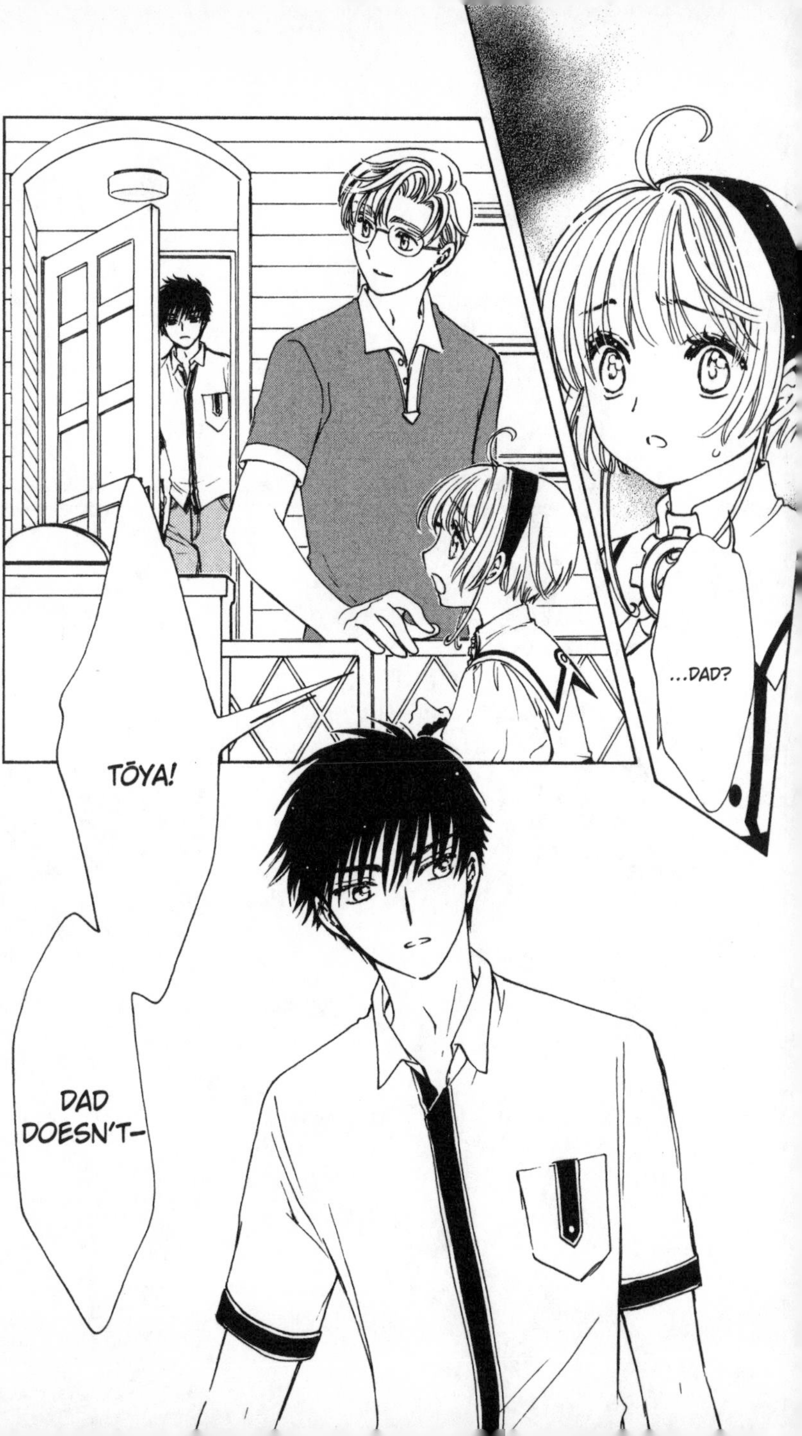
...DAD?
TŌYA!
DAD DOESN'T-

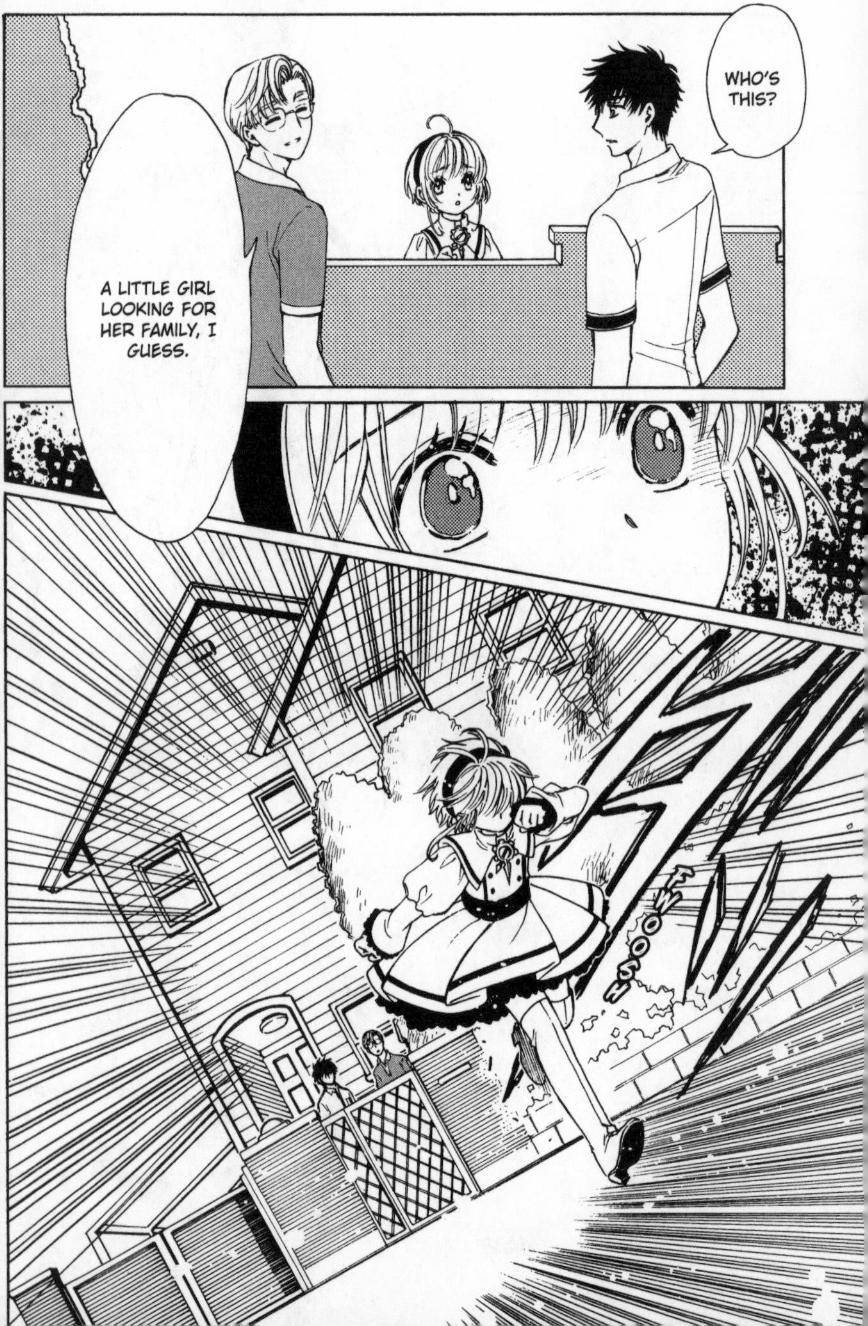
WHO'S THIS?
A LITTLE GIRL LOOKING FOR HER FAMILY, I GUESS.
WHOOSH

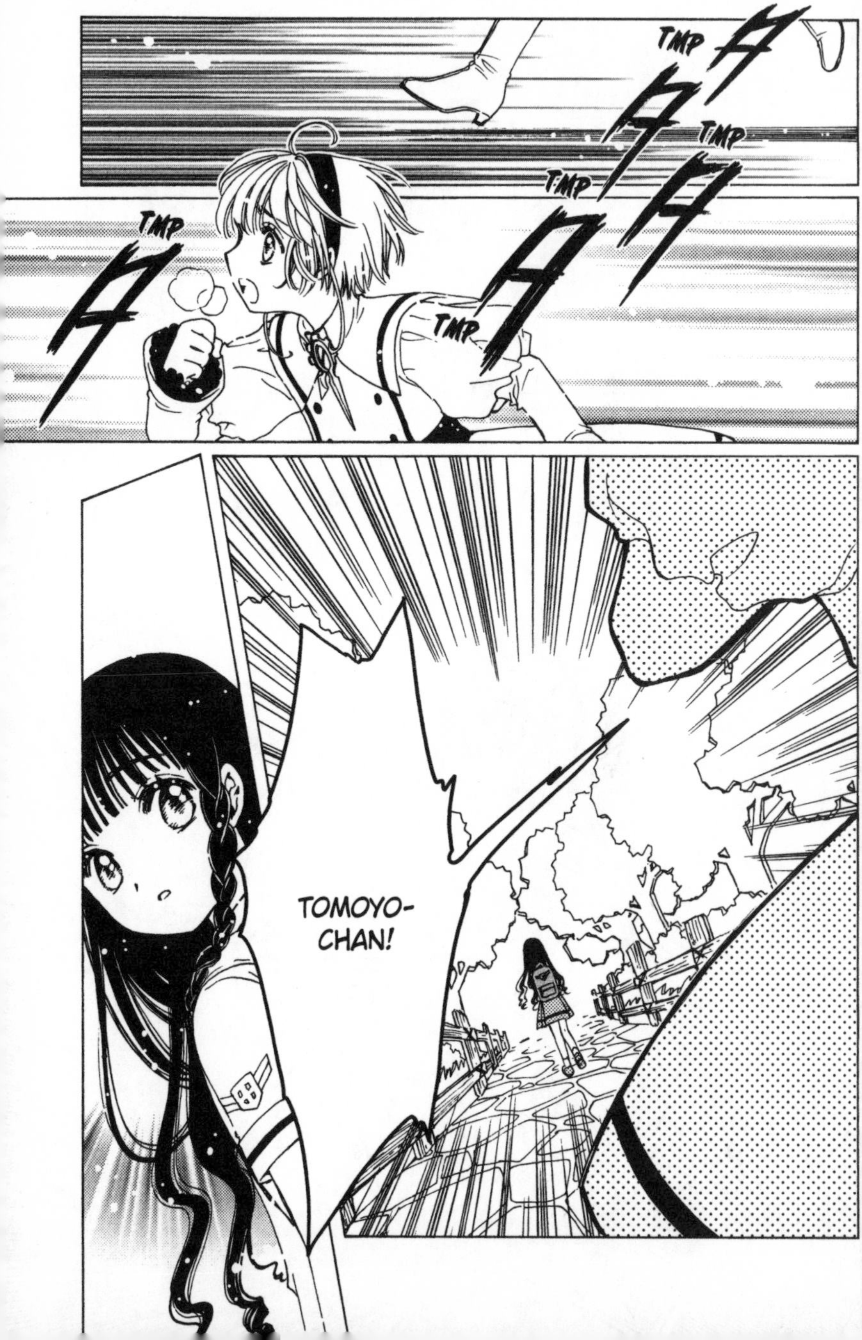
TMP
TMP
TMP
TMP
TMP
TOMOYO-CHAN!

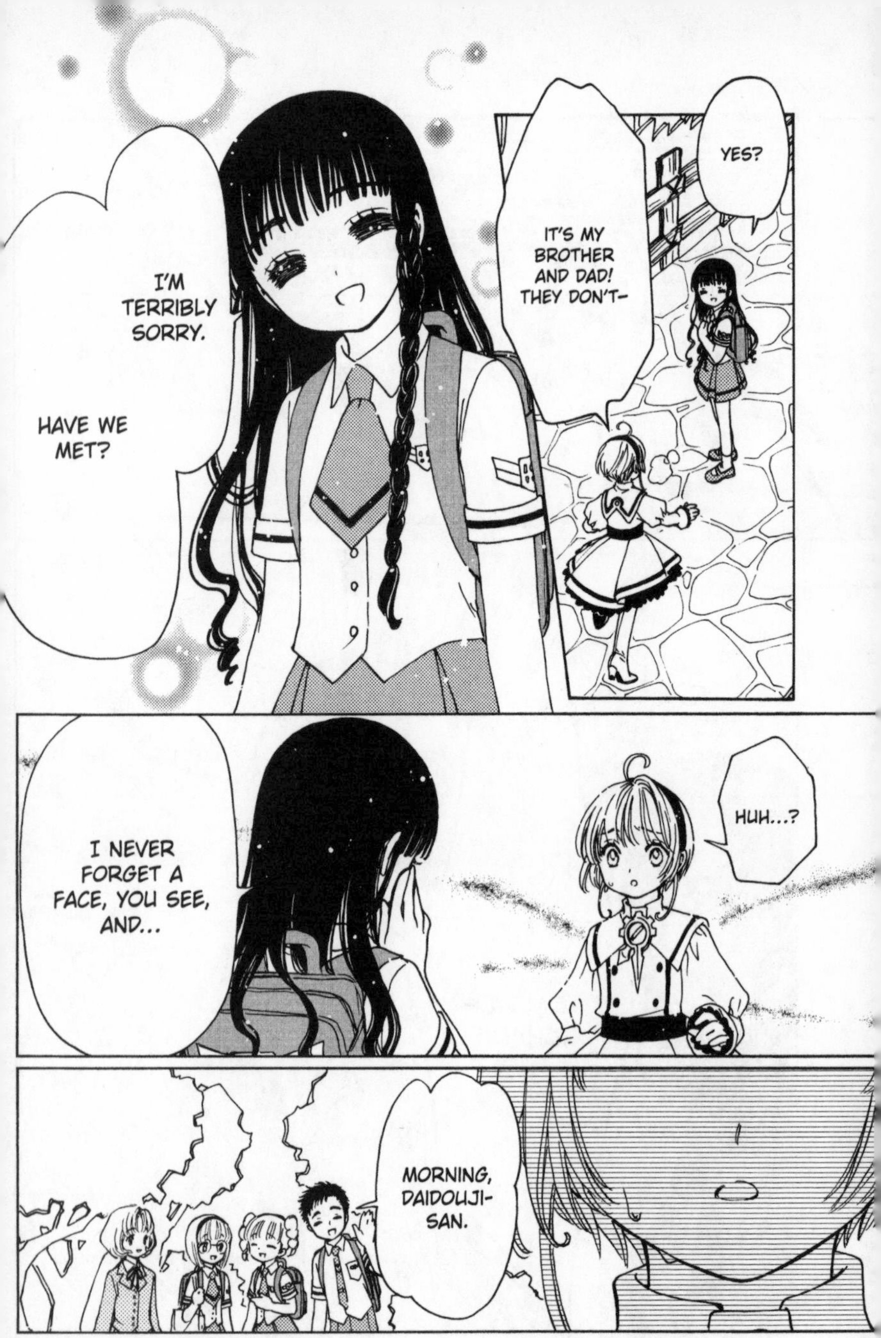
YES?
IT'S MY BROTHER AND DAD! THEY DON'T-
I'M TERRIBLY SORRY.
HAVE WE MET?
HUH...?
I NEVER FORGET A FACE, YOU SEE, AND...
MORNING, DAIDOUJI-SAN.

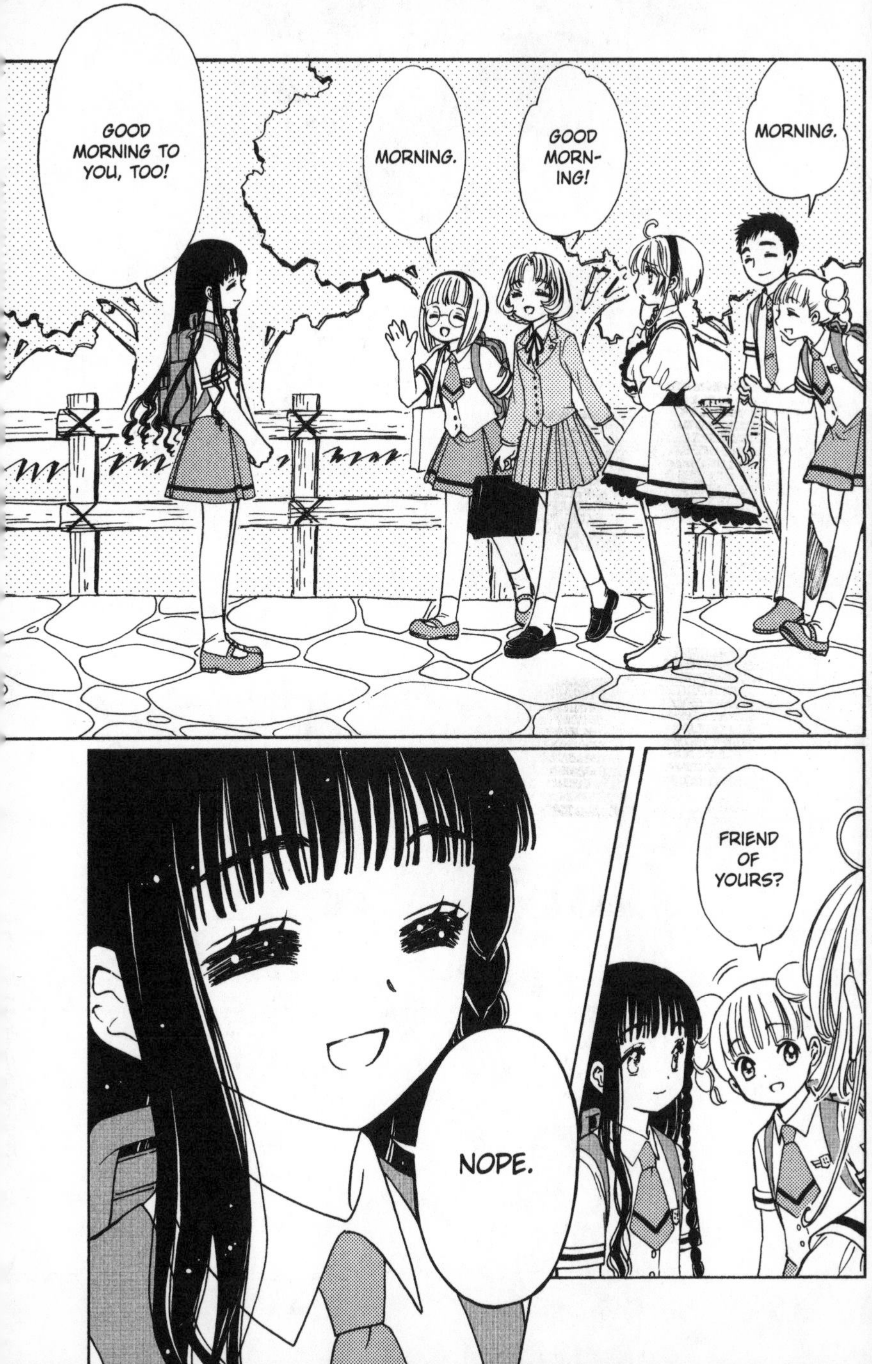
MORNING.
GOOD MORN-ING!
MORNING.
GOOD MORNING TO YOU, TOO!
FRIEND OF YOURS?
NOPE.

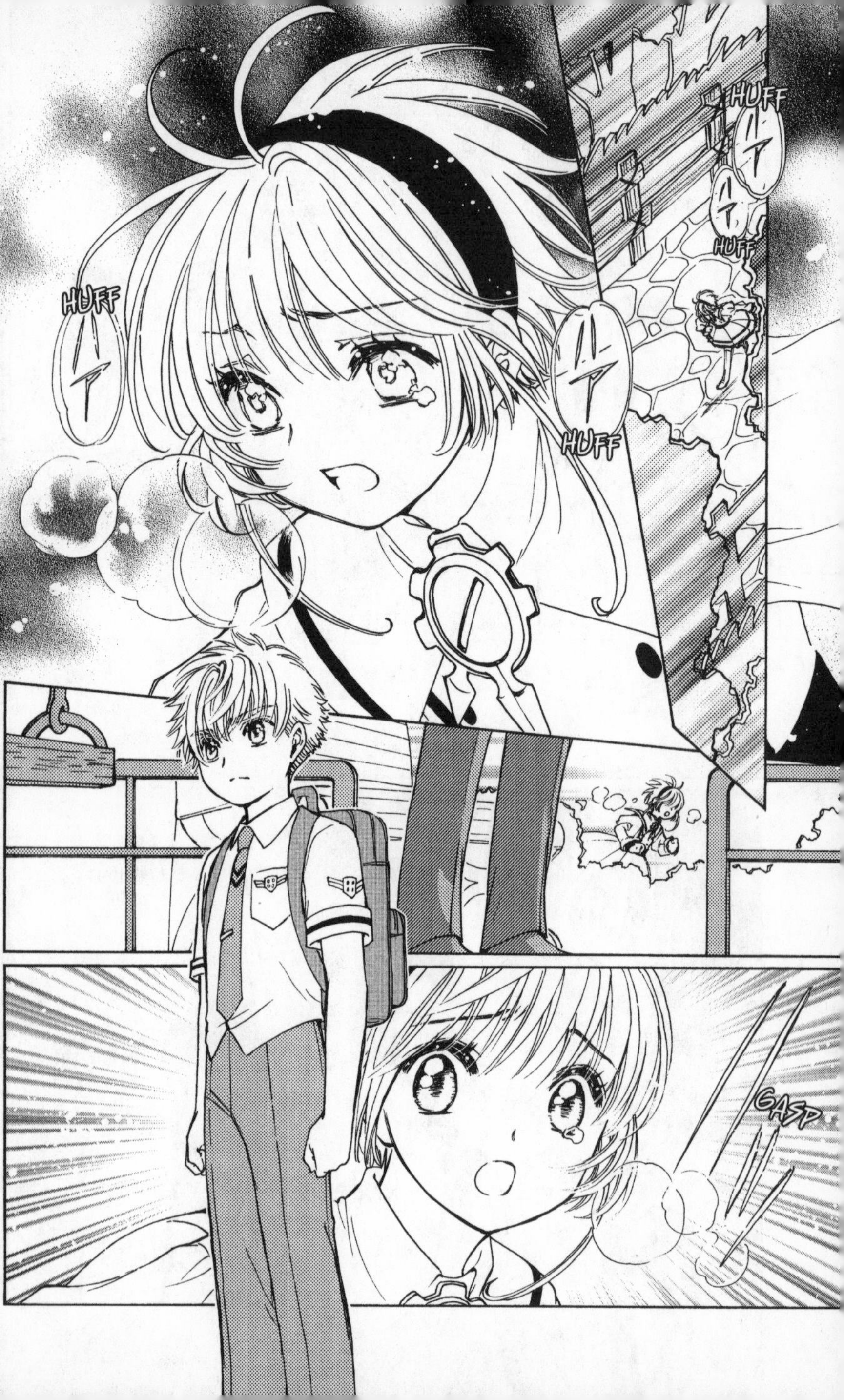
HUFF
ハァ
ハァ
HUFF
ハァ
HUFF
HUFF
ハァ
GASP

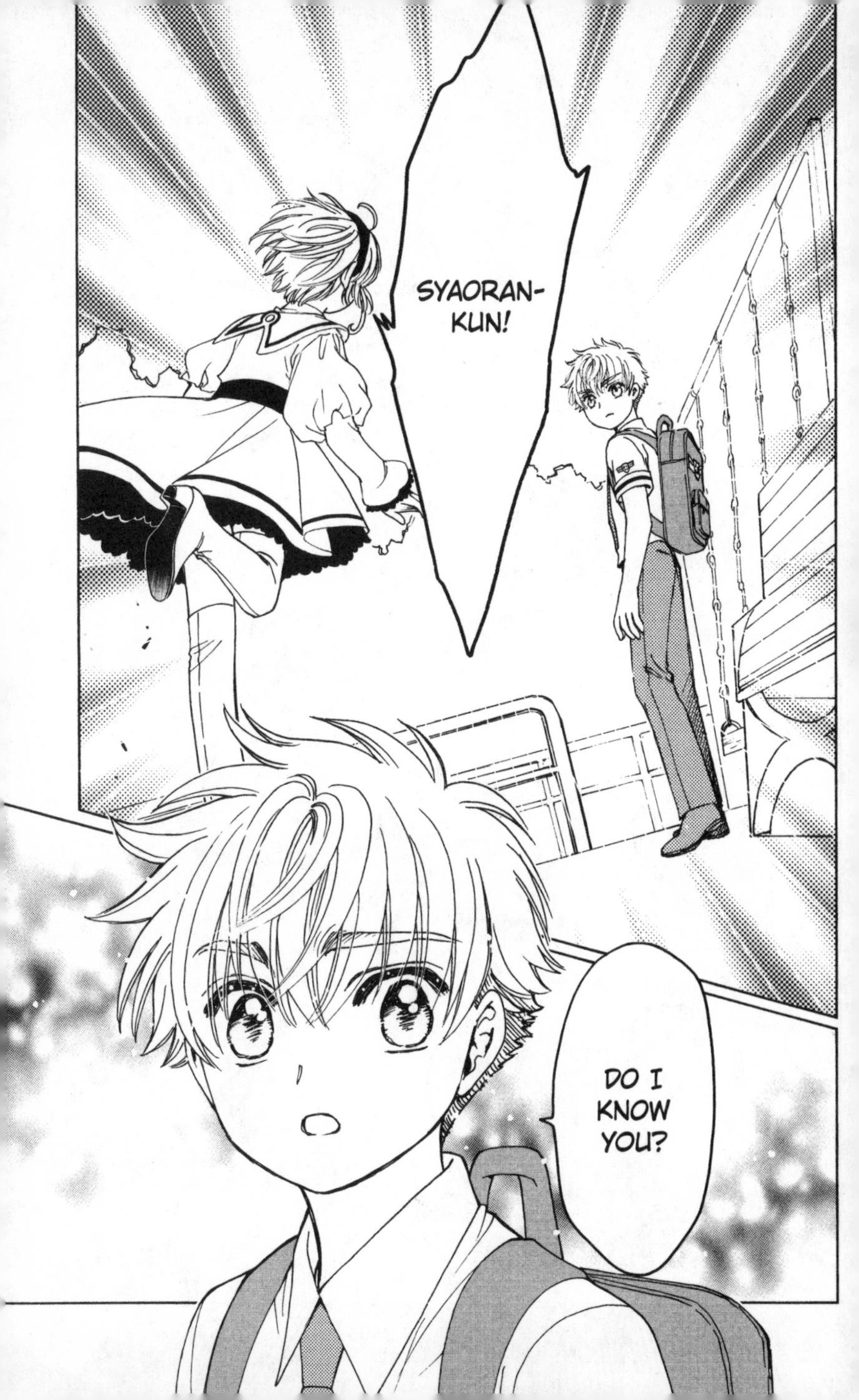
SYAORAN-KUN!
DO I KNOW YOU?

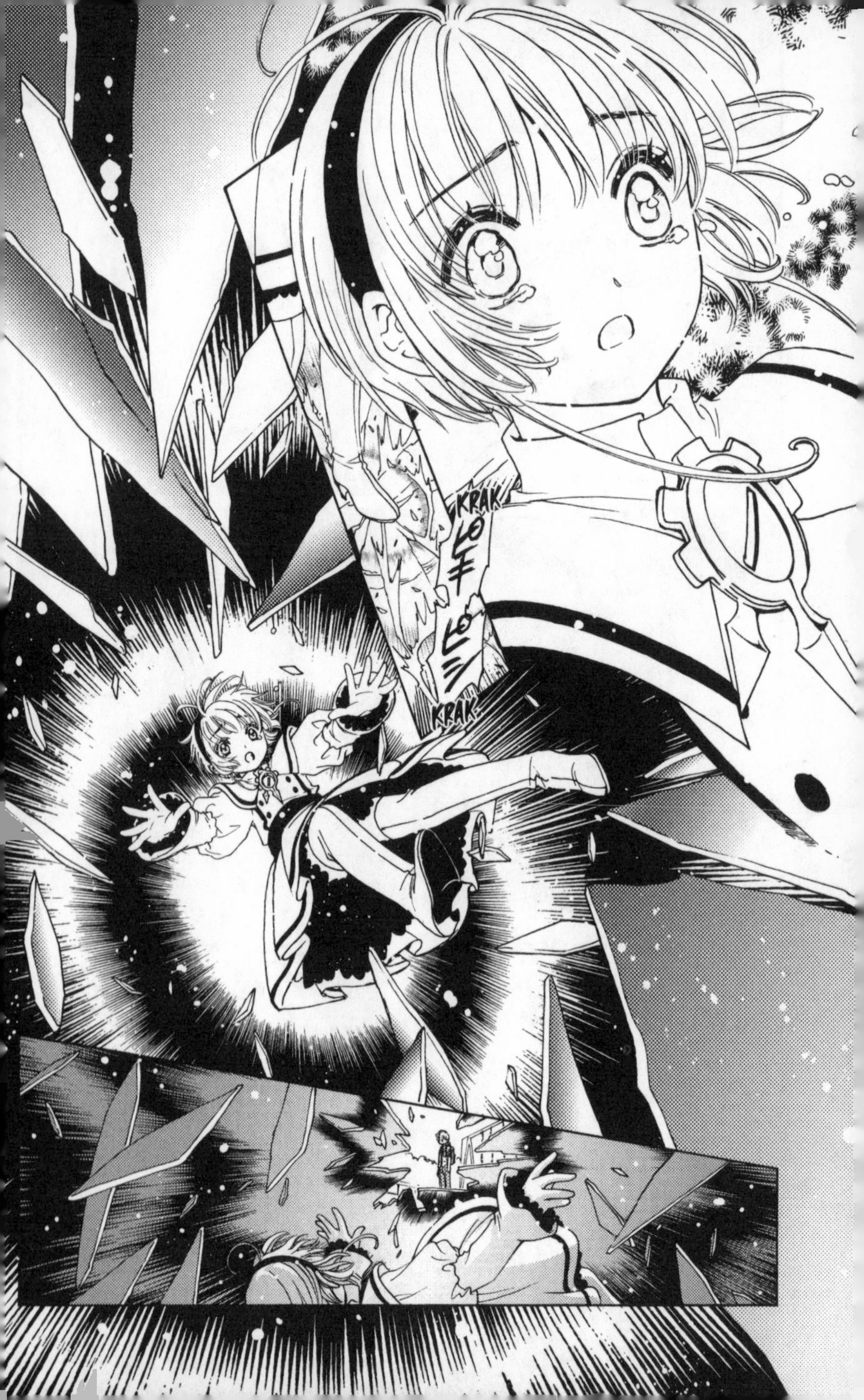
KRAK
KRAK

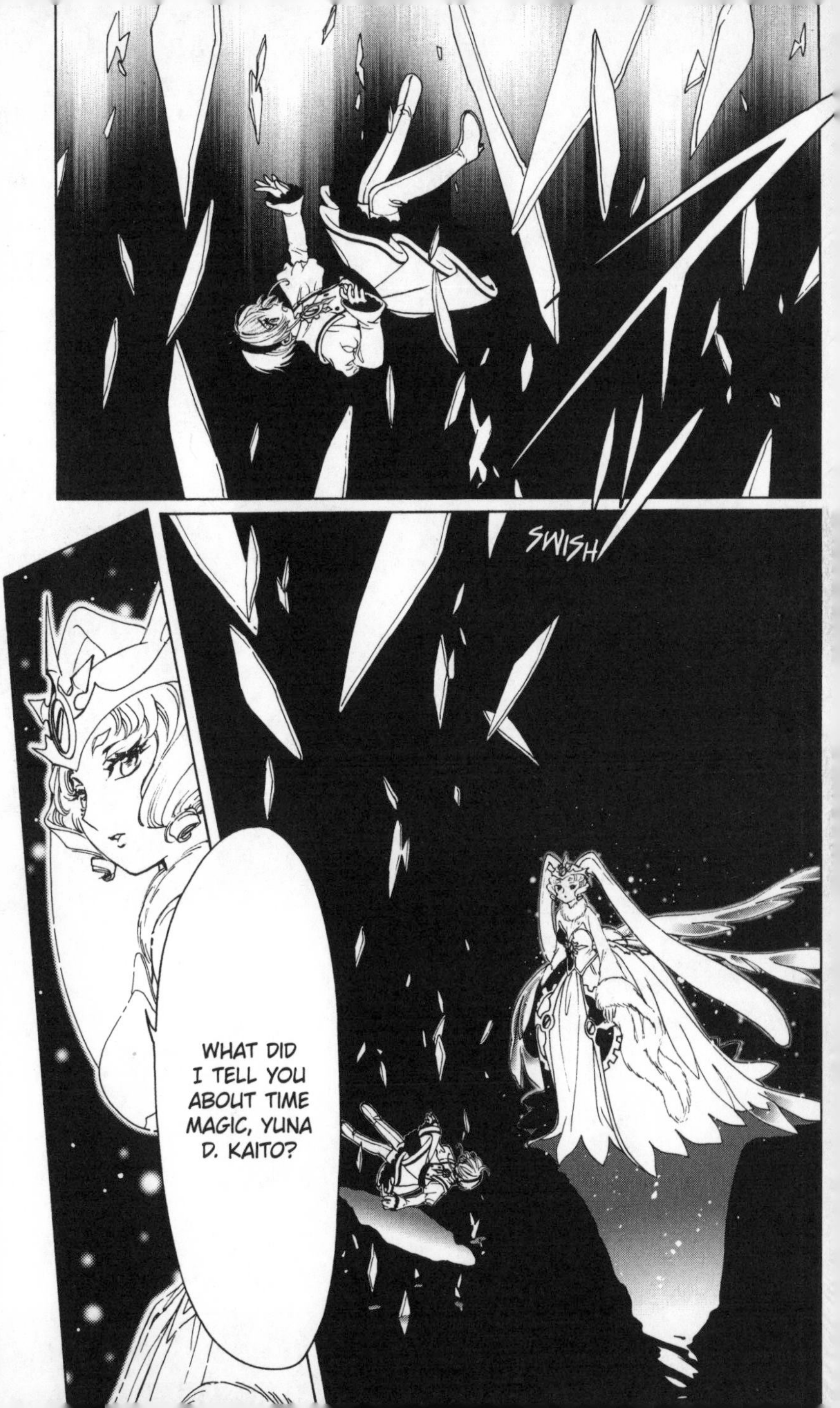
SWISH
WHAT DID I TELL YOU ABOUT TIME MAGIC, YUNA D. KAITO?

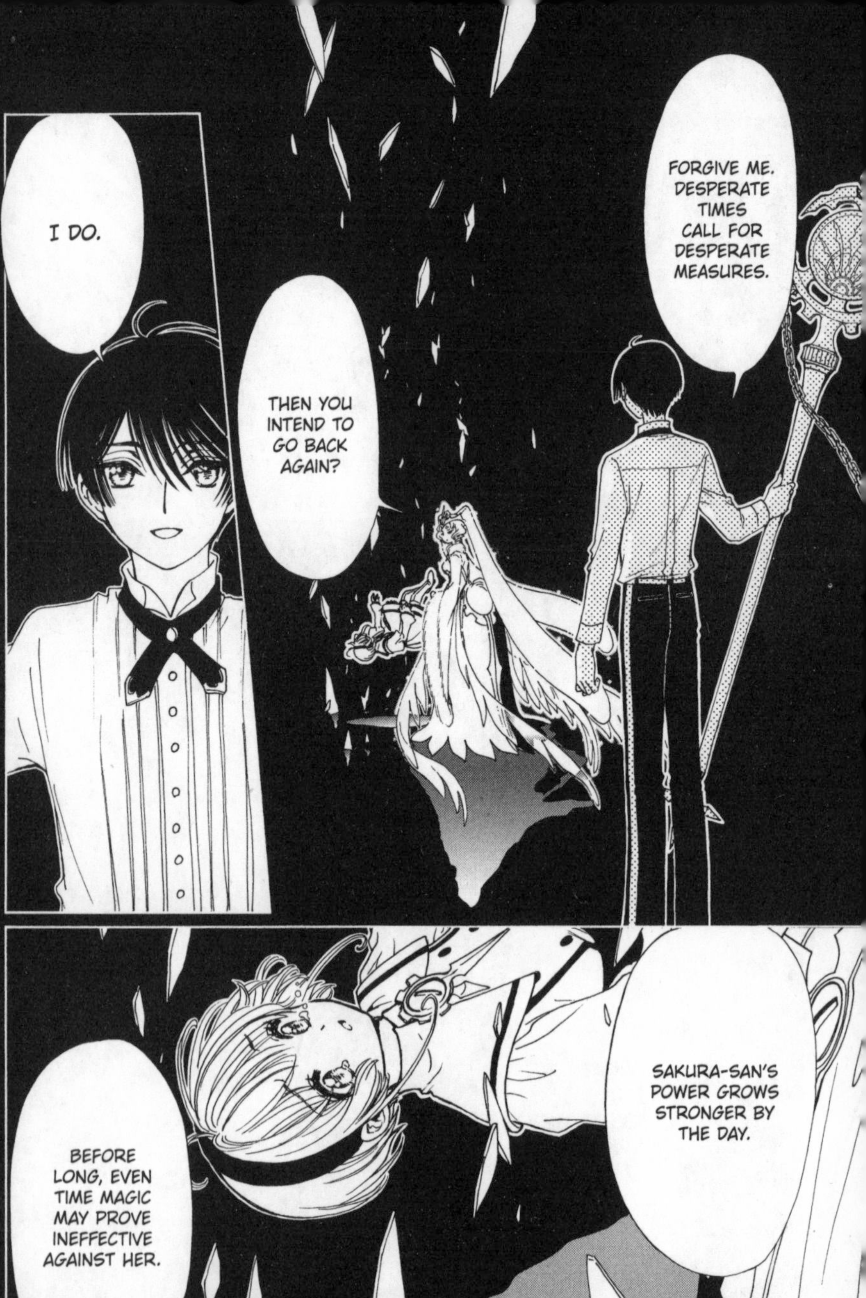
FORGIVE ME. DESPERATE TIMES CALL FOR DESPERATE MEASURES.
THEN YOU INTEND TO GO BACK AGAIN?
I DO.
SAKURA-SAN'S POWER GROWS STRONGER BY THE DAY.
BEFORE LONG, EVEN TIME MAGIC MAY PROVE INEFFECTIVE AGAINST HER.

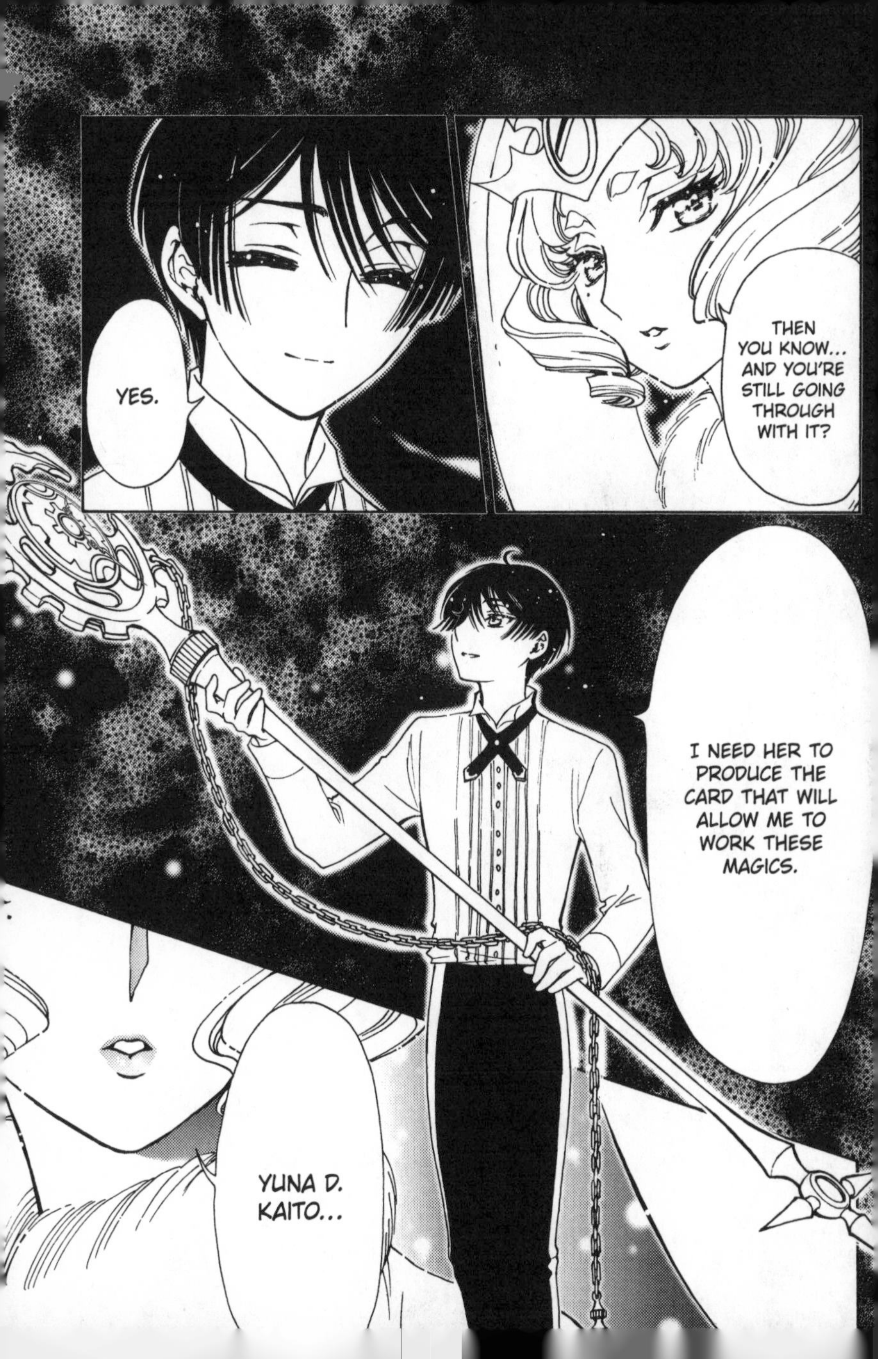
THEN YOU KNOW... AND YOU'RE STILL GOING THROUGH WITH IT?
YES.
I NEED HER TO PRODUCE THE CARD THAT WILL ALLOW ME TO WORK THESE MAGICS.
YUNA D. KAITO...

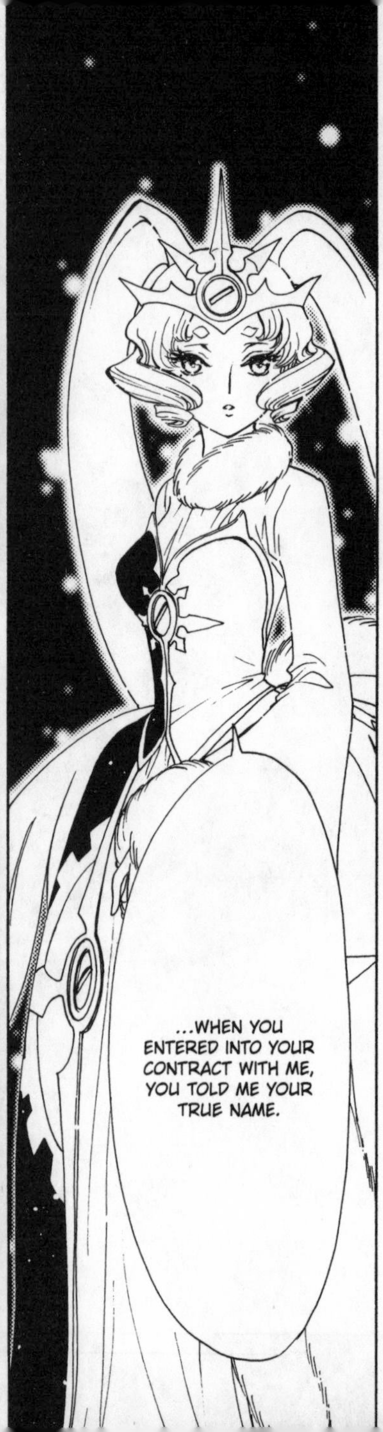
...WHEN YOU ENTERED INTO YOUR CONTRACT WITH ME, YOU TOLD ME YOUR TRUE NAME.

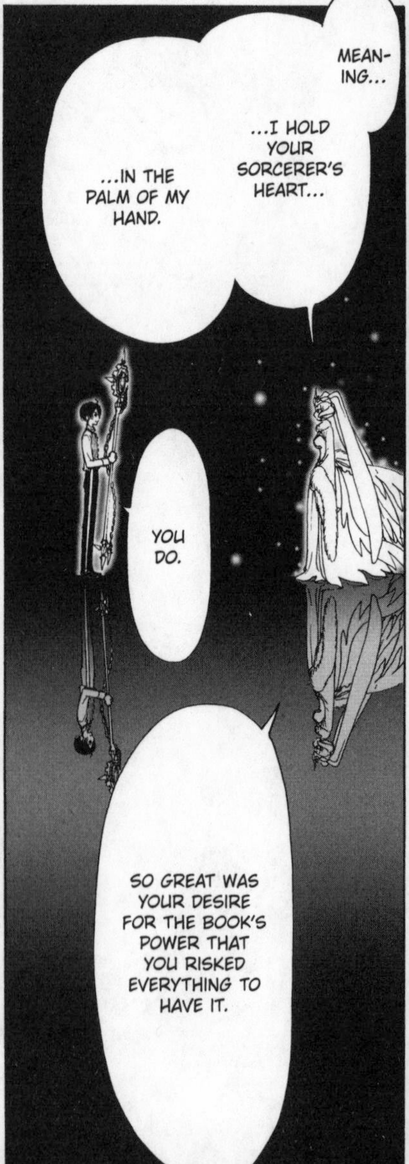
MEAN-ING...
...I HOLD YOUR SORCERER'S HEART...
...IN THE PALM OF MY HAND.
YOU DO.
SO GREAT WAS YOUR DESIRE FOR THE BOOK'S POWER THAT YOU RISKED EVERYTHING TO HAVE IT.

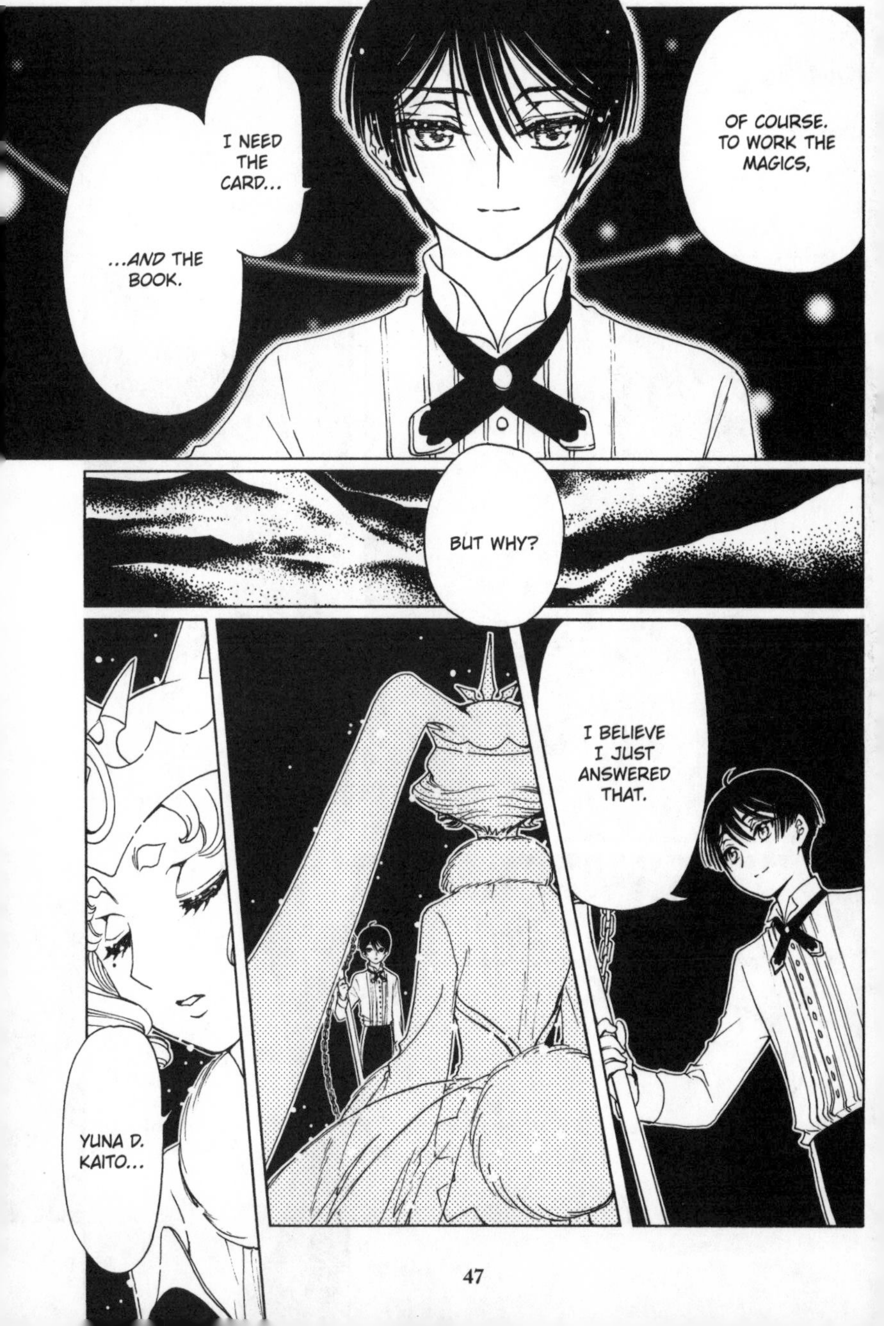
OF COURSE. TO WORK THE MAGICS,
I NEED THE CARD...
...AND THE BOOK.
BUT WHY?
I BELIEVE I JUST ANSWERED THAT.
YUNA D. KAITO...

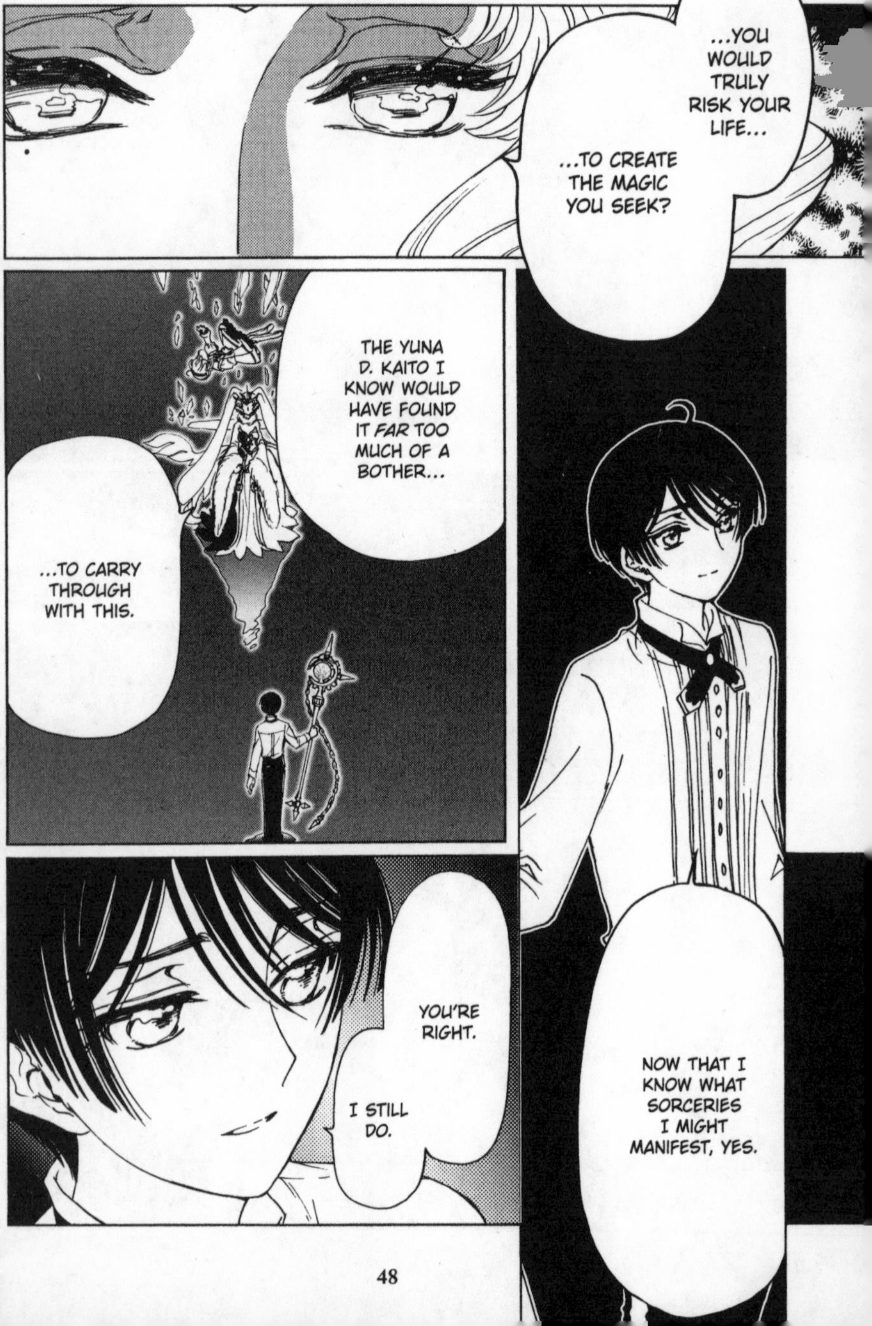

...YOU WOULD TRULY RISK YOUR LIFE...
...TO CREATE THE MAGIC YOU SEEK?
NOW THAT I KNOW WHAT SORCERIES I MIGHT MANIFEST, YES.
THE YUNA D. KAITO I KNOW WOULD HAVE FOUND IT *FAR* TOO MUCH OF A BOTHER...
...TO CARRY THROUGH WITH THIS.
YOU'RE RIGHT.
I STILL DO.

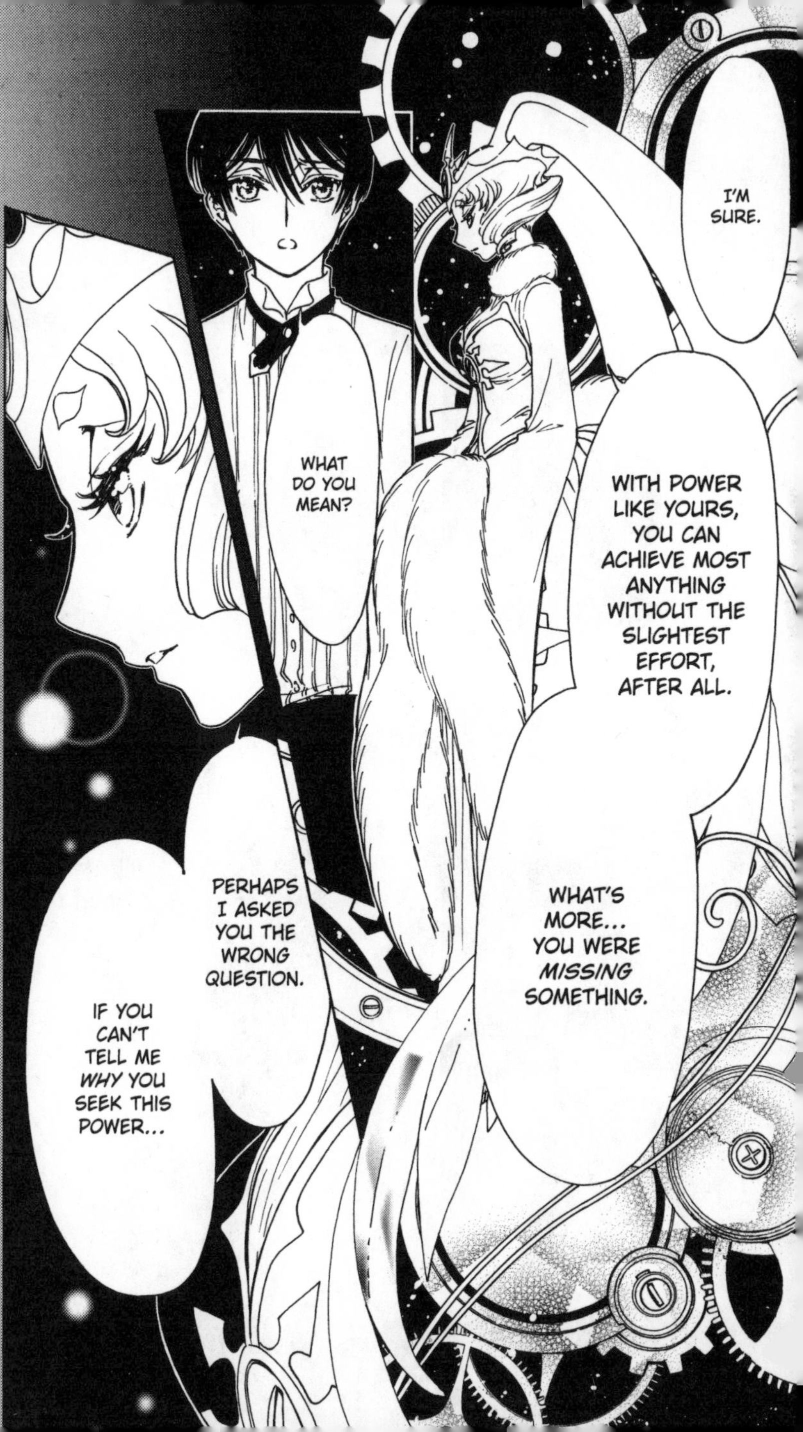
I'M SURE.
WITH POWER LIKE YOURS, YOU CAN ACHIEVE MOST ANYTHING WITHOUT THE SLIGHTEST EFFORT, AFTER ALL.
WHAT'S MORE... YOU WERE *MISSING* SOMETHING.
WHAT DO YOU MEAN?
PERHAPS I ASKED YOU THE WRONG QUESTION.
IF YOU CAN'T TELL ME *WHY* YOU SEEK THIS POWER...

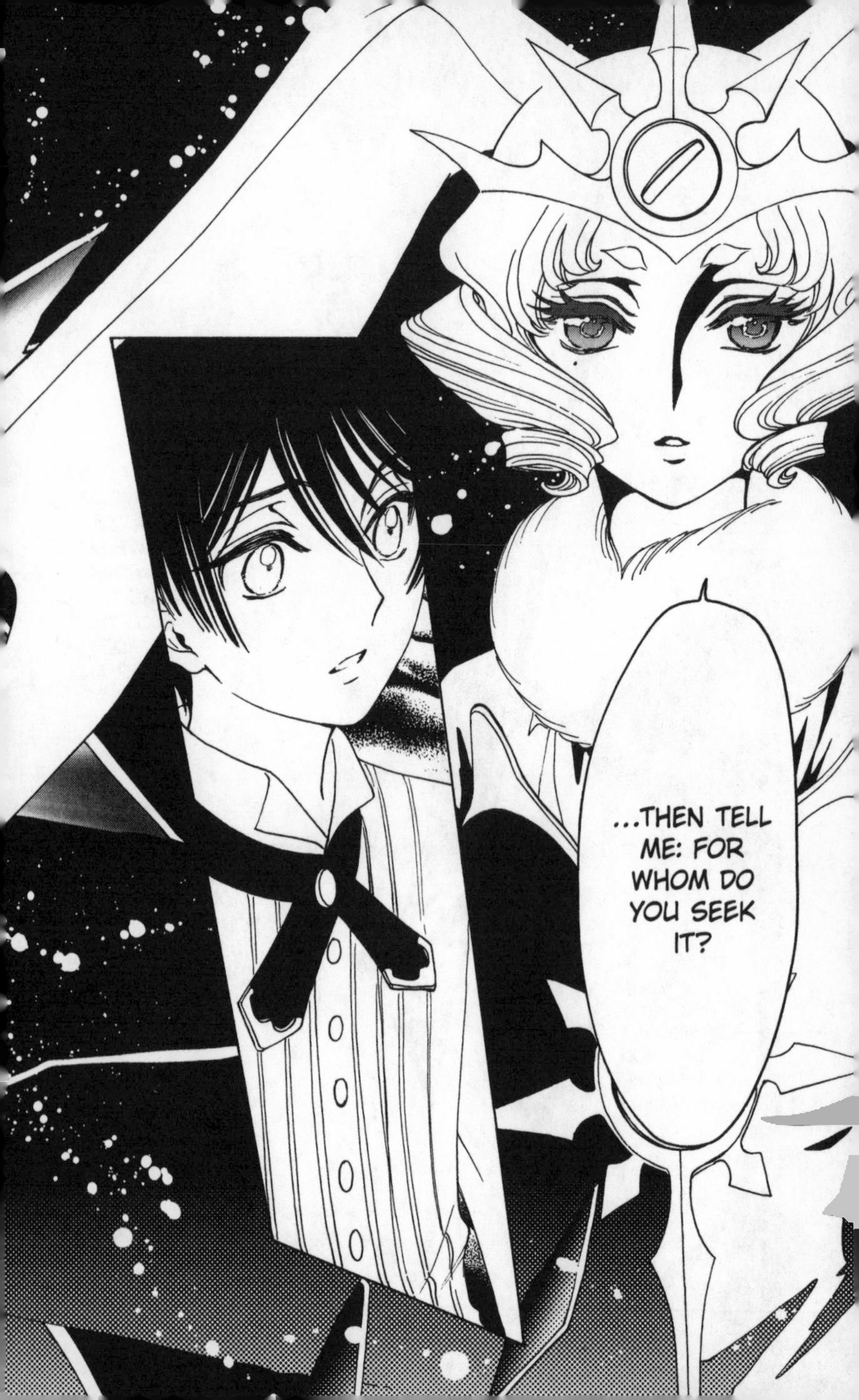
...THEN TELL ME: FOR WHOM DO YOU SEEK IT?

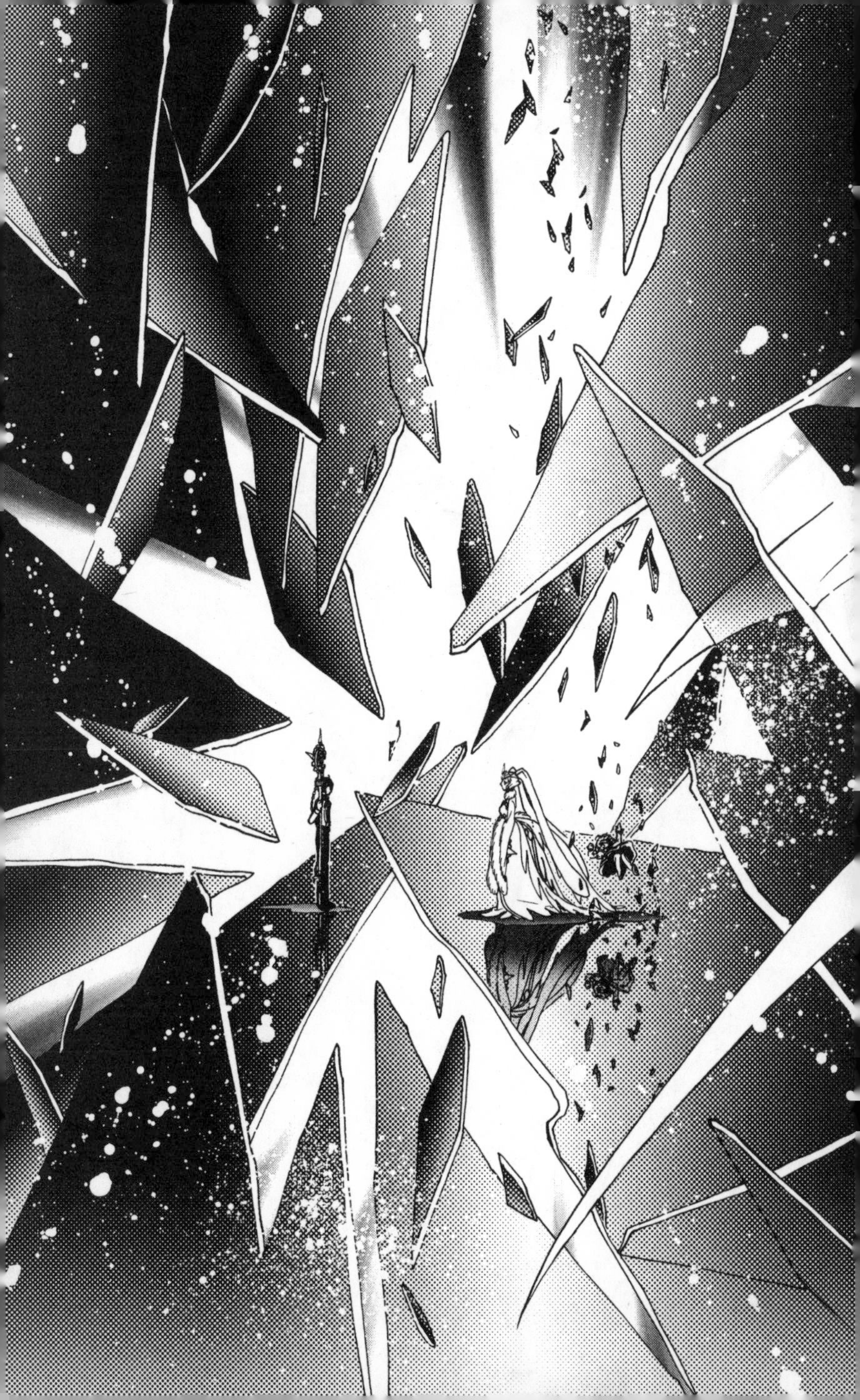

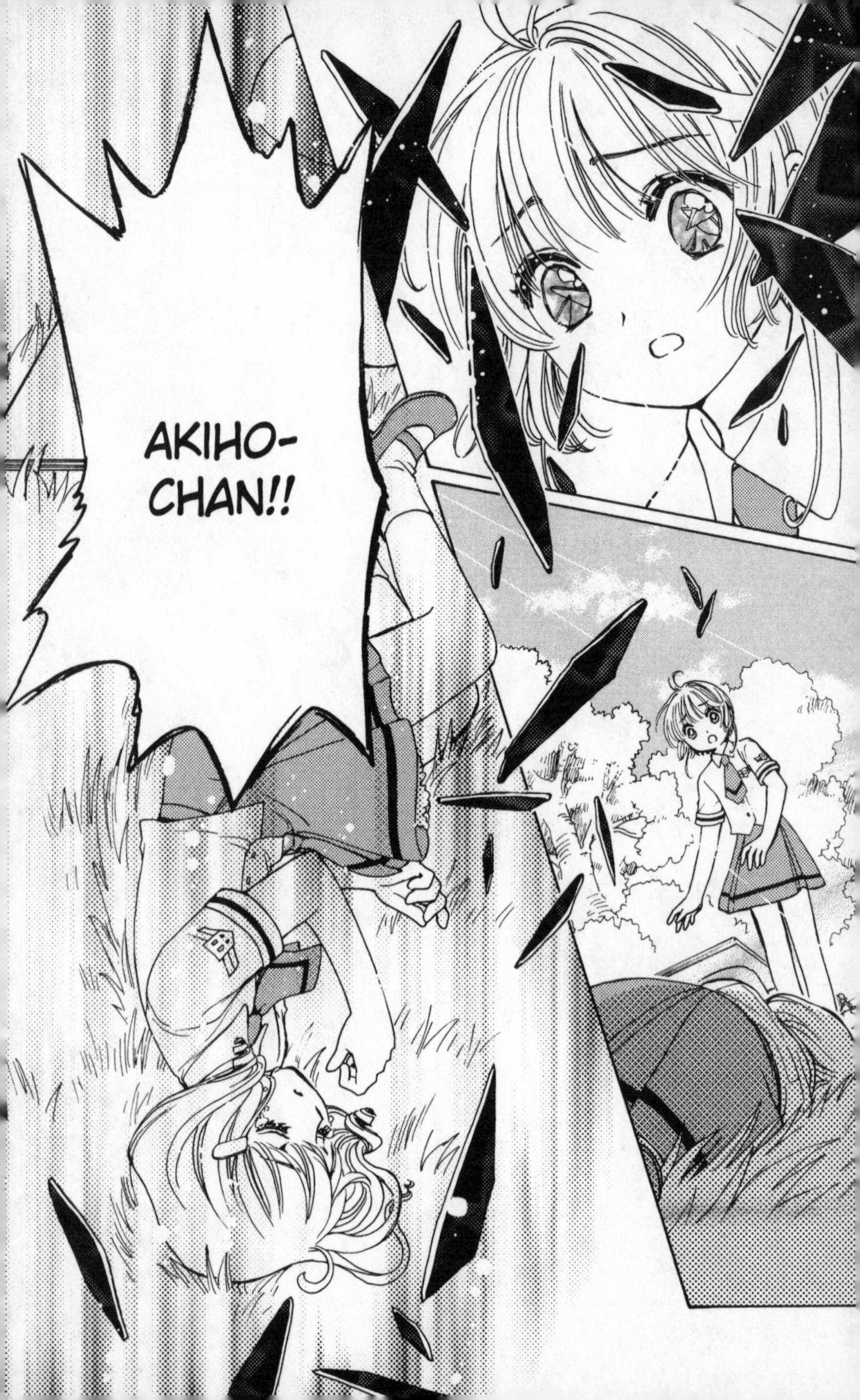
AKIHO-CHAN!!

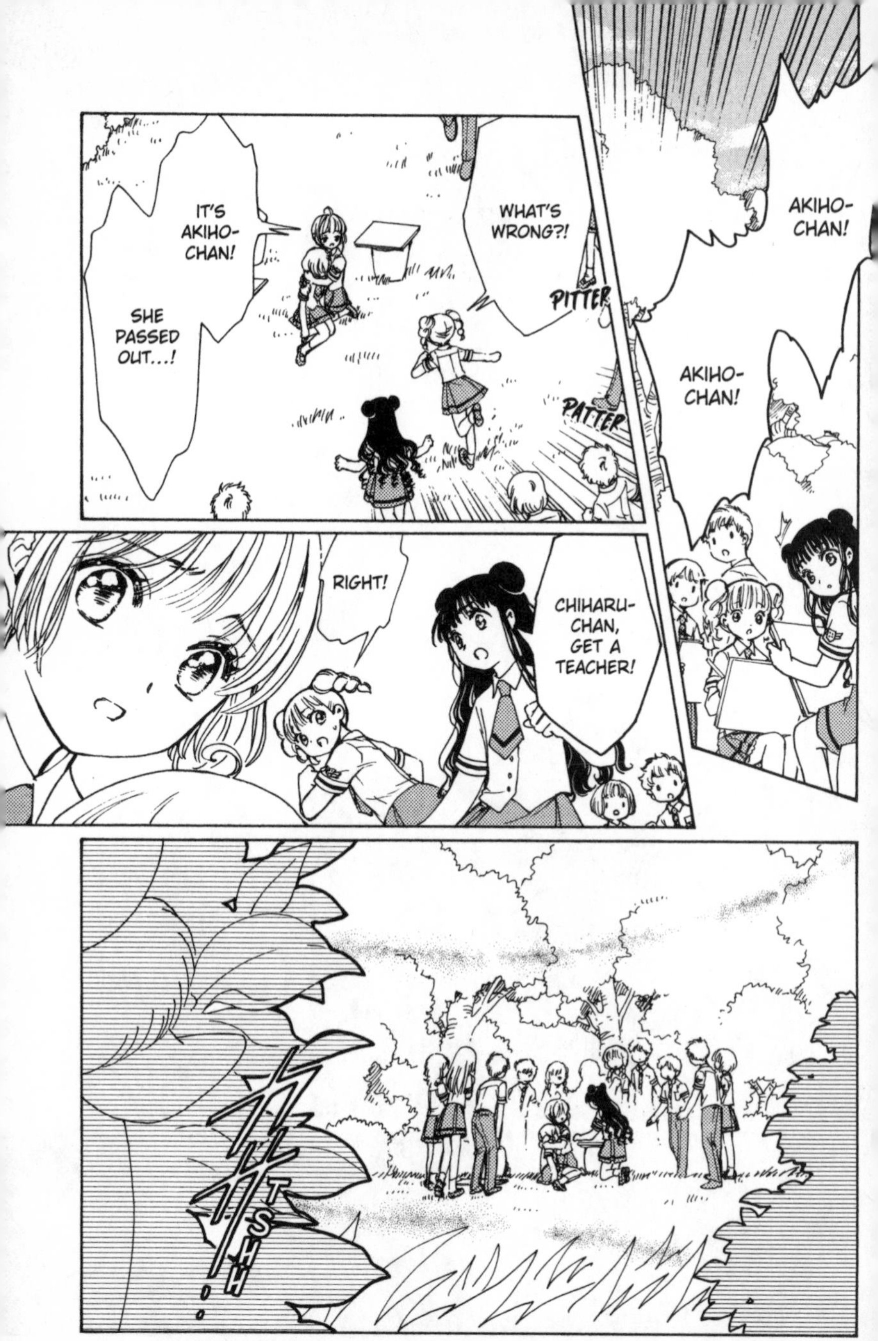
AKIHO-CHAN!
AKIHO-CHAN!
WHAT'S WRONG?!
PITTER
PATTER
IT'S AKIHO-CHAN!
SHE PASSED OUT...!
CHIHARU-CHAN, GET A TEACHER!
RIGHT!
TSHH!!

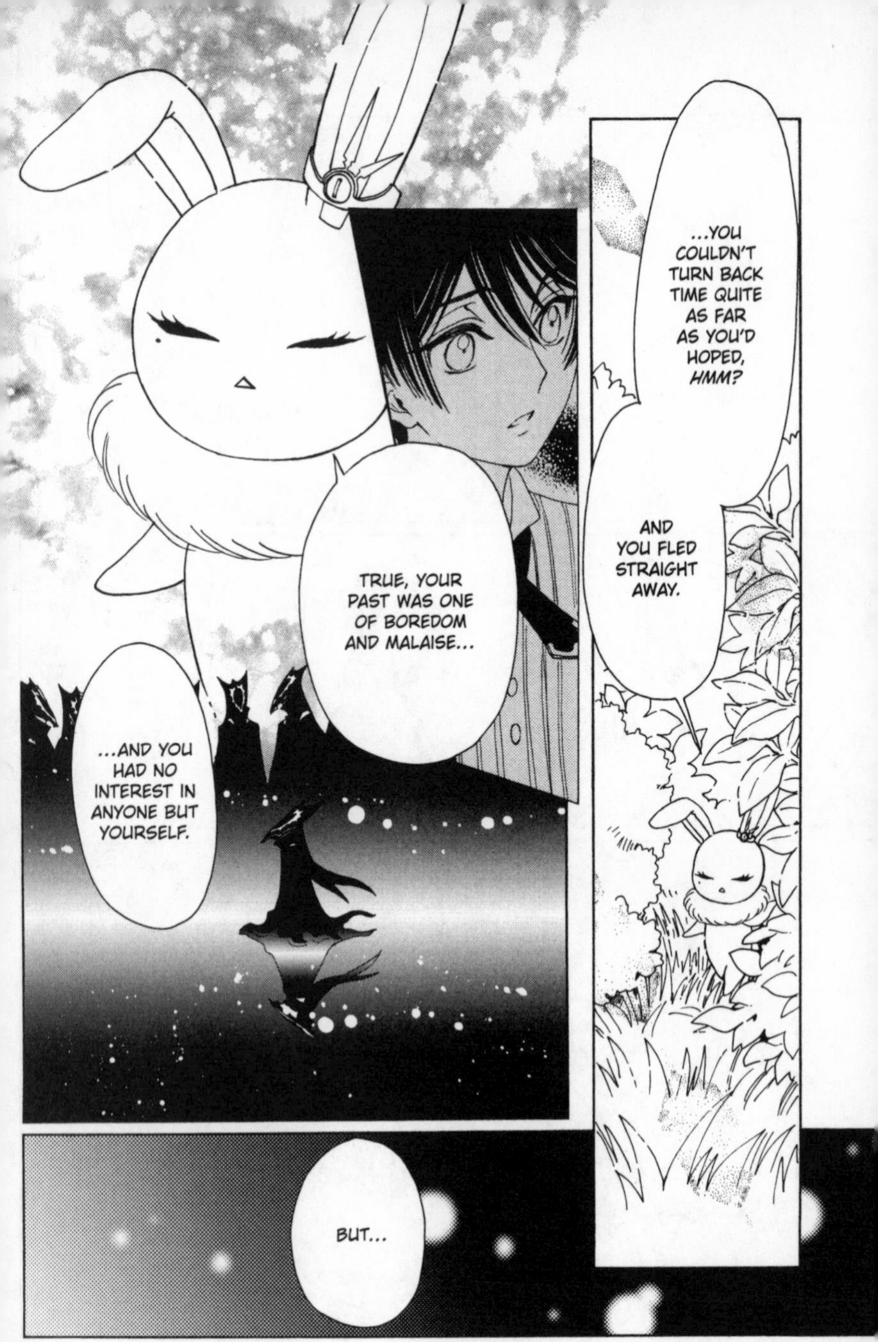
...YOU COULDN'T TURN BACK TIME QUITE AS FAR AS YOU'D HOPED, *HMM?*
AND YOU FLED STRAIGHT AWAY.
TRUE, YOUR PAST WAS ONE OF BOREDOM AND MALAISE...
...AND YOU HAD NO INTEREST IN ANYONE BUT YOURSELF.
BUT...

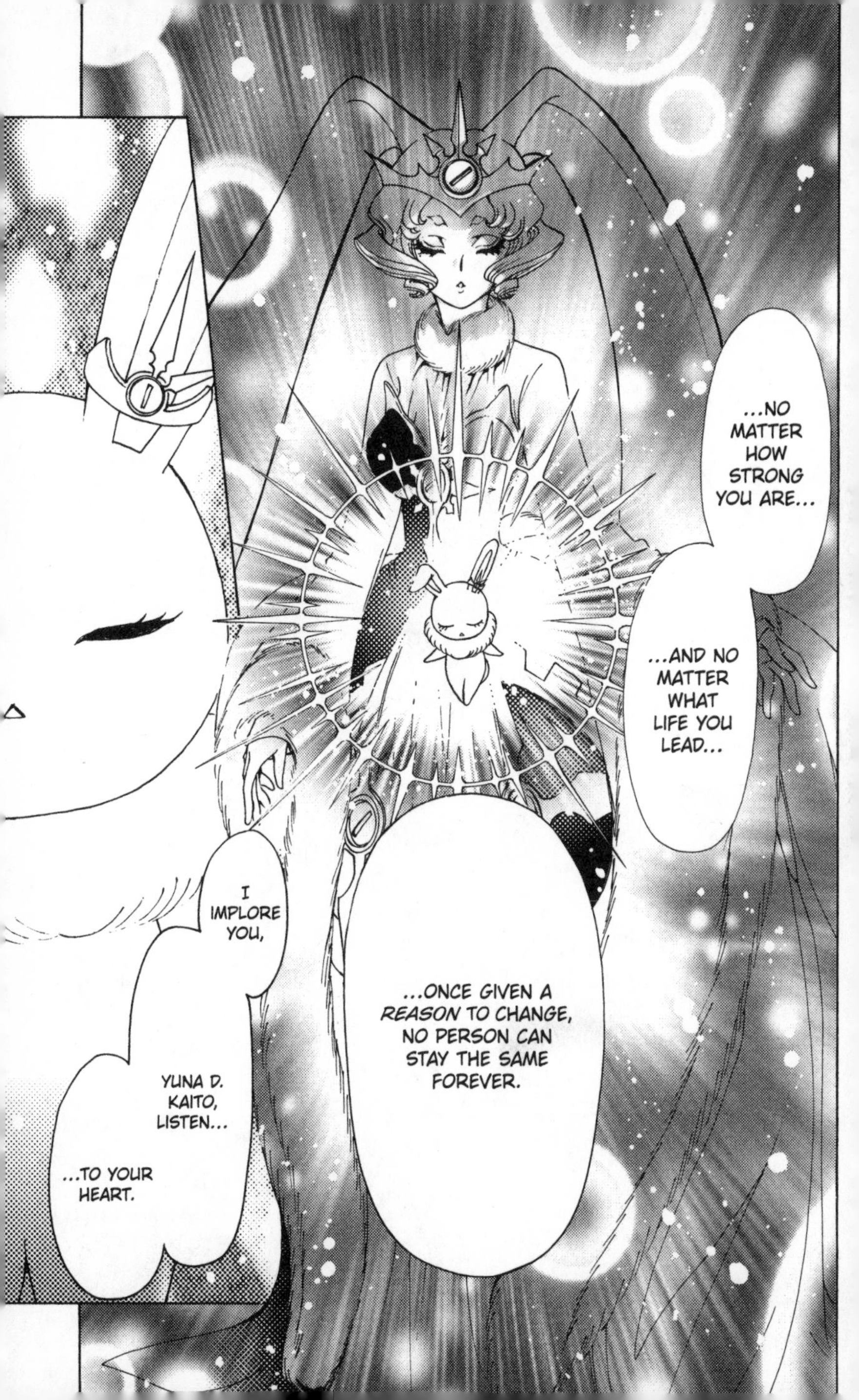
...NO MATTER HOW STRONG YOU ARE...
...AND NO MATTER WHAT LIFE YOU LEAD...
...ONCE GIVEN A *REASON* TO CHANGE, NO PERSON CAN STAY THE SAME FOREVER.
I IMPLORE YOU,
YUNA D. KAITO, LISTEN...
...TO YOUR HEART.

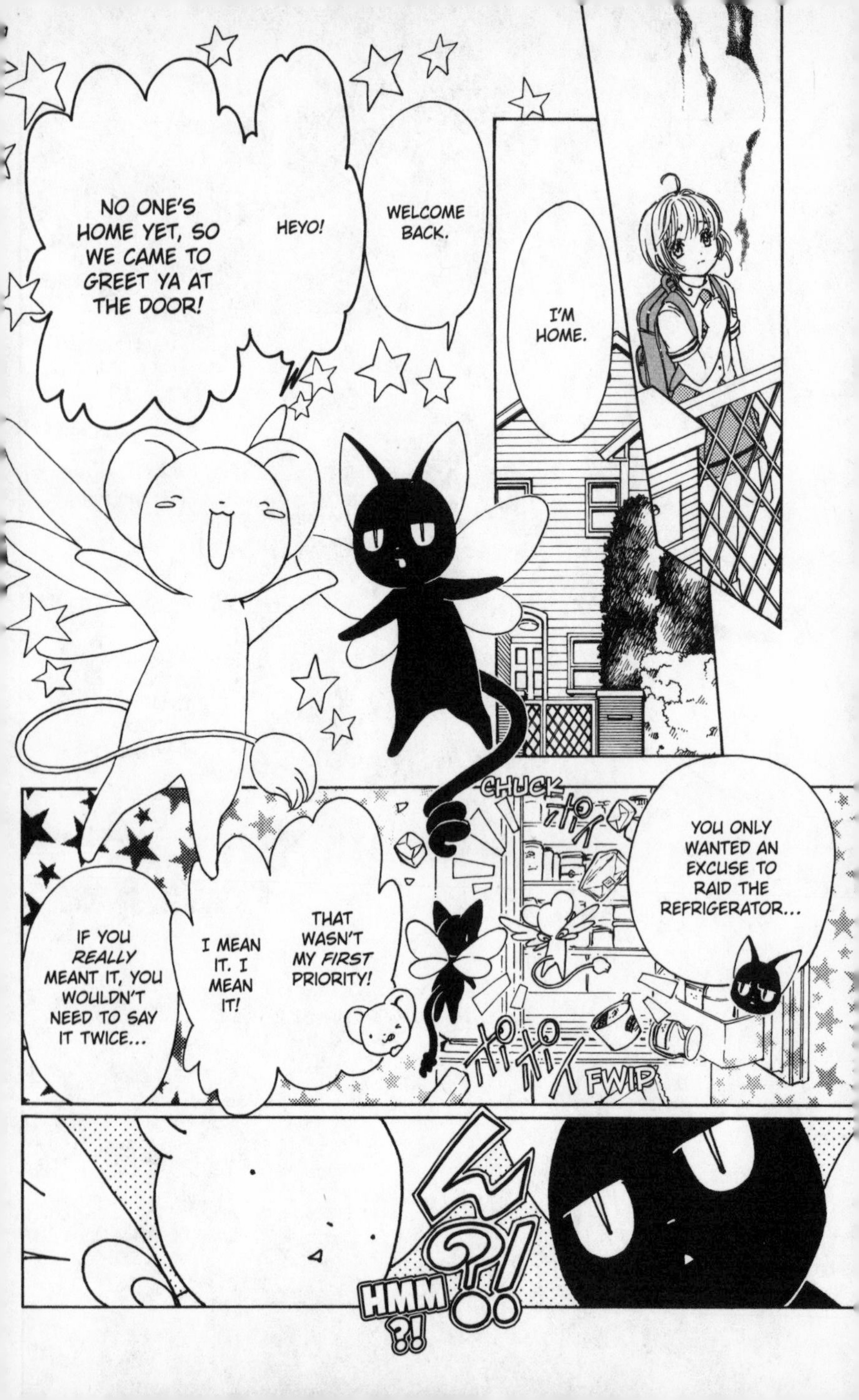
I'M HOME.
WELCOME BACK.
HEYO!
NO ONE'S HOME YET, SO WE CAME TO GREET YA AT THE DOOR!
YOU ONLY WANTED AN EXCUSE TO RAID THE REFRIGERATOR...
CHUCK
ポイ
ポイポイ
FWIP
THAT WASN'T MY *FIRST* PRIORITY!
I MEAN IT. I MEAN IT!
IF YOU *REALLY* MEANT IT, YOU WOULDN'T NEED TO SAY IT TWICE...
HMM?!

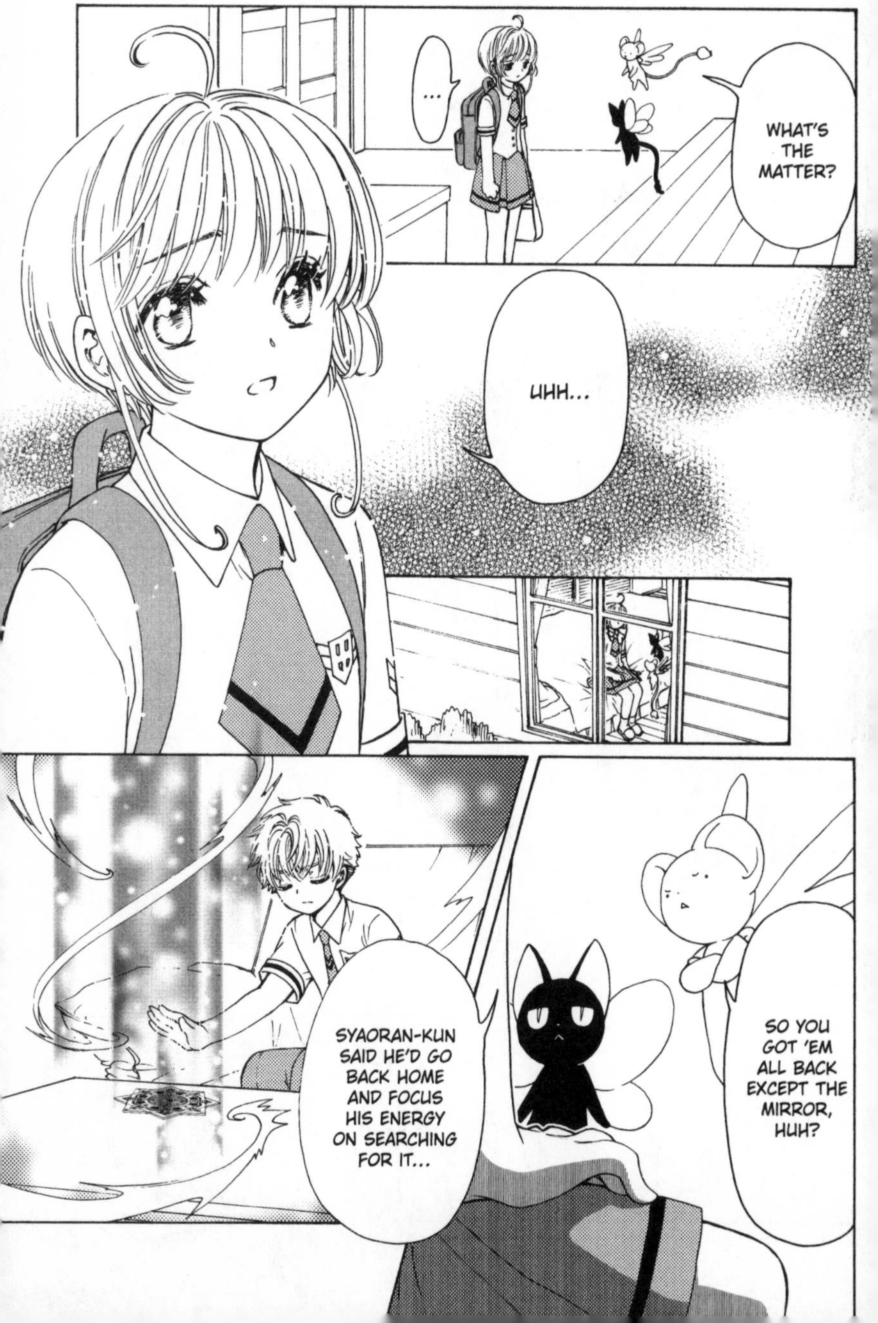
WHAT'S THE MATTER?
...
UHH...
SO YOU GOT 'EM ALL BACK EXCEPT THE MIRROR, HUH?
SYAORAN-KUN SAID HE'D GO BACK HOME AND FOCUS HIS ENERGY ON SEARCHING FOR IT...

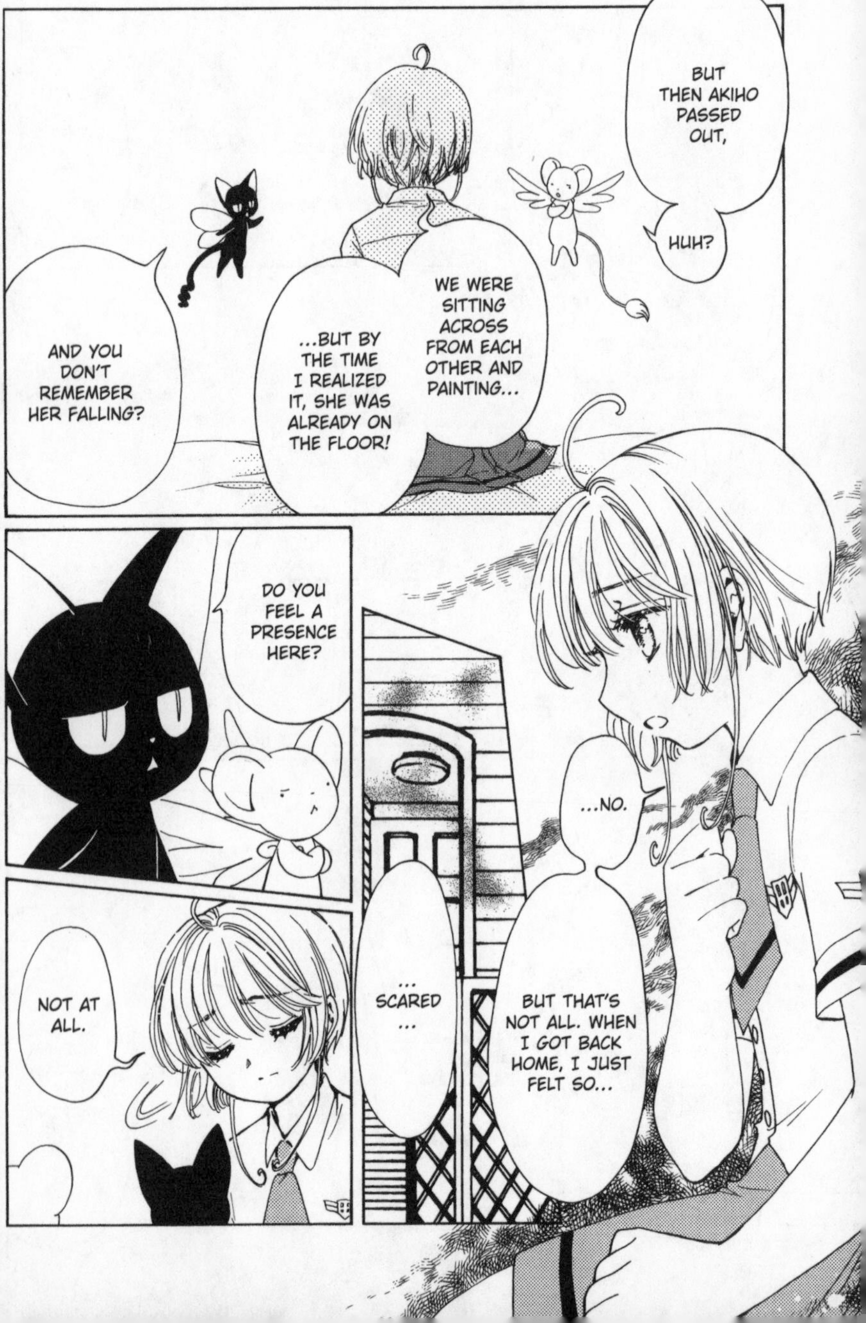
BUT THEN AKIHO PASSED OUT,
HUH?
WE WERE SITTING ACROSS FROM EACH OTHER AND PAINTING...
...BUT BY THE TIME I REALIZED IT, SHE WAS ALREADY ON THE FLOOR!
AND YOU DON'T REMEMBER HER FALLING?
...NO.
BUT THAT'S NOT ALL. WHEN I GOT BACK HOME, I JUST FELT SO...
...SCARED...
DO YOU FEEL A PRESENCE HERE?
NOT AT ALL.

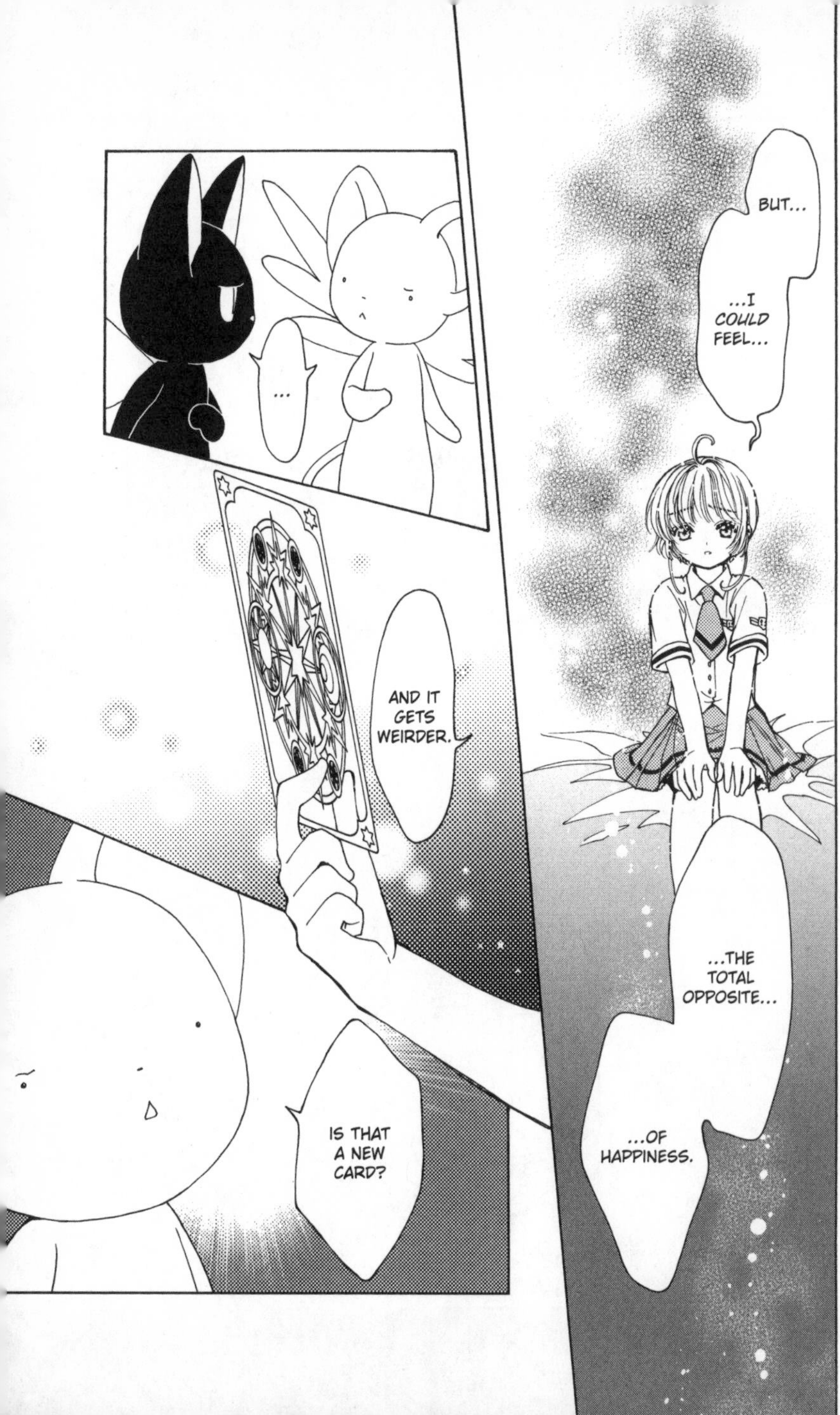
BUT...
...I COULD FEEL...
...THE TOTAL OPPOSITE...
...OF HAPPINESS.
...
AND IT GETS WEIRDER.
IS THAT A NEW CARD?

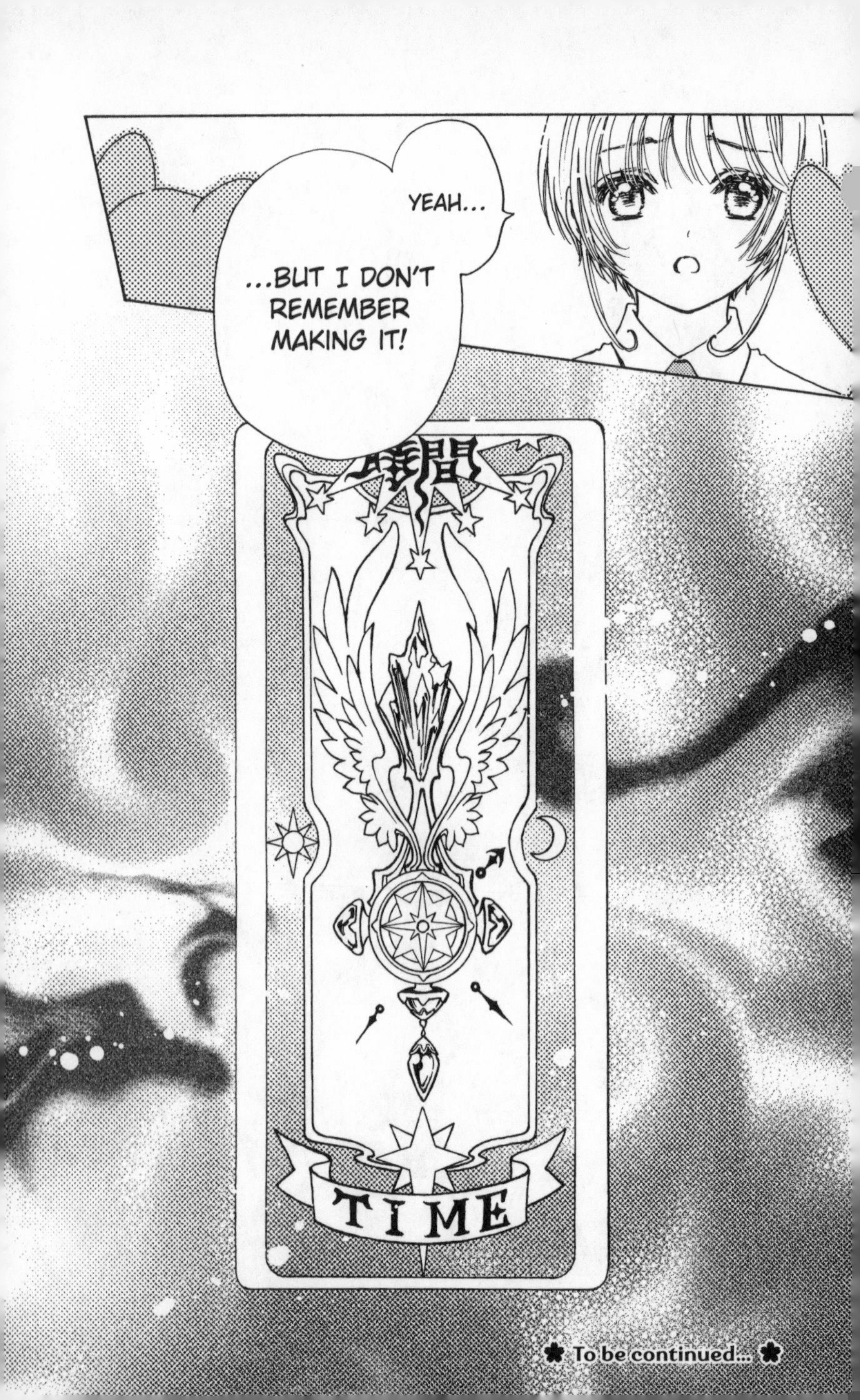
YEAH...
...BUT I DON'T REMEMBER MAKING IT!
TIME
To be continued...

Cardcaptor Sakura
CLEAR CARD

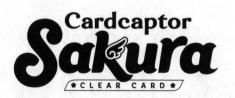

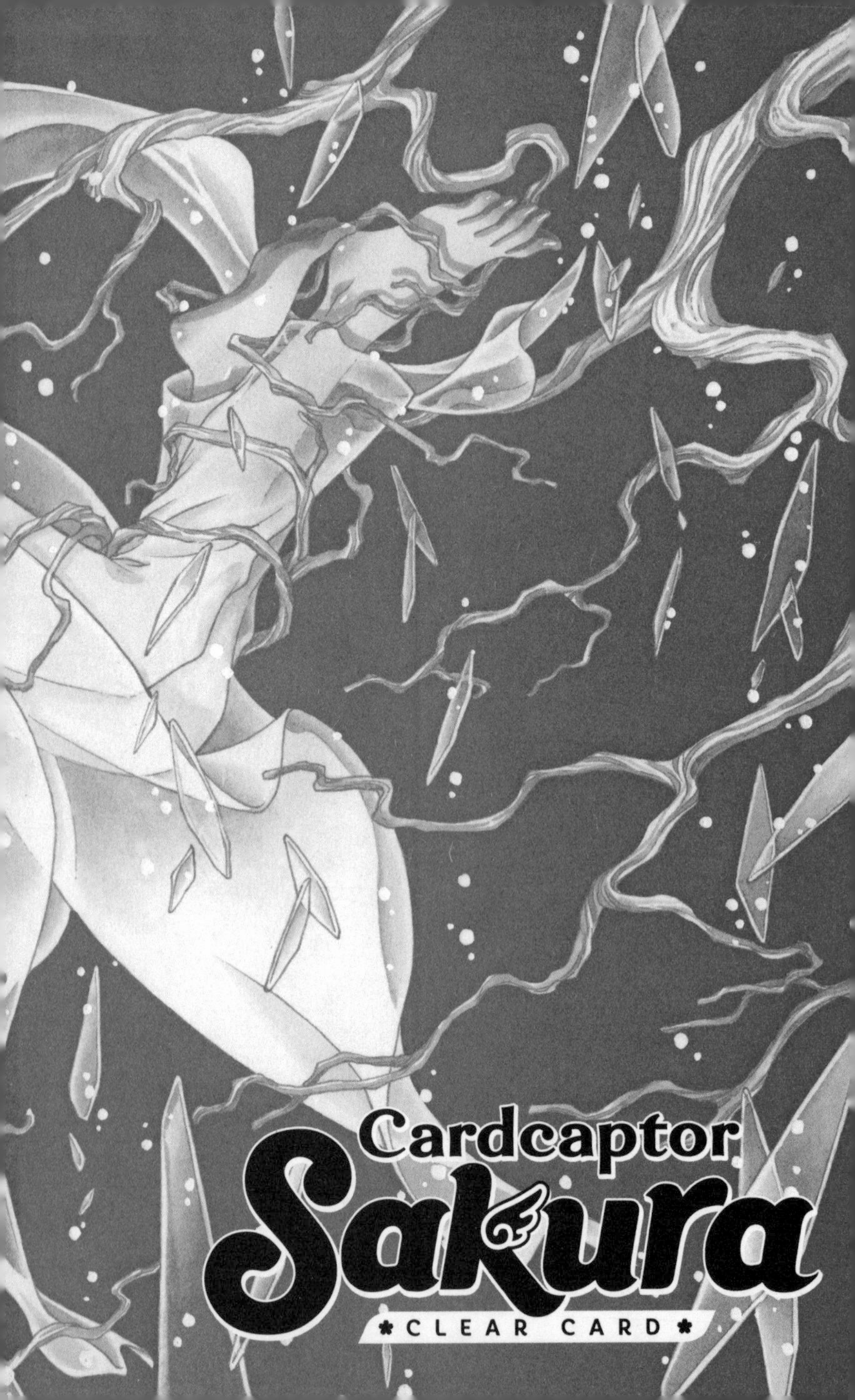
Cardcaptor
Sakura
CLEAR CARD

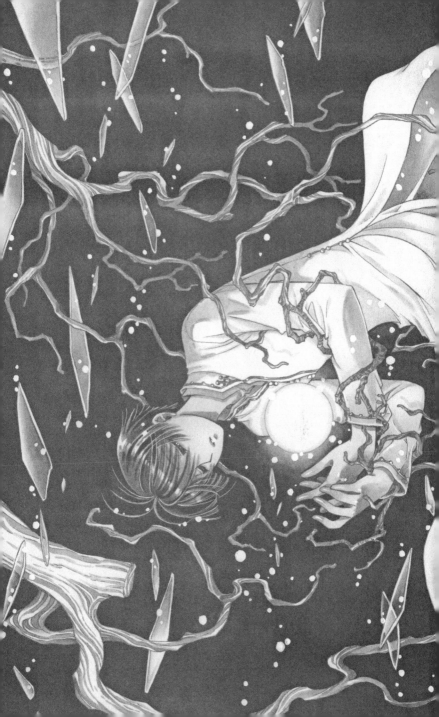

Cardcaptor Sakura
CLEAR CARD

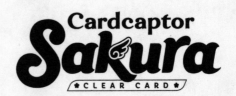

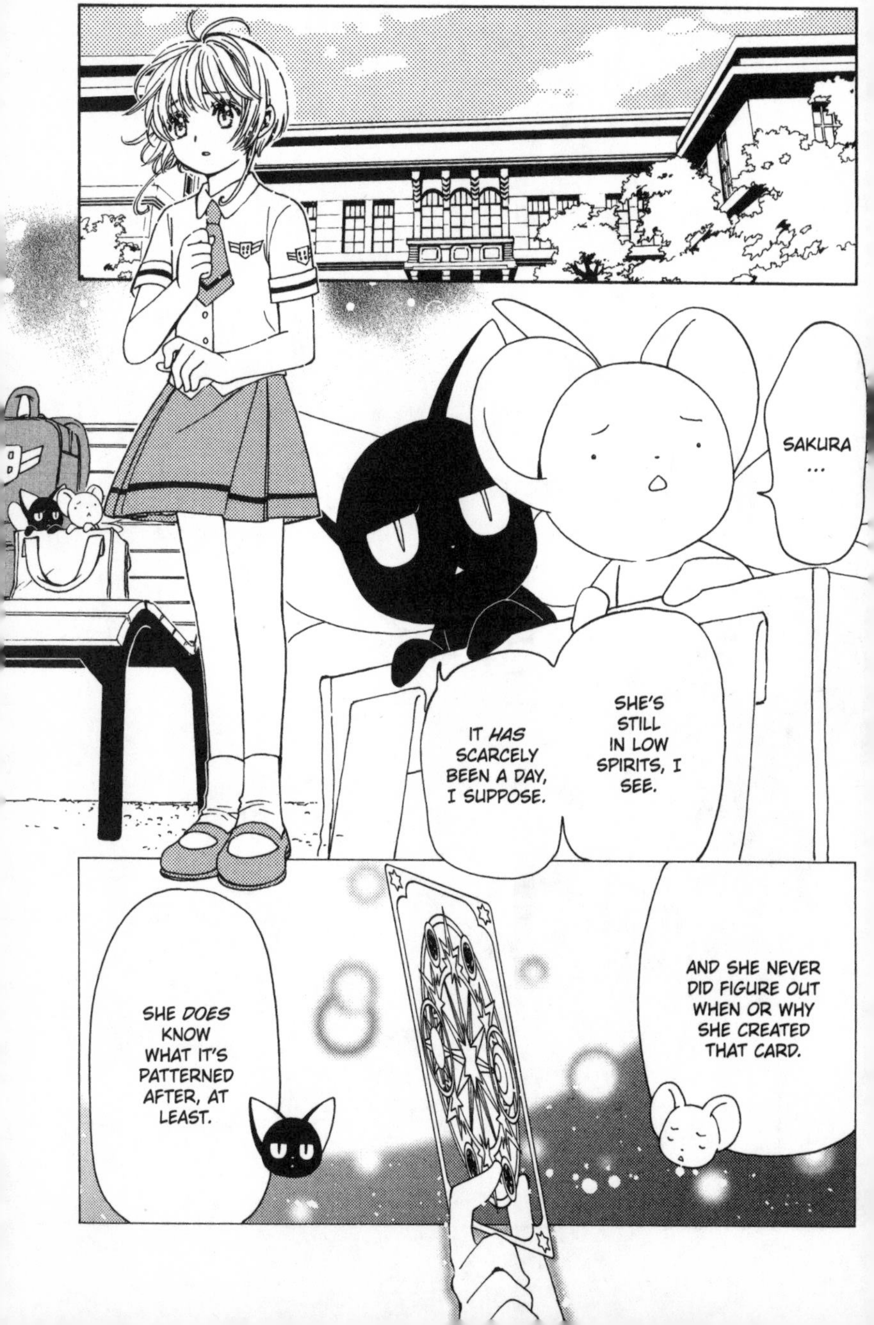
SAKURA …
SHE'S STILL IN LOW SPIRITS, I SEE.
IT *HAS* SCARCELY BEEN A DAY, I SUPPOSE.
AND SHE NEVER DID FIGURE OUT WHEN OR WHY SHE CREATED THAT CARD.
SHE *DOES* KNOW WHAT IT'S PATTERNED AFTER, AT LEAST.

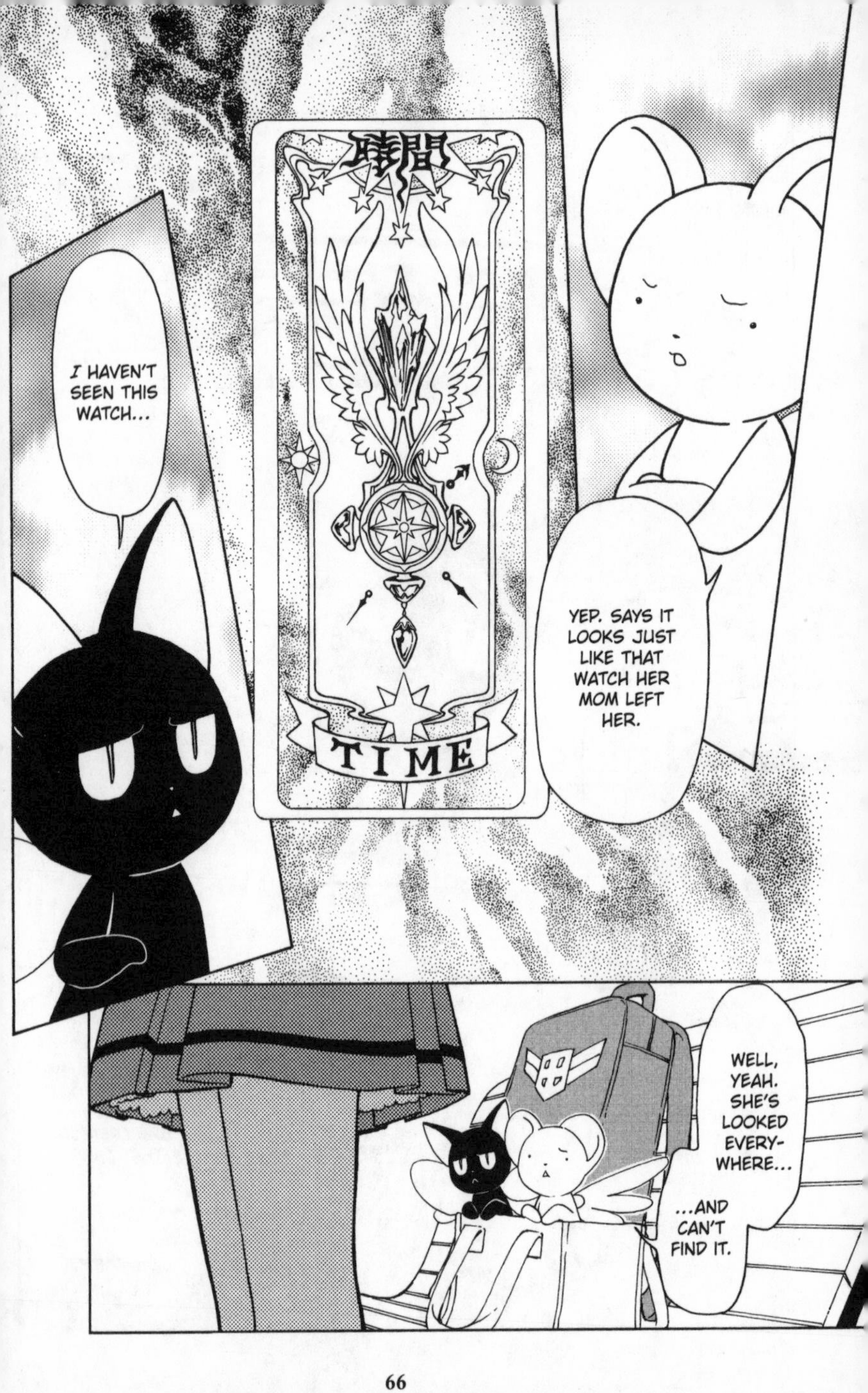
I HAVEN'T SEEN THIS WATCH...
YEP. SAYS IT LOOKS JUST LIKE THAT WATCH HER MOM LEFT HER.
時間
TIME
WELL, YEAH. SHE'S LOOKED EVERY-WHERE...
...AND CAN'T FIND IT.

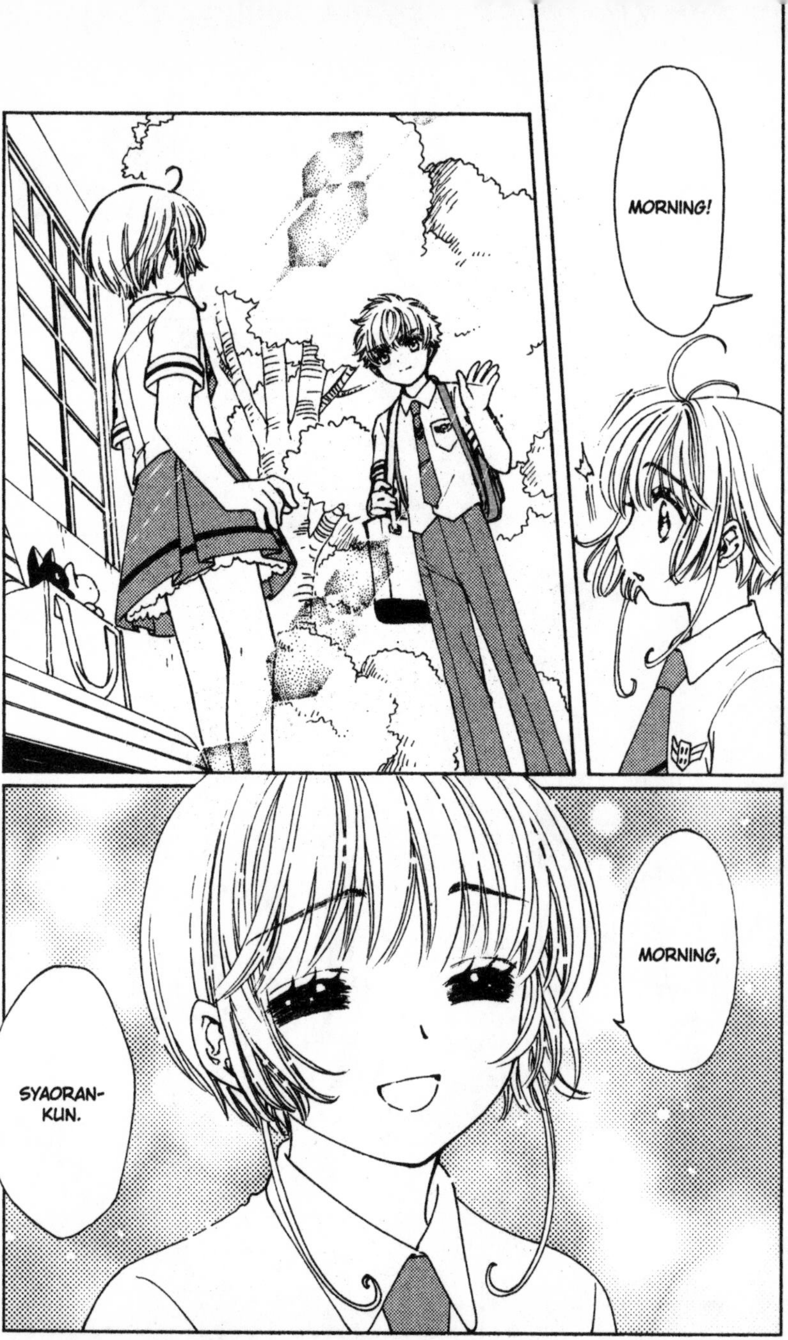
MORNING!
MORNING,
SYAORAN-KUN.

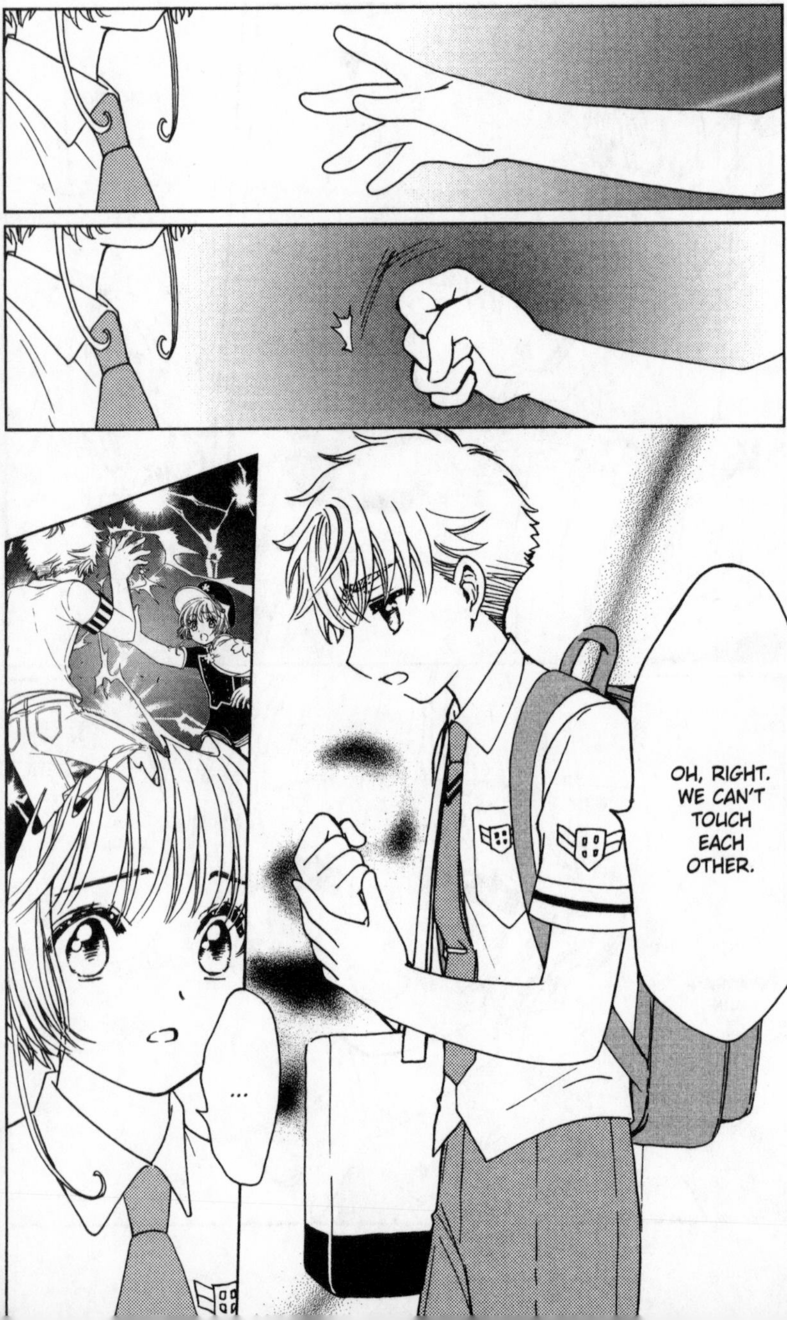
OH, RIGHT. WE CAN'T TOUCH EACH OTHER.
...

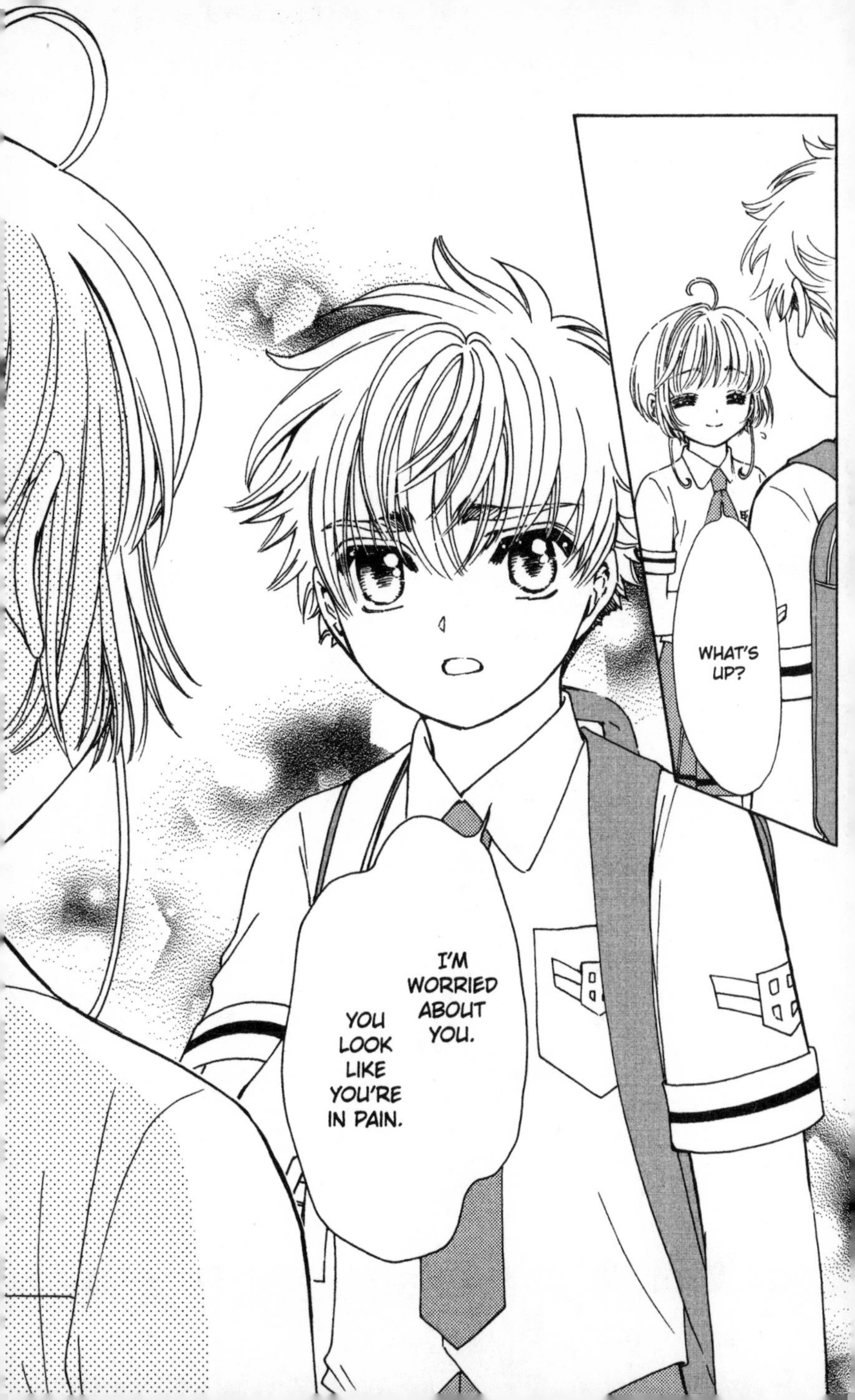
WHAT'S UP?
I'M WORRIED ABOUT YOU.
YOU LOOK LIKE YOU'RE IN PAIN.

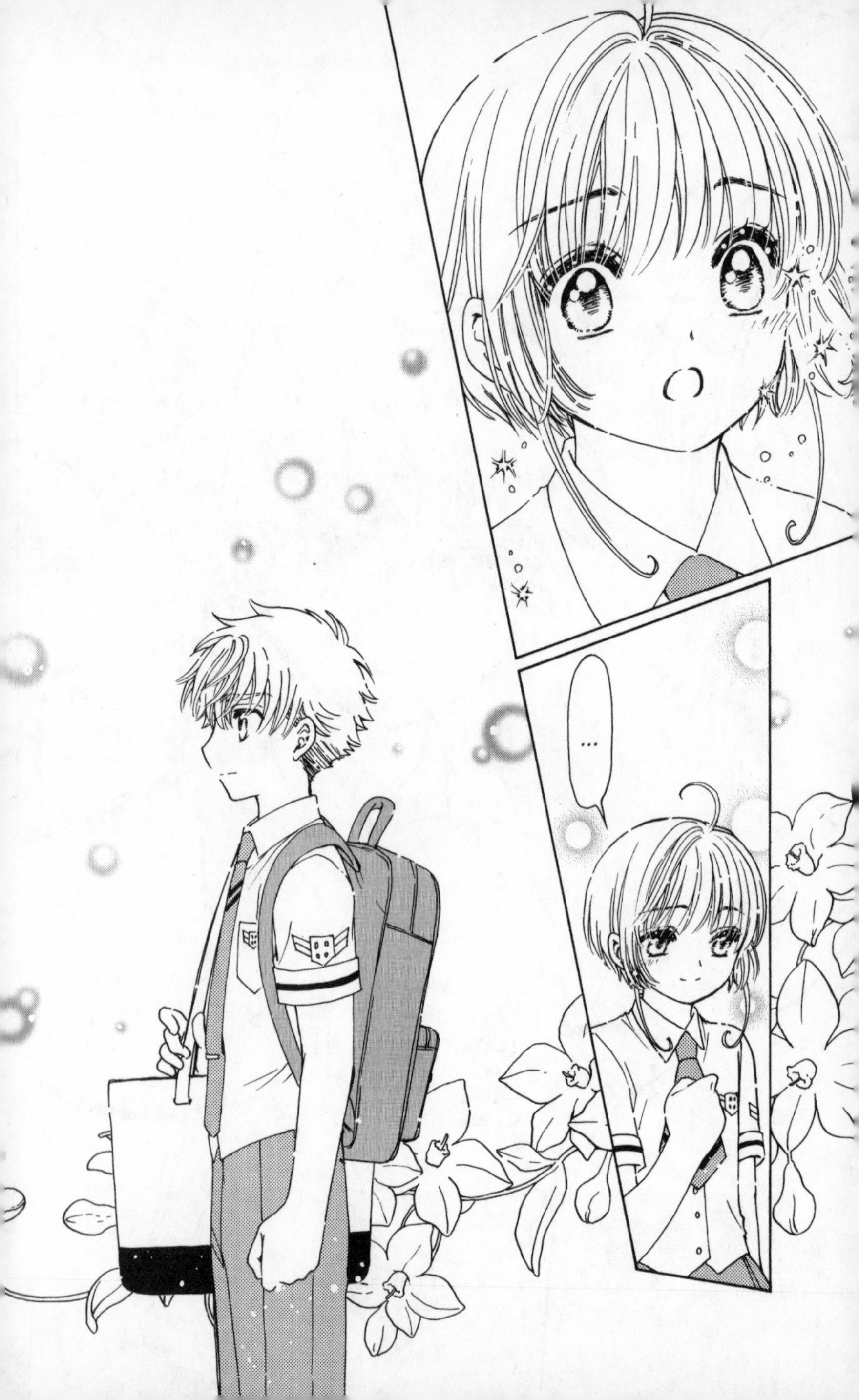
...

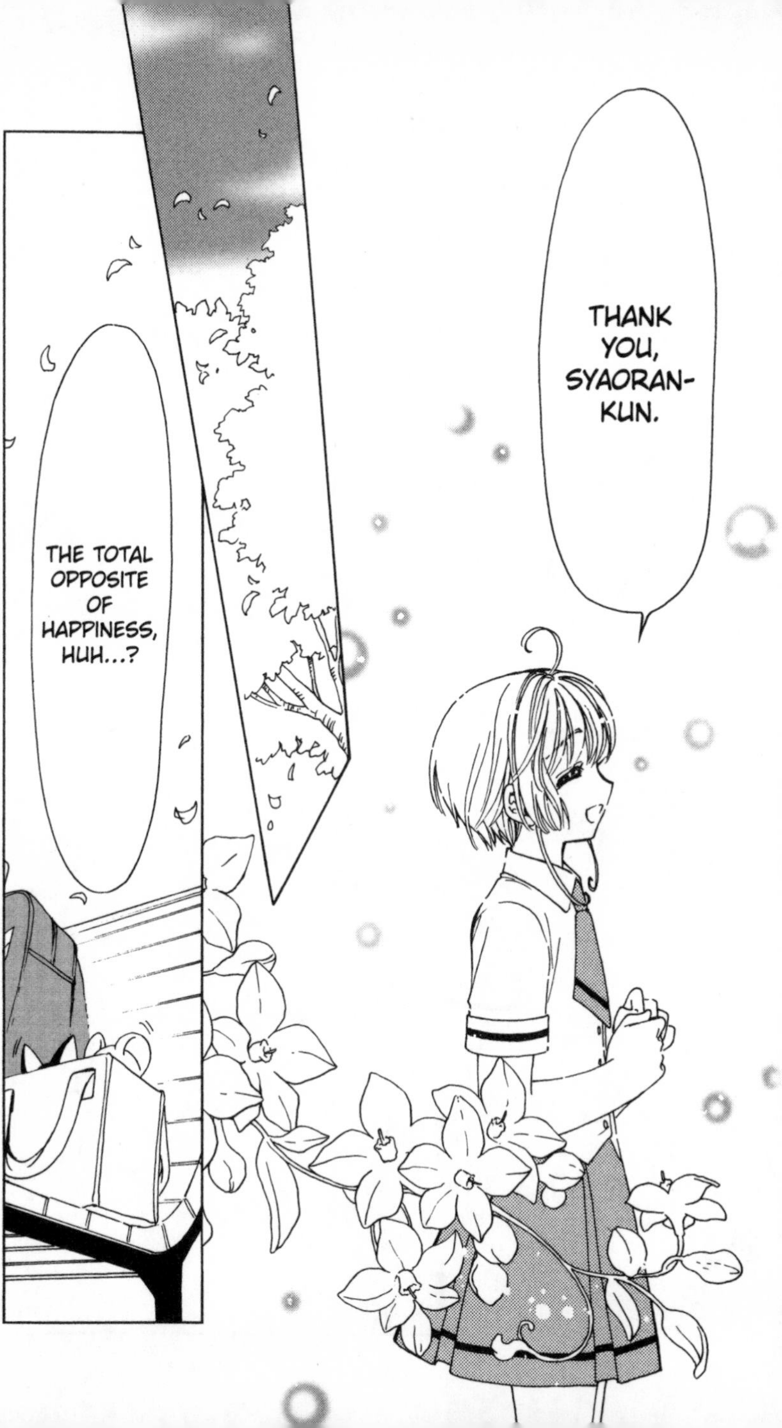
THANK YOU, SYAORAN-KUN.
THE TOTAL OPPOSITE OF HAPPINESS, HUH...?

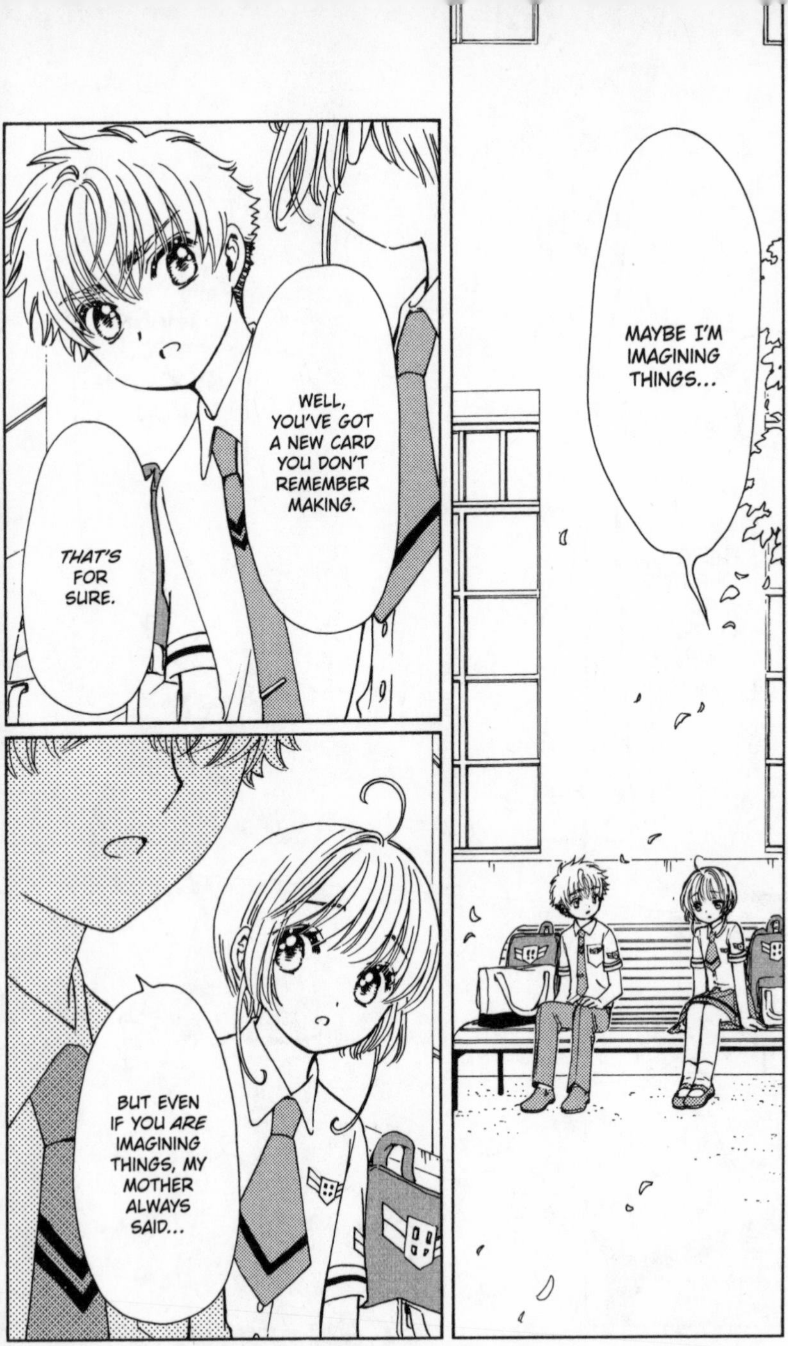
MAYBE I'M IMAGINING THINGS...
WELL, YOU'VE GOT A NEW CARD YOU DON'T REMEMBER MAKING.
THAT'S FOR SURE.
BUT EVEN IF YOU *ARE* IMAGINING THINGS, MY MOTHER ALWAYS SAID...

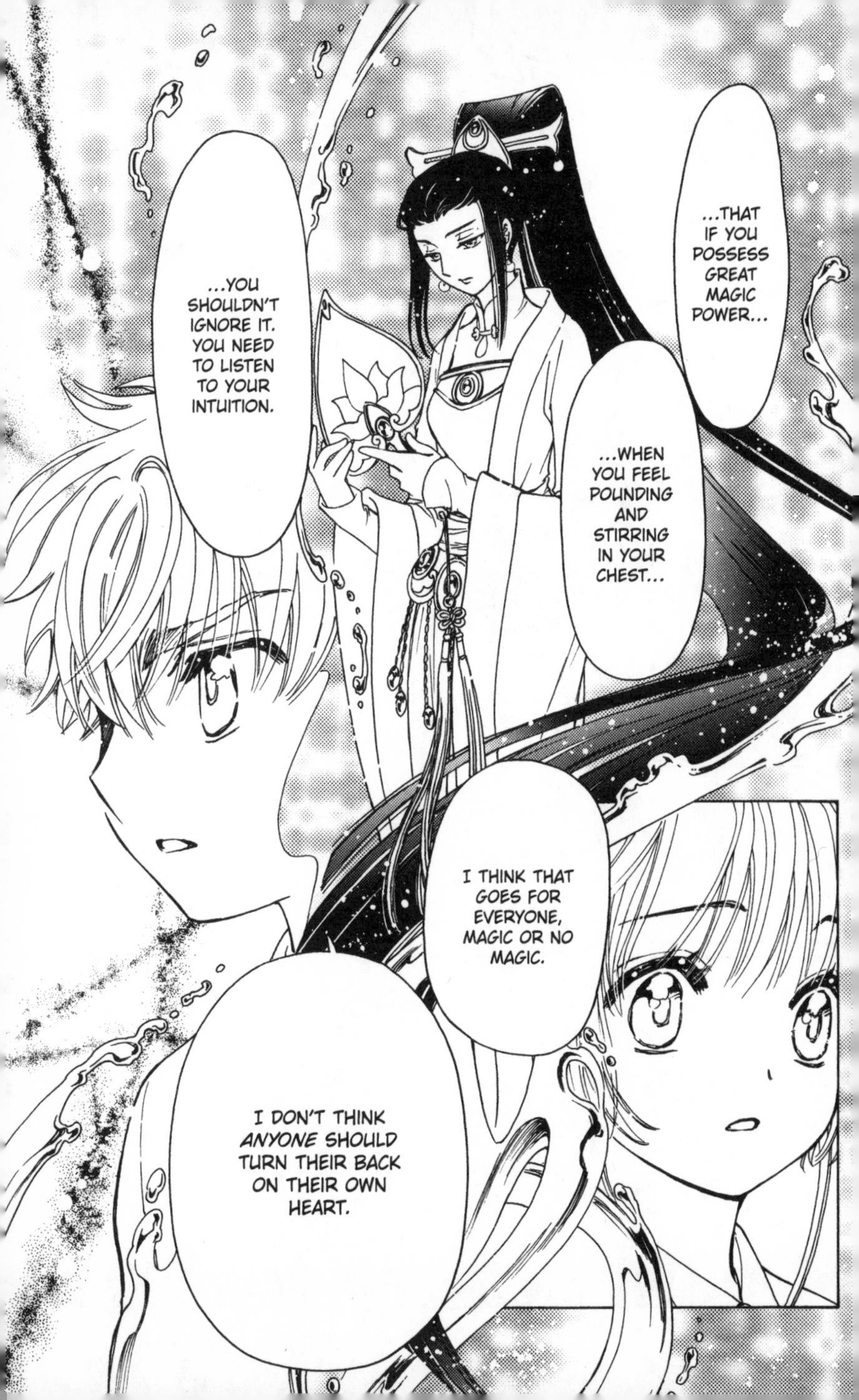
...THAT IF YOU POSSESS GREAT MAGIC POWER...
...WHEN YOU FEEL POUNDING AND STIRRING IN YOUR CHEST...
...YOU SHOULDN'T IGNORE IT. YOU NEED TO LISTEN TO YOUR INTUITION.
I THINK THAT GOES FOR EVERYONE, MAGIC OR NO MAGIC.
I DON'T THINK *ANYONE* SHOULD TURN THEIR BACK ON THEIR OWN HEART.

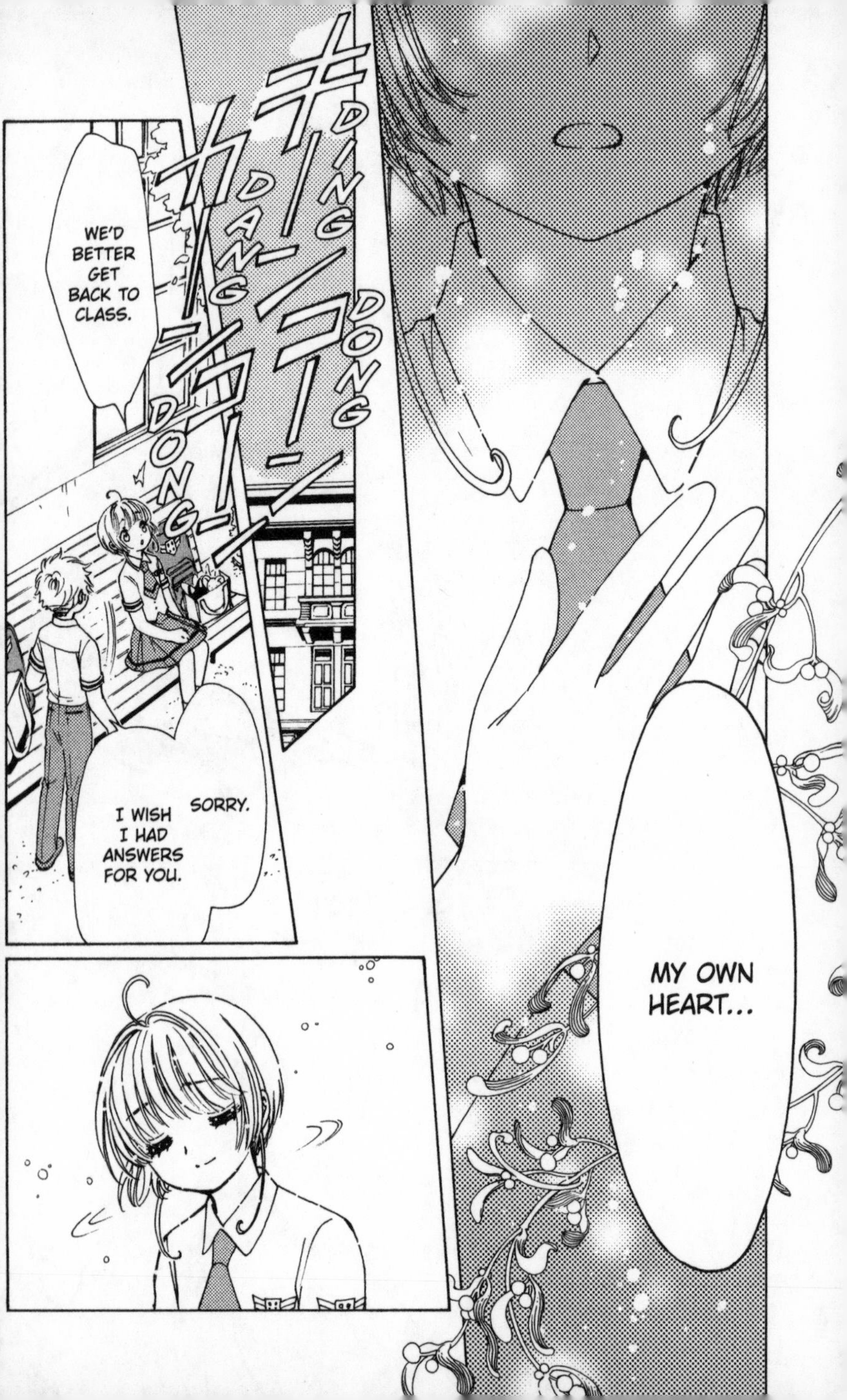
MY OWN HEART...
DING DONG
DANG DONG
WE'D BETTER GET BACK TO CLASS.
SORRY.
I WISH I HAD ANSWERS FOR YOU.

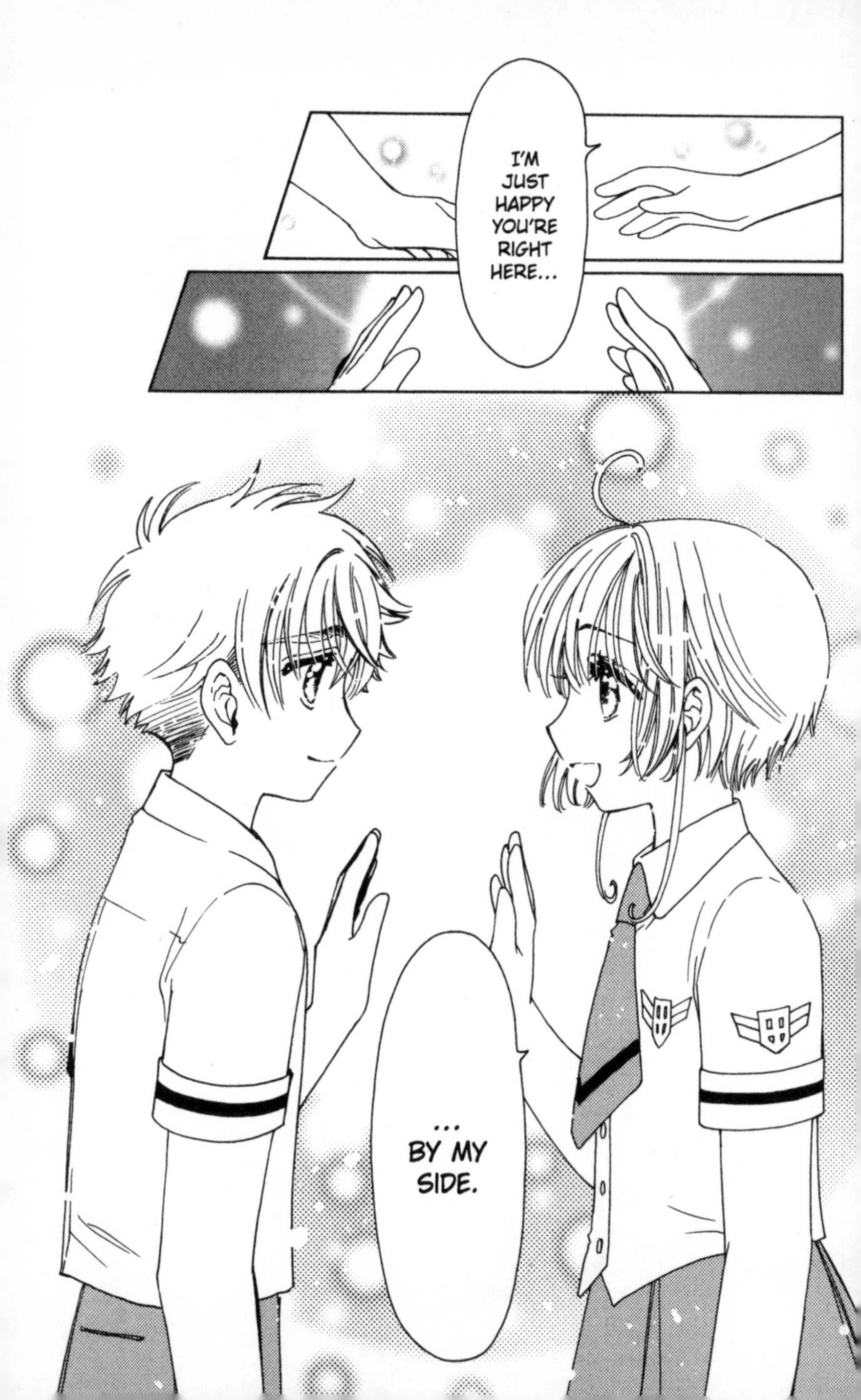
I'M JUST HAPPY YOU'RE RIGHT HERE...
...BY MY SIDE.

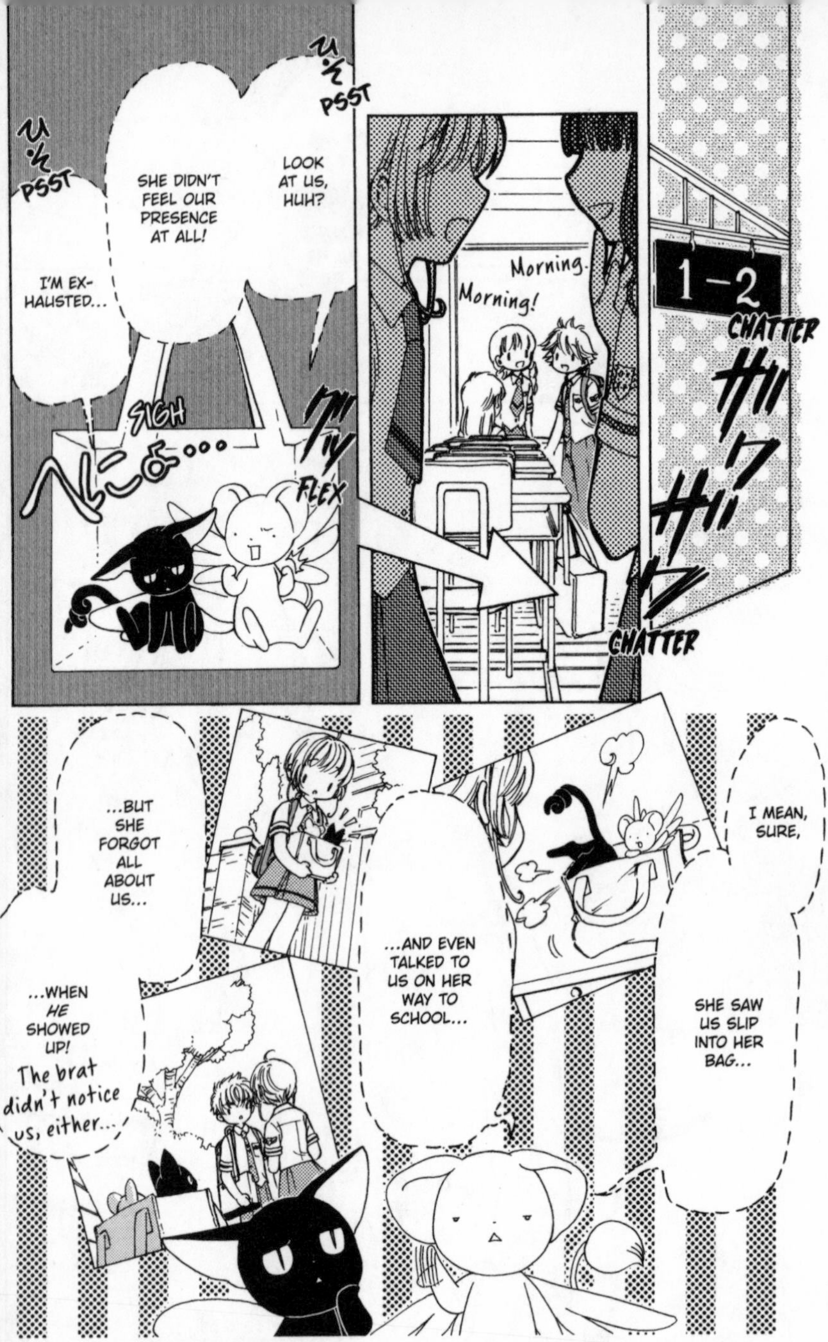
1—2
CHATTER
ザワザワ
CHATTER
Morning.
Morning!
ひそ
PSST
LOOK AT US, HUH?
SHE DIDN'T FEEL OUR PRESENCE AT ALL!
ひそ
PSST
I'M EX- HAUSTED...
SIGH
へにょ・・・
FLEX
I MEAN, SURE,
SHE SAW US SLIP INTO HER BAG...
...AND EVEN TALKED TO US ON HER WAY TO SCHOOL...
...BUT SHE FORGOT ALL ABOUT US...
...WHEN *HE* SHOWED UP!
The brat didn't notice us, either...

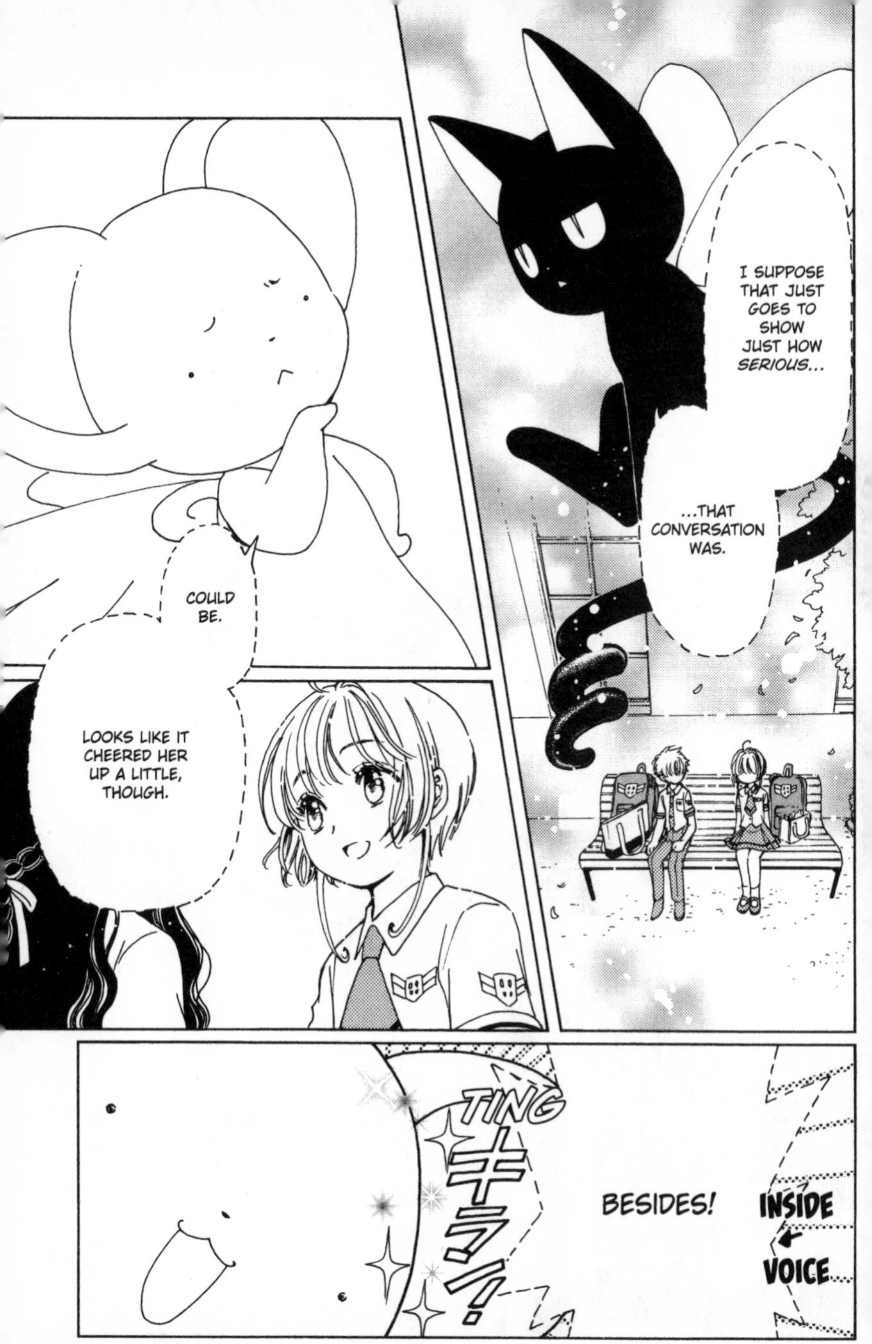
I SUPPOSE THAT JUST GOES TO SHOW JUST HOW *SERIOUS*...
...THAT CONVERSATION WAS.
COULD BE.
LOOKS LIKE IT CHEERED HER UP A LITTLE, THOUGH.
INSIDE VOICE
BESIDES!
TING
キラ!!

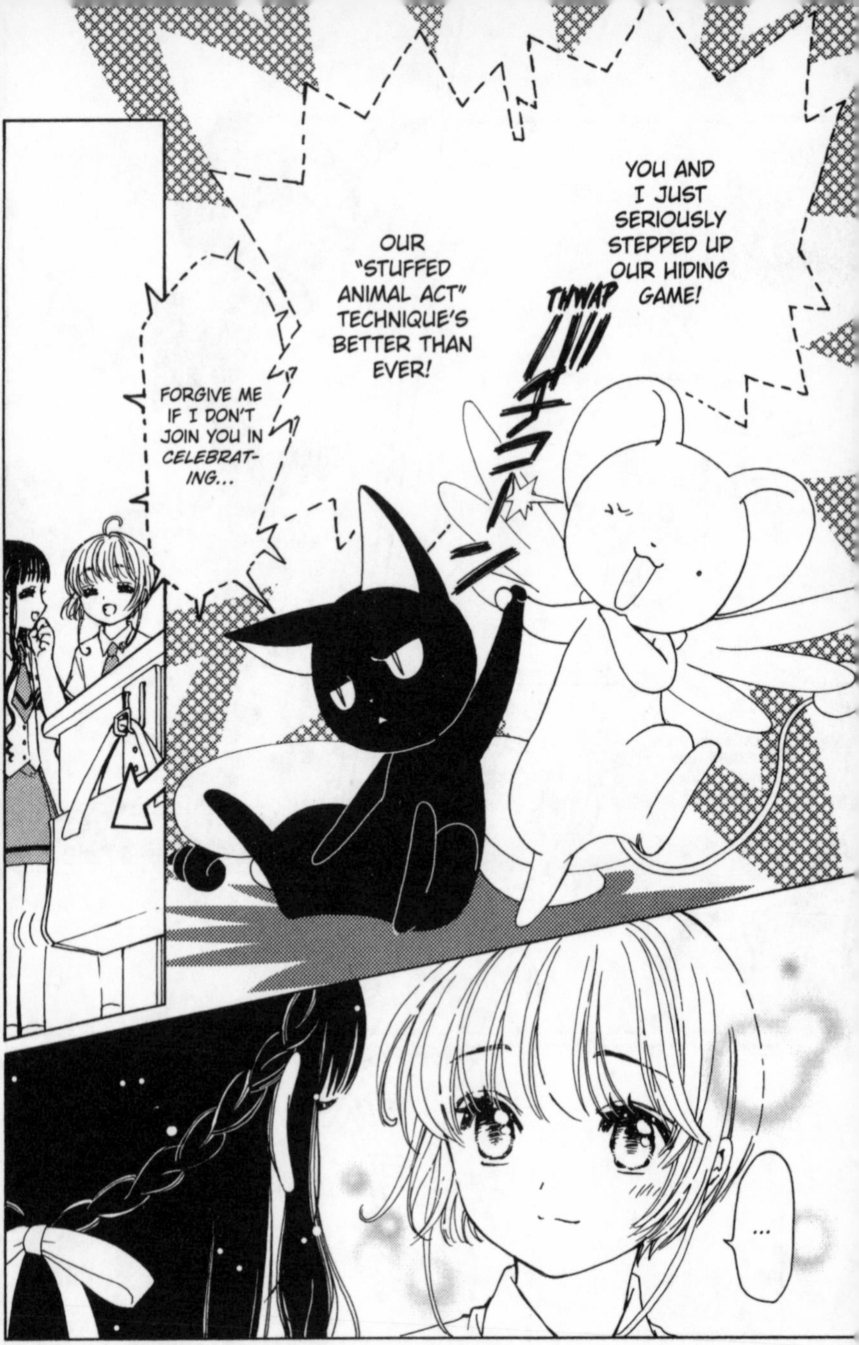
YOU AND I JUST SERIOUSLY STEPPED UP OUR HIDING GAME!
THWAP
OUR "STUFFED ANIMAL ACT" TECHNIQUE'S BETTER THAN EVER!
FORGIVE ME IF I DON'T JOIN YOU IN CELEBRATING...
...

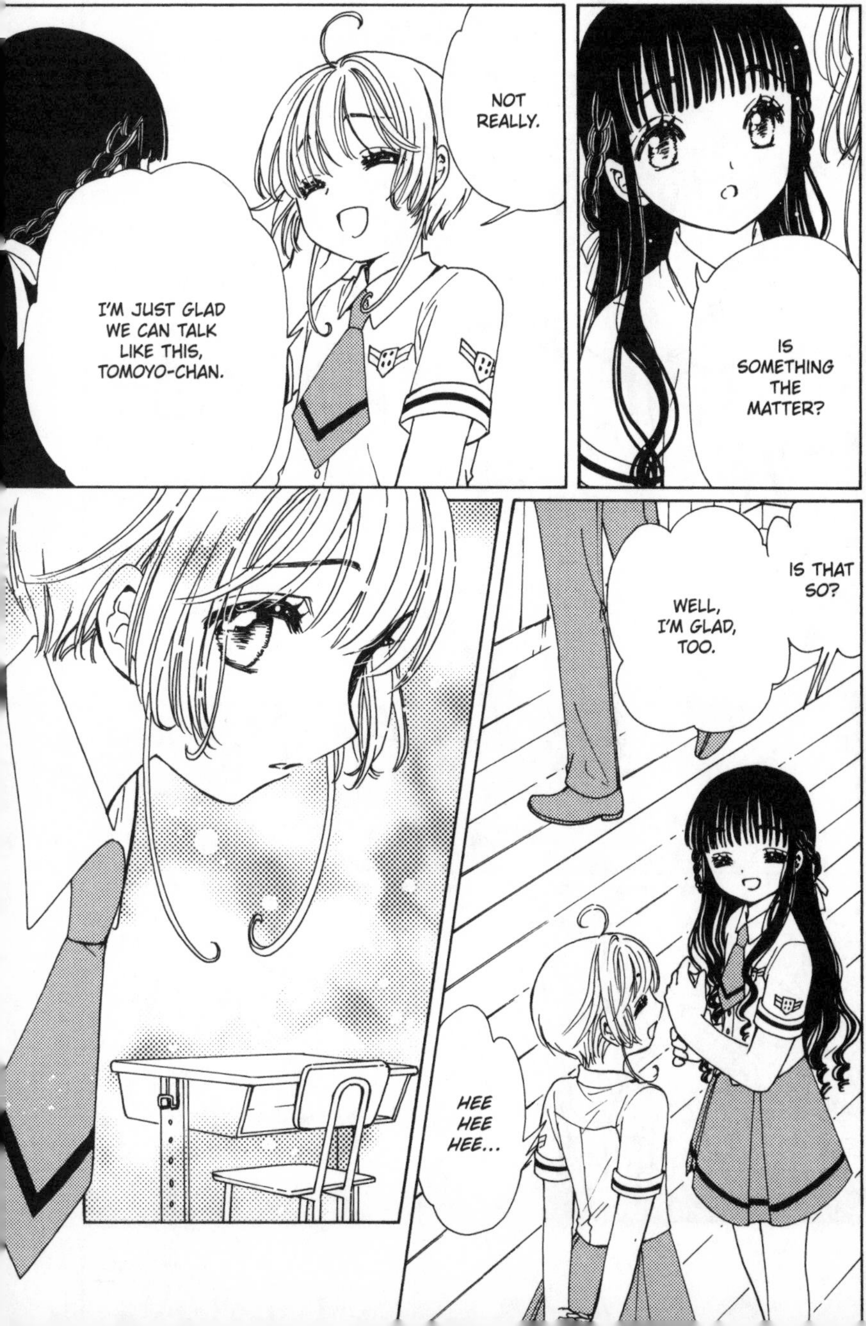
IS SOMETHING THE MATTER?
NOT REALLY.
I'M JUST GLAD WE CAN TALK LIKE THIS, TOMOYO-CHAN.
IS THAT SO?
WELL, I'M GLAD, TOO.
HEE HEE HEE...

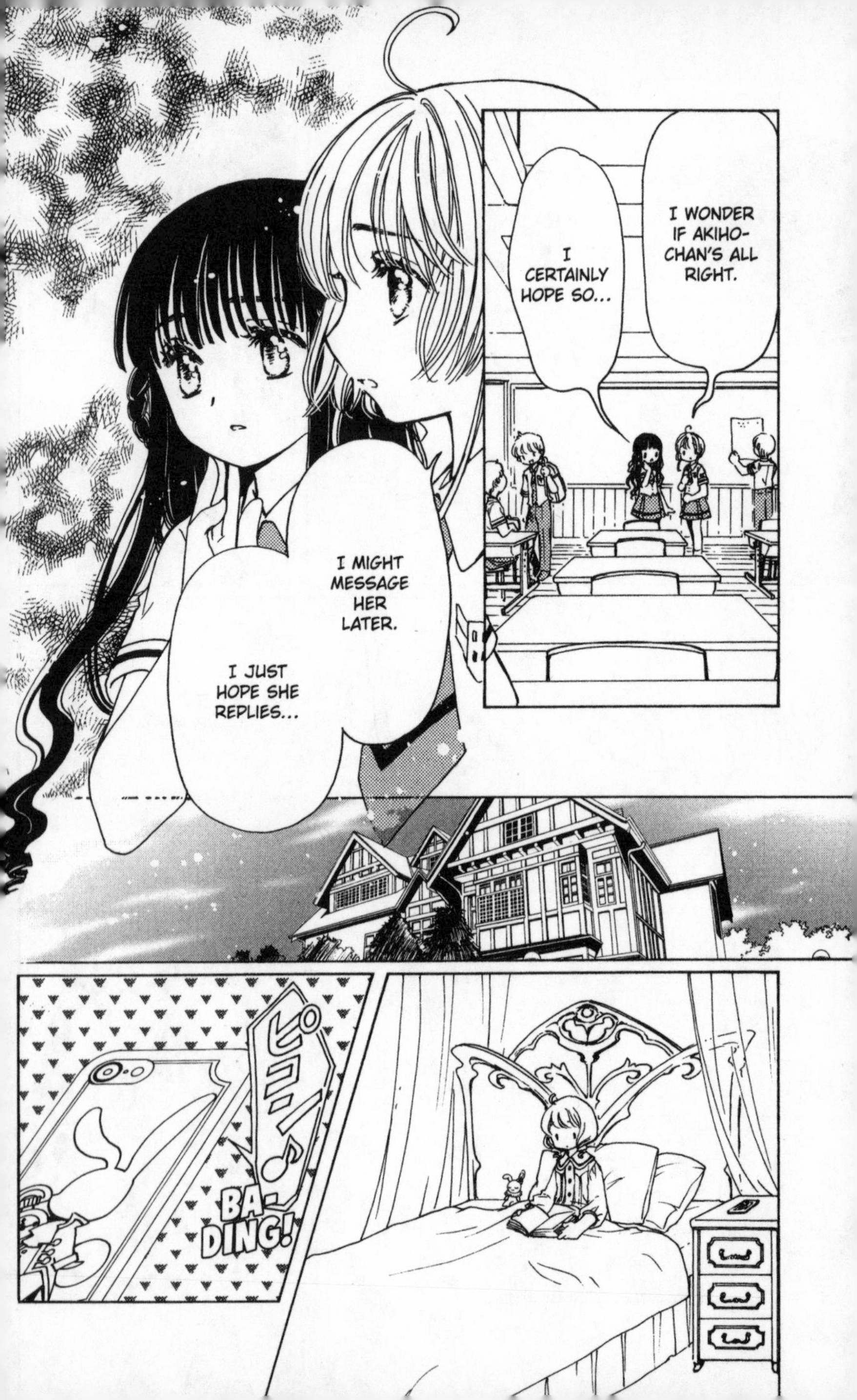
I WONDER IF AKIHO-CHAN'S ALL RIGHT.
I CERTAINLY HOPE SO...
I MIGHT MESSAGE HER LATER.
I JUST HOPE SHE REPLIES...
ピコン♪
BA-DING!

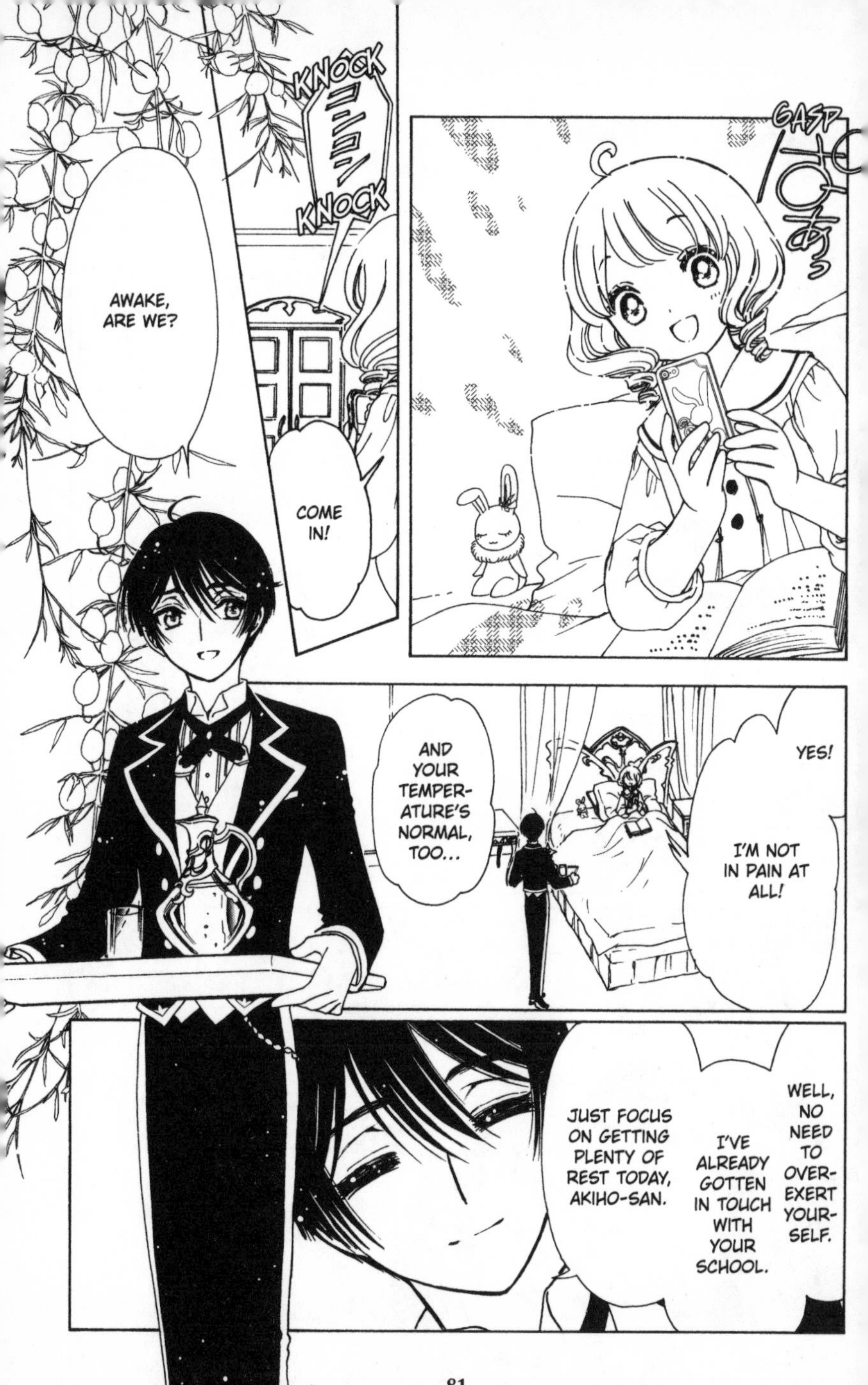
GASP
KNOCK
KNOCK
COME IN!
AWAKE, ARE WE?
YES!
I'M NOT IN PAIN AT ALL!
AND YOUR TEMPERATURE'S NORMAL, TOO...
WELL, NO NEED TO OVEREXERT YOURSELF.
I'VE ALREADY GOTTEN IN TOUCH WITH YOUR SCHOOL.
JUST FOCUS ON GETTING PLENTY OF REST TODAY, AKIHO-SAN.

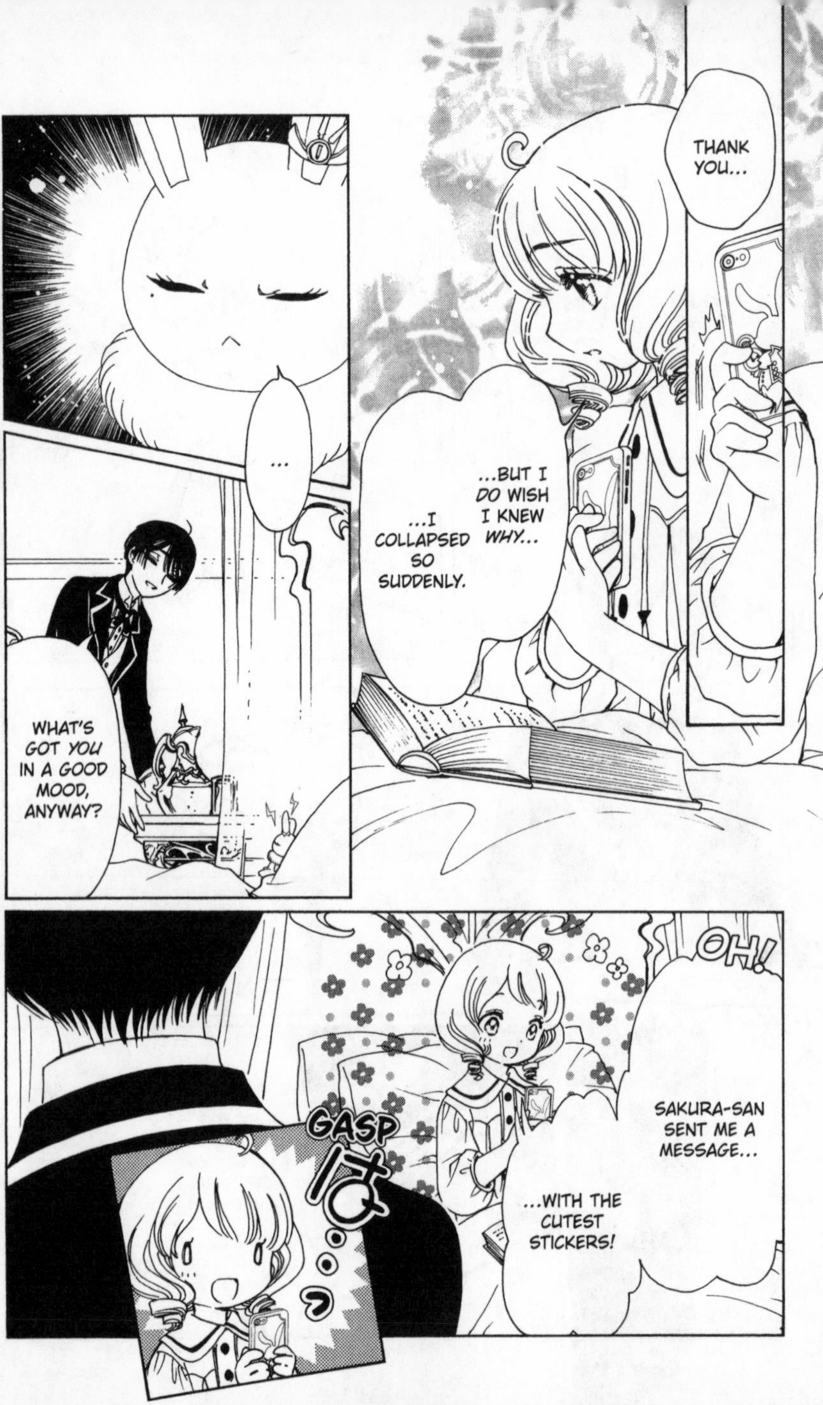
THANK YOU...
...BUT I DO WISH I KNEW WHY...
...I COLLAPSED SO SUDDENLY.
...
WHAT'S GOT YOU IN A GOOD MOOD, ANYWAY?
OH!
SAKURA-SAN SENT ME A MESSAGE...
...WITH THE CUTEST STICKERS!
GASP
は

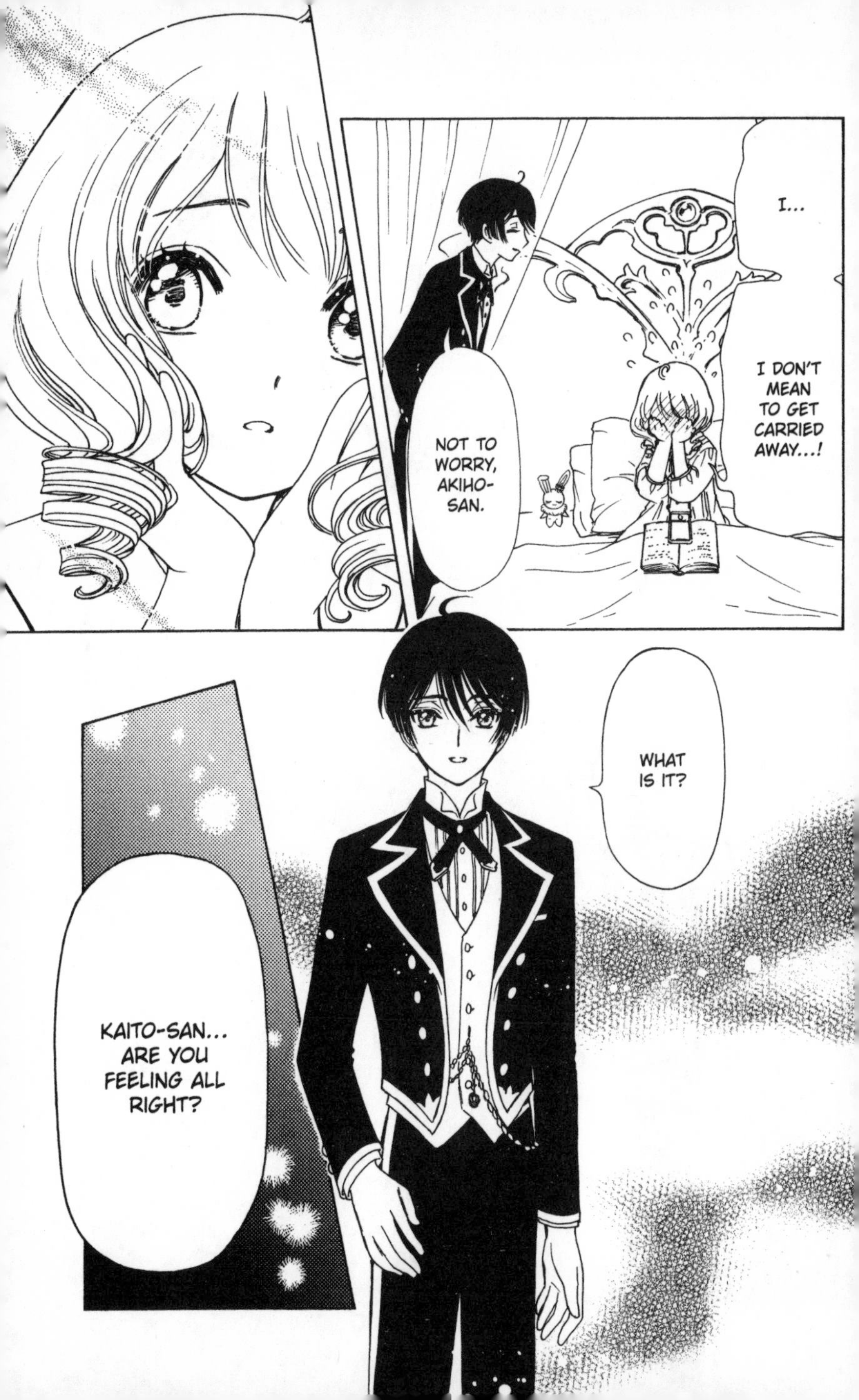
I...
I DON'T MEAN TO GET CARRIED AWAY...!
NOT TO WORRY, AKIHO-SAN.
WHAT IS IT?
KAITO-SAN... ARE YOU FEELING ALL RIGHT?

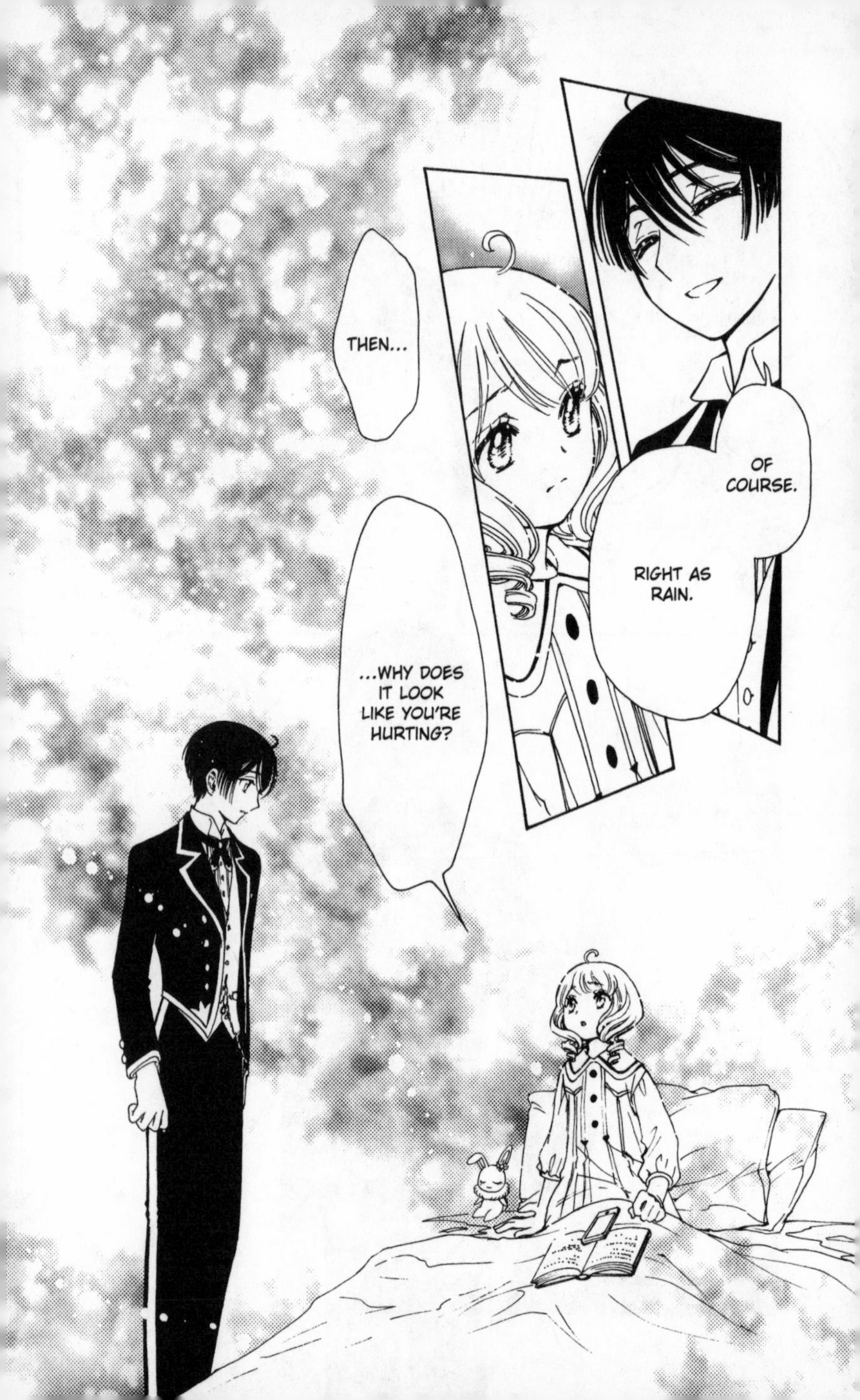
OF COURSE.
RIGHT AS RAIN.
THEN...
...WHY DOES IT LOOK LIKE YOU'RE HURTING?

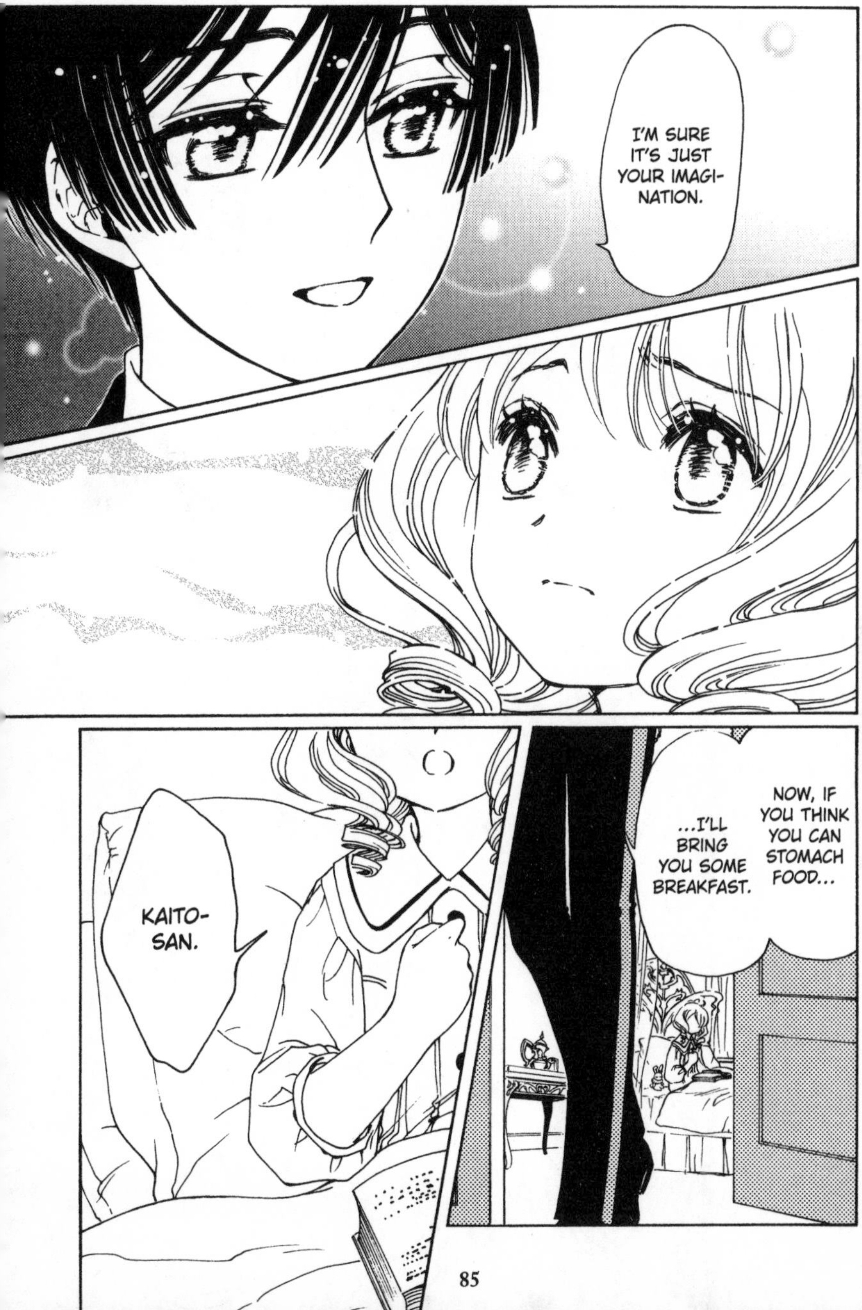
I'M SURE IT'S JUST YOUR IMAGI-NATION.
NOW, IF YOU THINK YOU CAN STOMACH FOOD...
...I'LL BRING YOU SOME BREAKFAST.
KAITO-SAN.

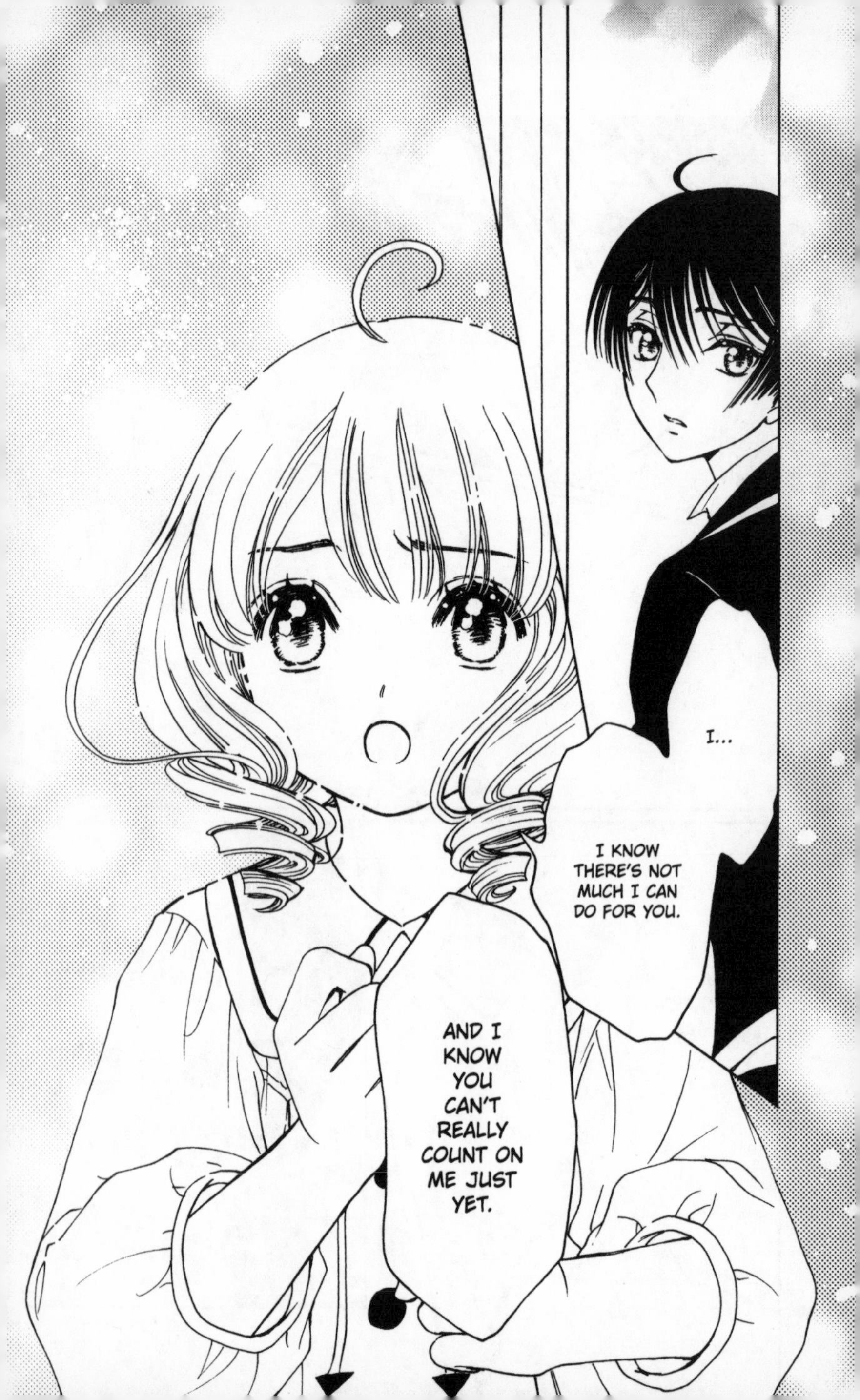
I...
I KNOW THERE'S NOT MUCH I CAN DO FOR YOU.
AND I KNOW YOU CAN'T REALLY COUNT ON ME JUST YET.

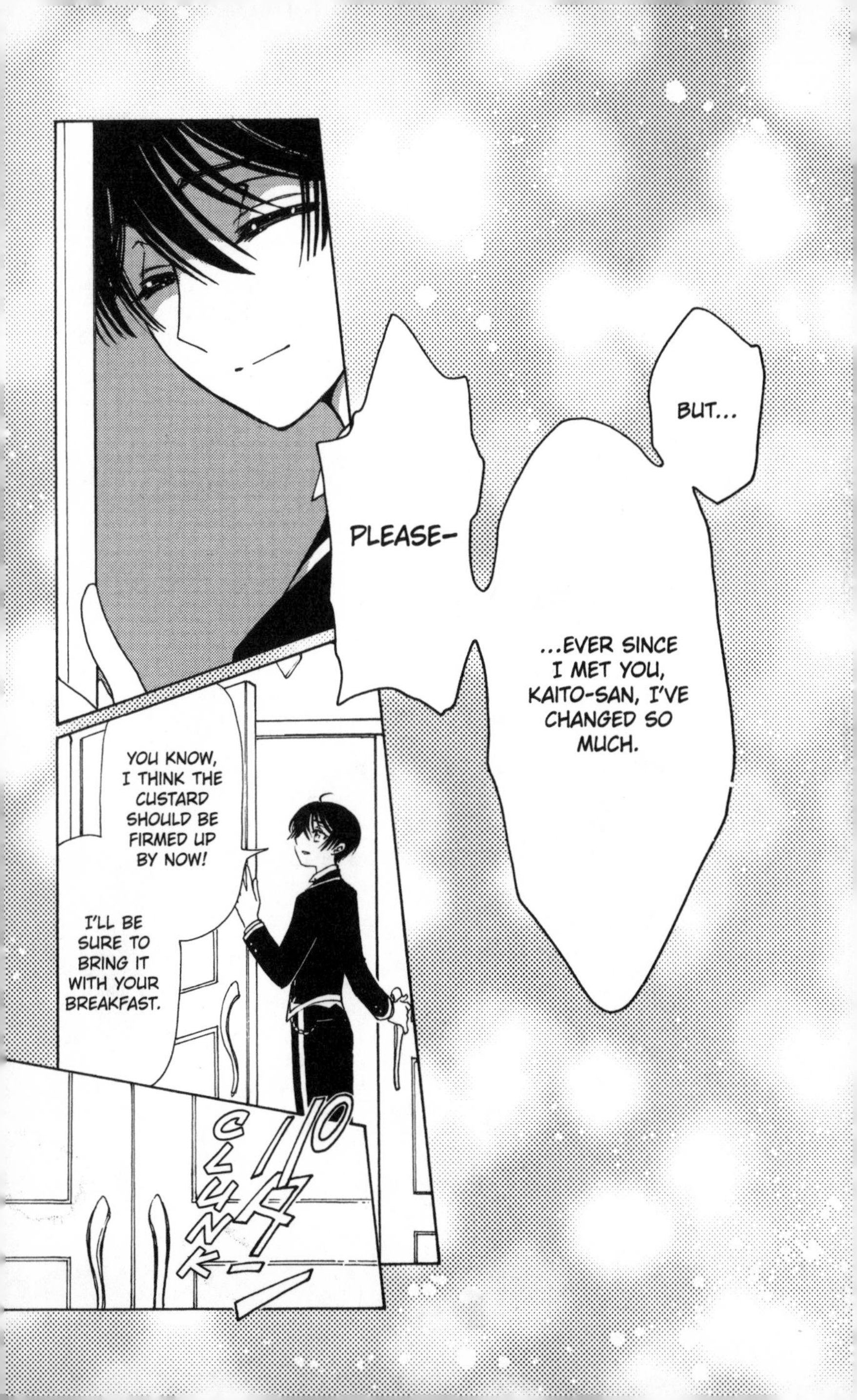

BUT...
PLEASE-
...EVER SINCE I MET YOU, KAITO-SAN, I'VE CHANGED SO MUCH.
YOU KNOW, I THINK THE CUSTARD SHOULD BE FIRMED UP BY NOW!
I'LL BE SURE TO BRING IT WITH YOUR BREAKFAST.
CLUNK-

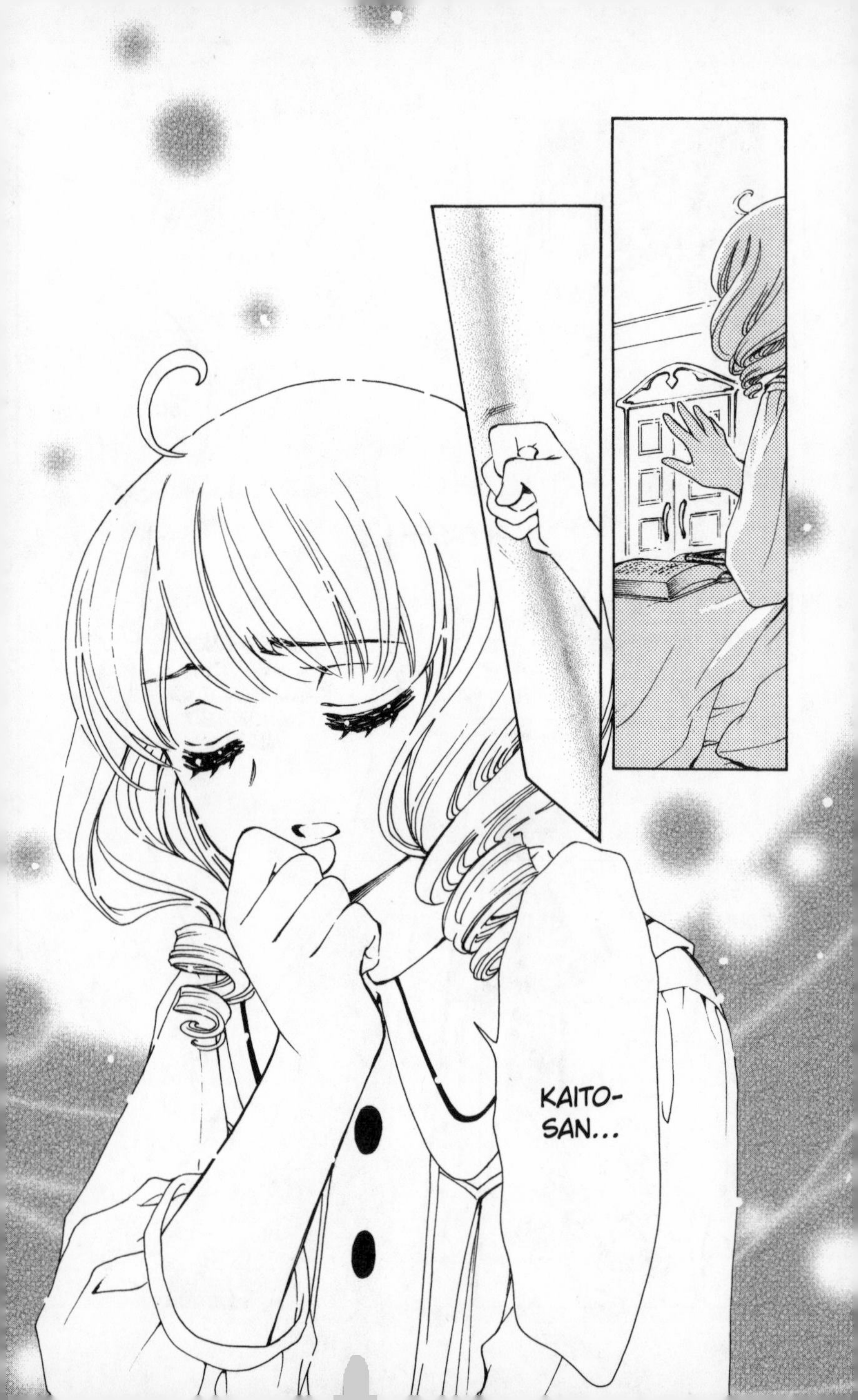
KAITO-
SAN...

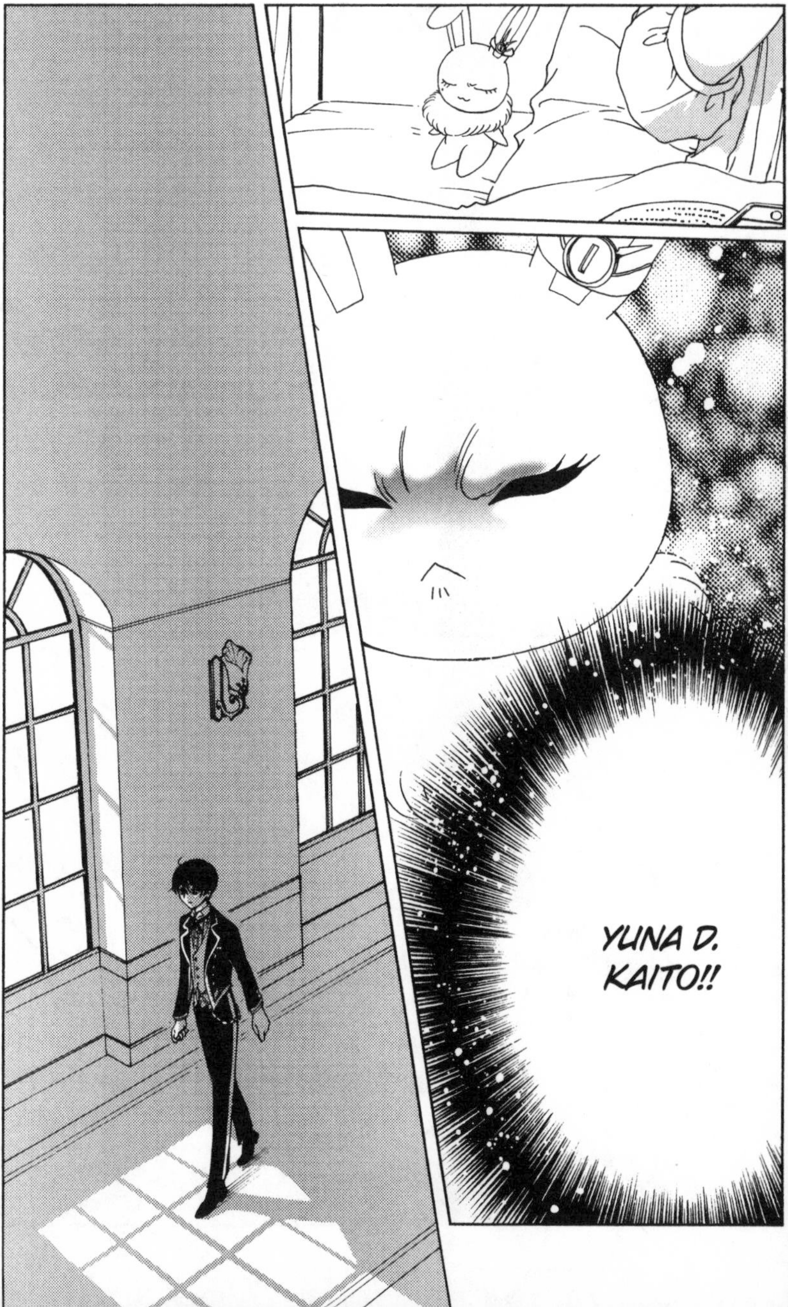
YUNA D. KAITO!!

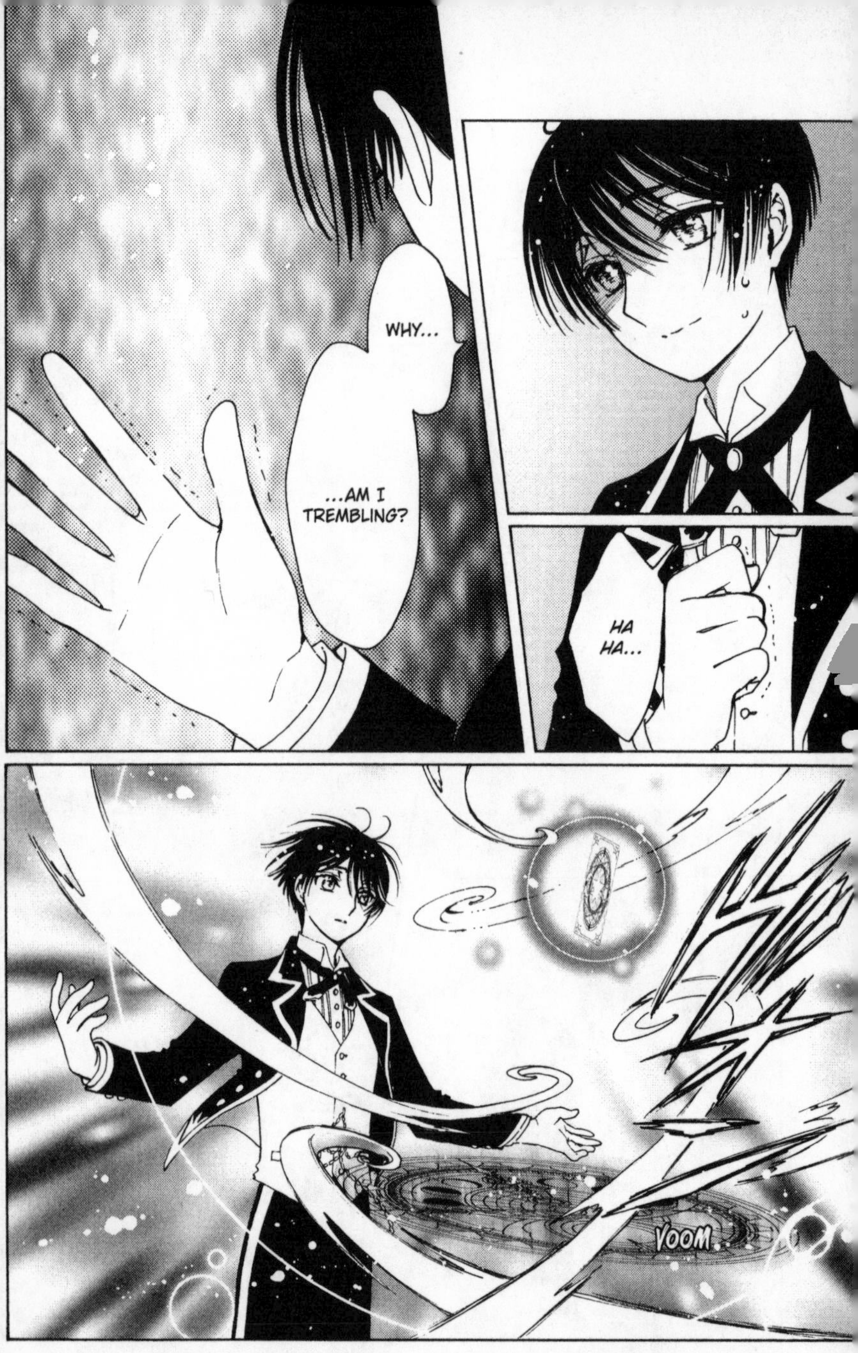
HA HA...
WHY...
...AM I TREMBLING?
VOOM

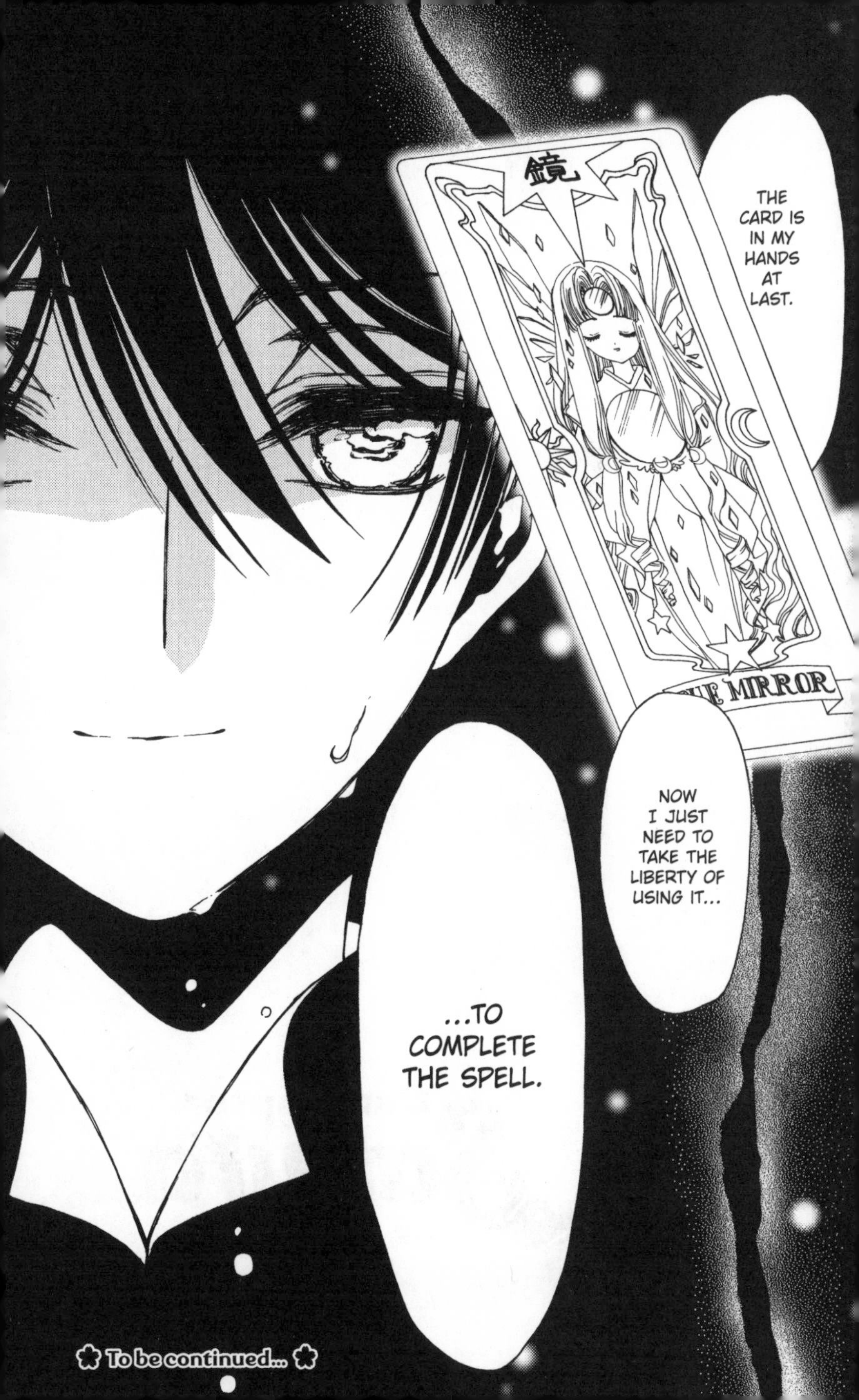
鏡
MIRROR
THE CARD IS IN MY HANDS AT LAST.
NOW I JUST NEED TO TAKE THE LIBERTY OF USING IT...
...TO COMPLETE THE SPELL.
To be continued...

Cardcaptor
Sakura
CLEAR CARD

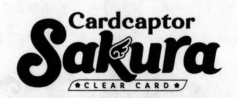

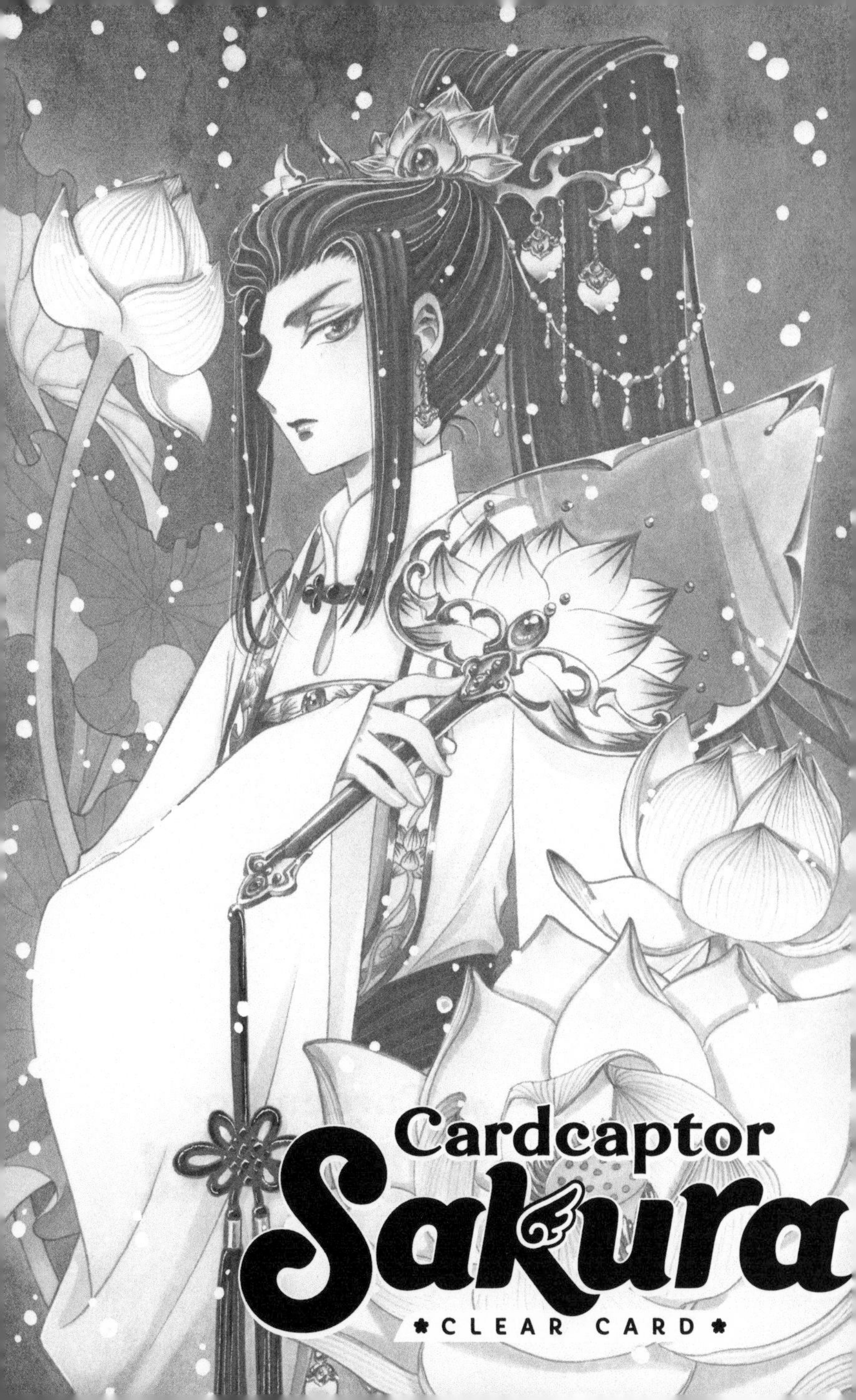
Cardcaptor
Sakura
CLEAR CARD

Cardcaptor Sakura

CLEAR CARD

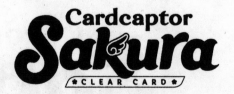

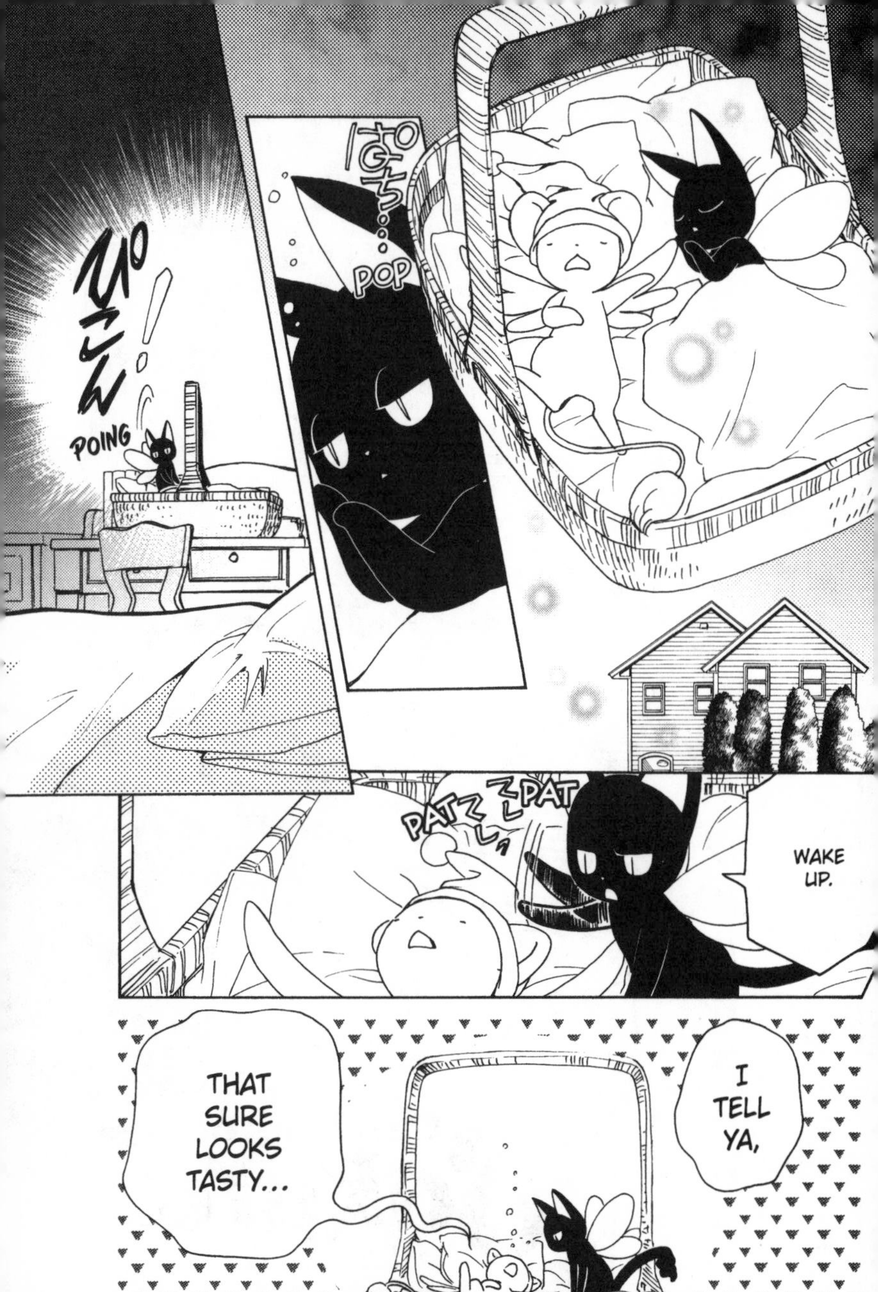
POP
POING
PAT PAT
WAKE UP.
I TELL YA,
THAT SURE LOOKS TASTY...

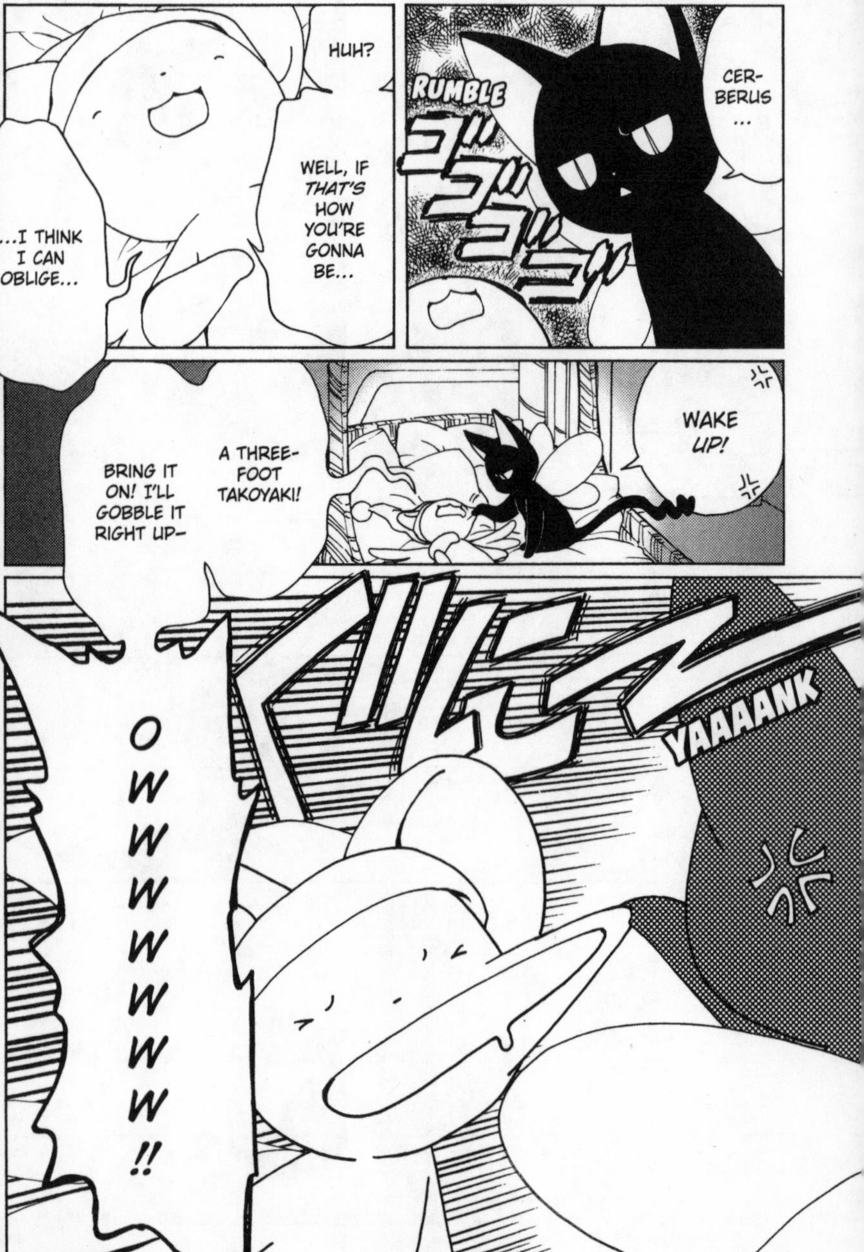
RUMBLE
CER-BERUS...
HUH?
WELL, IF THAT'S HOW YOU'RE GONNA BE...
...I THINK I CAN OBLIGE...
WAKE UP!
A THREE-FOOT TAKOYAKI!
BRING IT ON! I'LL GOBBLE IT RIGHT UP-
YAAAANK
OWWWWWWW!!

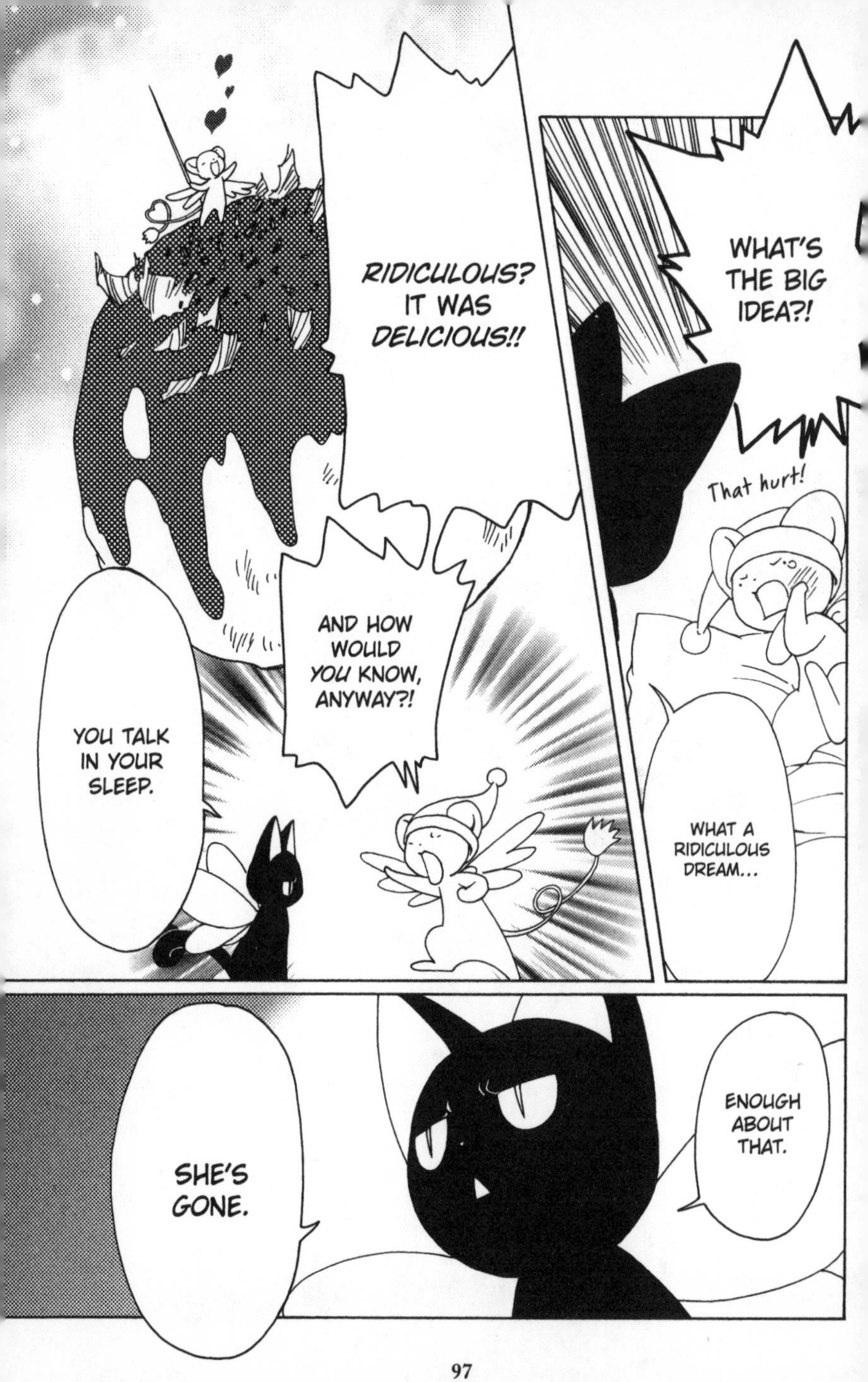

WHAT'S THE BIG IDEA?!
That hurt!
WHAT A RIDICULOUS DREAM...
*RIDICULOUS?* IT WAS *DELICIOUS!!*
AND HOW WOULD *YOU* KNOW, ANYWAY?!
YOU TALK IN YOUR SLEEP.
ENOUGH ABOUT THAT.
SHE'S GONE.

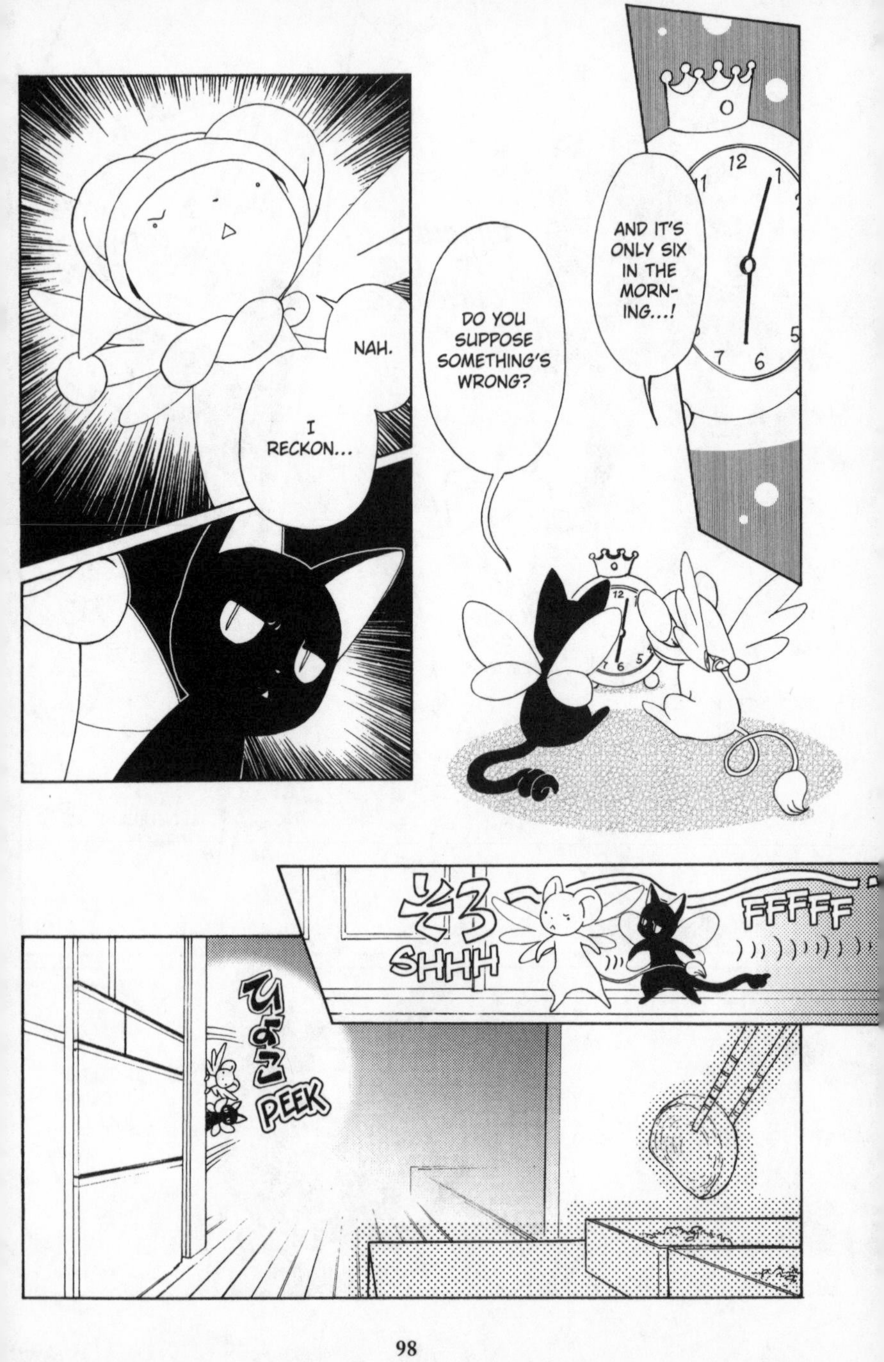
AND IT'S ONLY SIX IN THE MORNING...!
DO YOU SUPPOSE SOMETHING'S WRONG?
NAH.
I RECKON...
FFFFF
そろ~
SHHH
ひょこ
PEEK

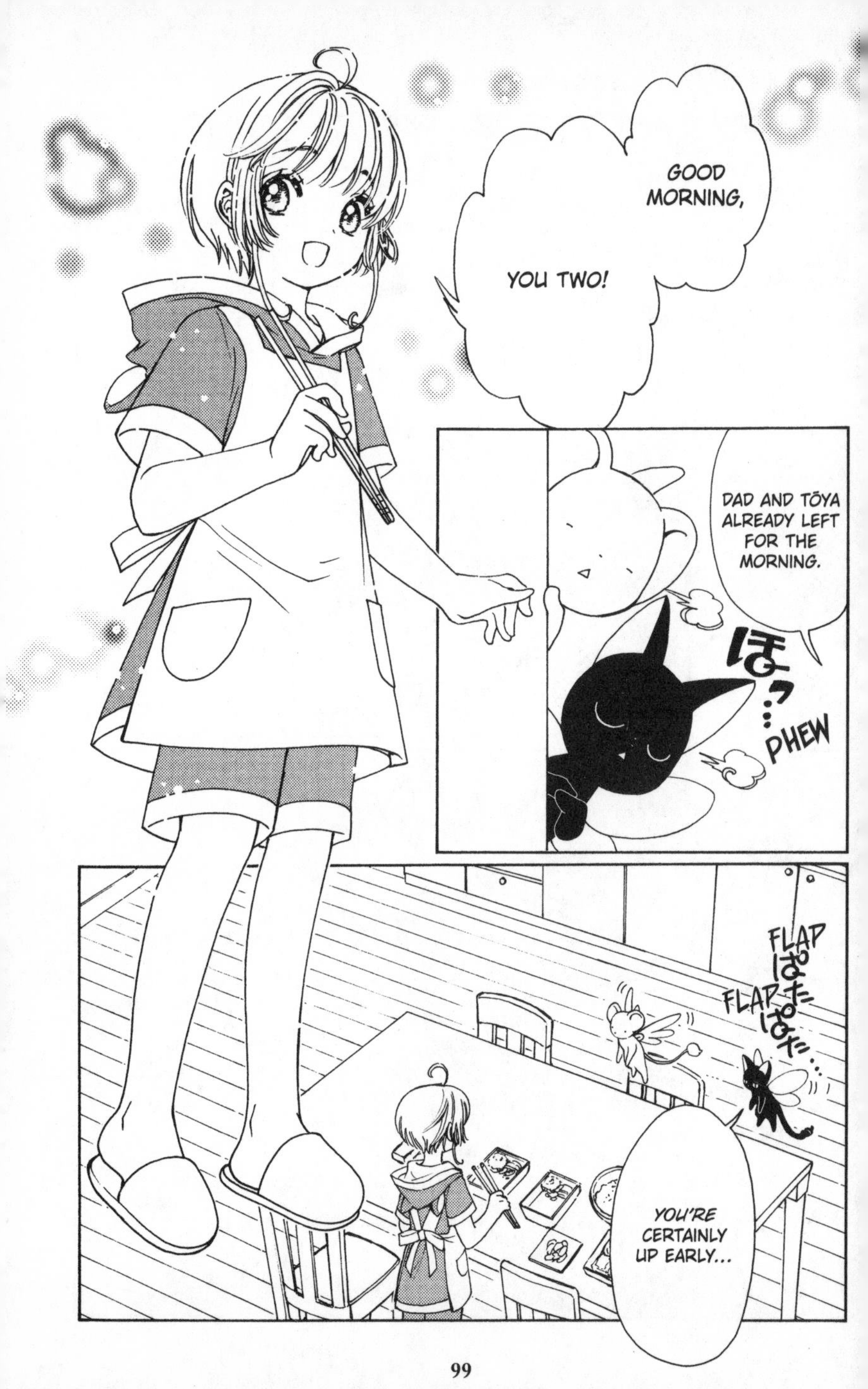
GOOD MORNING, YOU TWO!
DAD AND TŌYA ALREADY LEFT FOR THE MORNING.
ほっ… PHEW
FLAP ぱた FLAP ぱた…
YOU'RE CERTAINLY UP EARLY…

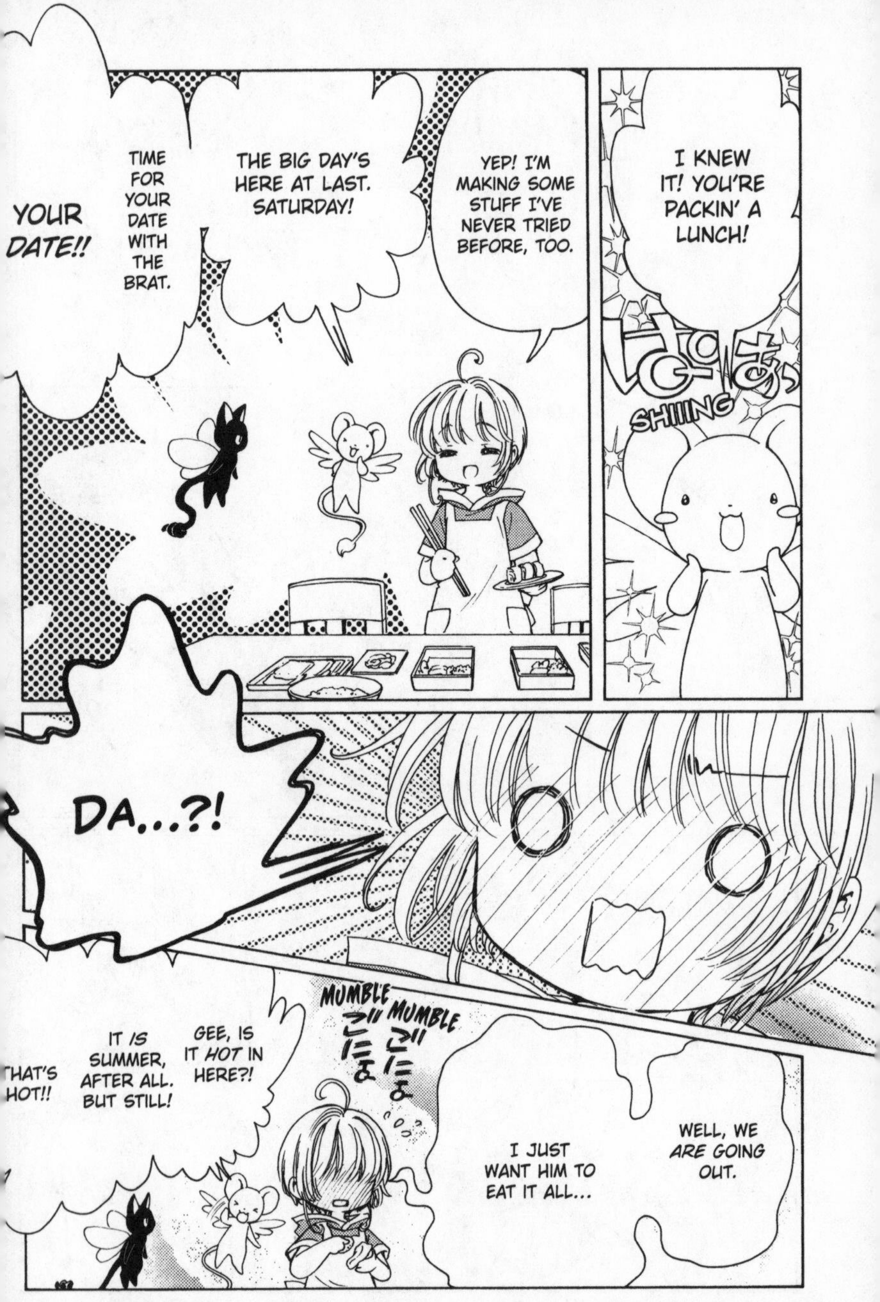
I KNEW IT! YOU'RE PACKIN' A LUNCH!
SHIIING
YEP! I'M MAKING SOME STUFF I'VE NEVER TRIED BEFORE, TOO.
THE BIG DAY'S HERE AT LAST. SATURDAY!
TIME FOR YOUR DATE WITH THE BRAT.
YOUR *DATE!!*
DA...?!
WELL, WE *ARE GOING* OUT.
I JUST WANT HIM TO EAT IT ALL...
MUMBLE MUMBLE
GEE, IS IT *HOT* IN HERE?!
IT *IS* SUMMER, AFTER ALL. BUT STILL!
THAT'S HOT!!

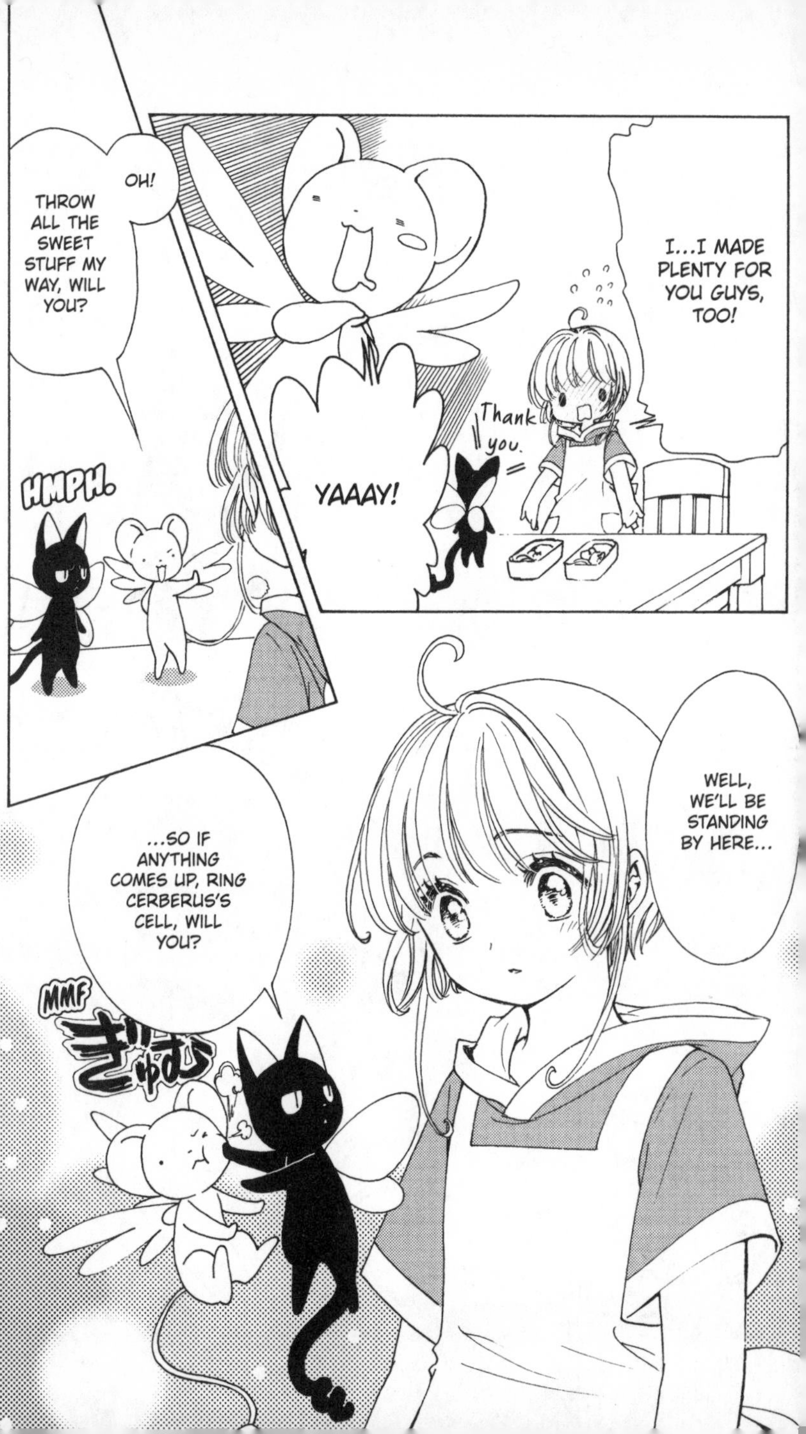

I...I MADE PLENTY FOR YOU GUYS, TOO!
Thank you.
YAAAY!
OH!
THROW ALL THE SWEET STUFF MY WAY, WILL YOU?
HMPH.
WELL, WE'LL BE STANDING BY HERE...
...SO IF ANYTHING COMES UP, RING CERBERUS'S CELL, WILL YOU?
MMF
ぎゅむ

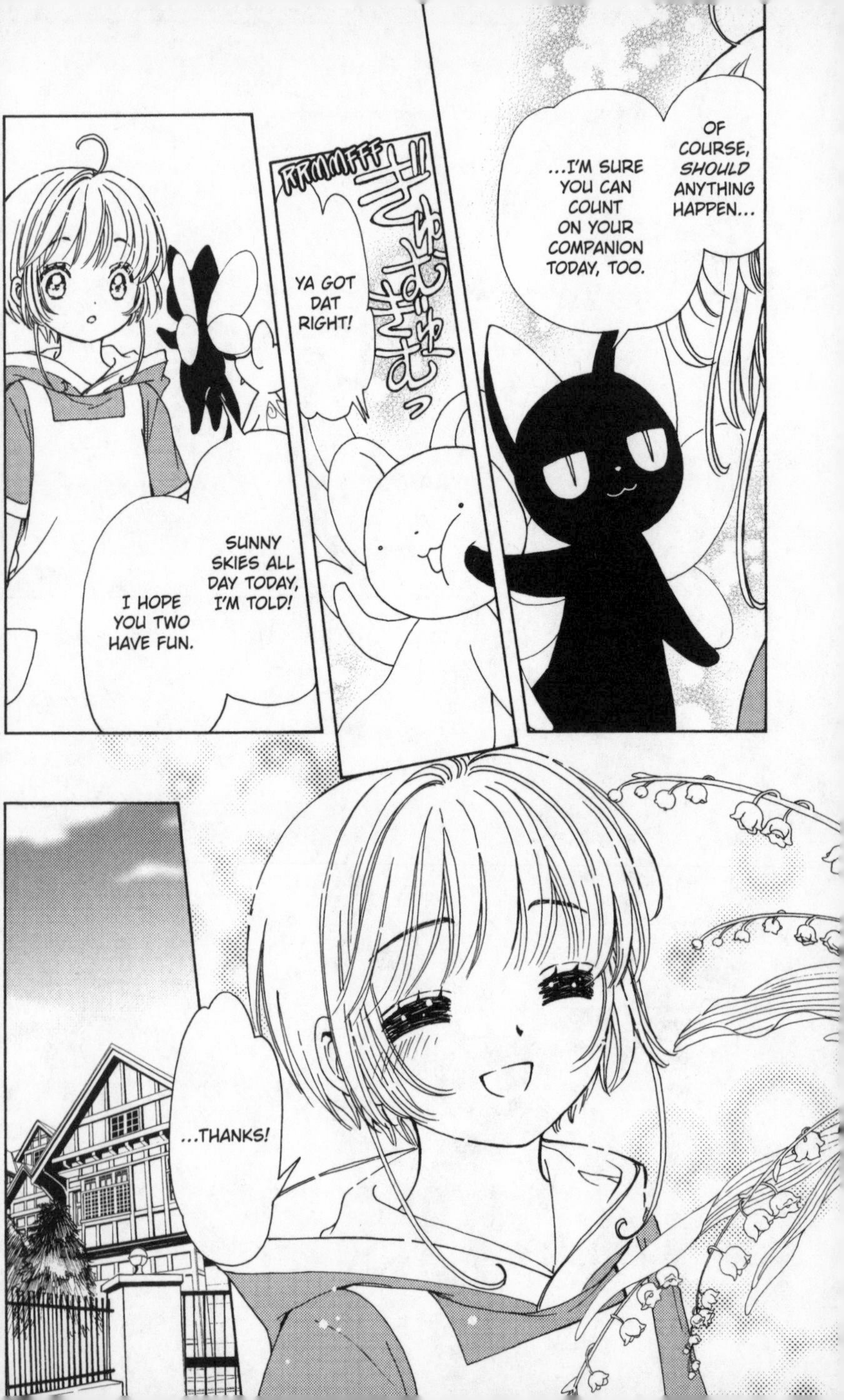
OF COURSE, SHOULD ANYTHING HAPPEN...
...I'M SURE YOU CAN COUNT ON YOUR COMPANION TODAY, TOO.
RRMMFFF
ぎゅむぎゅむっ
YA GOT DAT RIGHT!
SUNNY SKIES ALL DAY TODAY, I'M TOLD!
I HOPE YOU TWO HAVE FUN.
...THANKS!

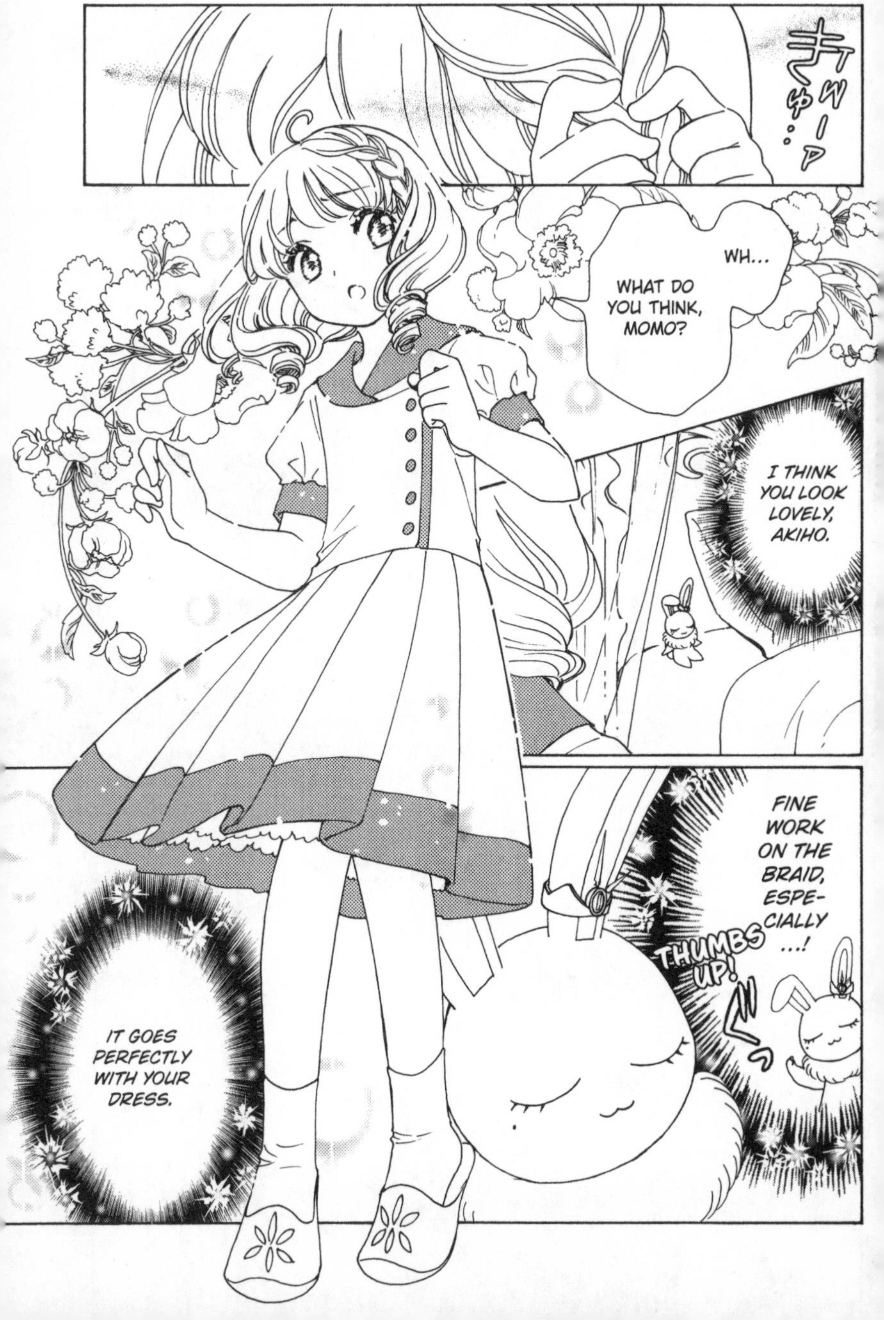
きゅ…
TWIP
WH…
WHAT DO YOU THINK, MOMO?
I THINK YOU LOOK LOVELY, AKIHO.
FINE WORK ON THE BRAID, ESPECIALLY …!
THUMBS UP!
IT GOES PERFECTLY WITH YOUR DRESS.

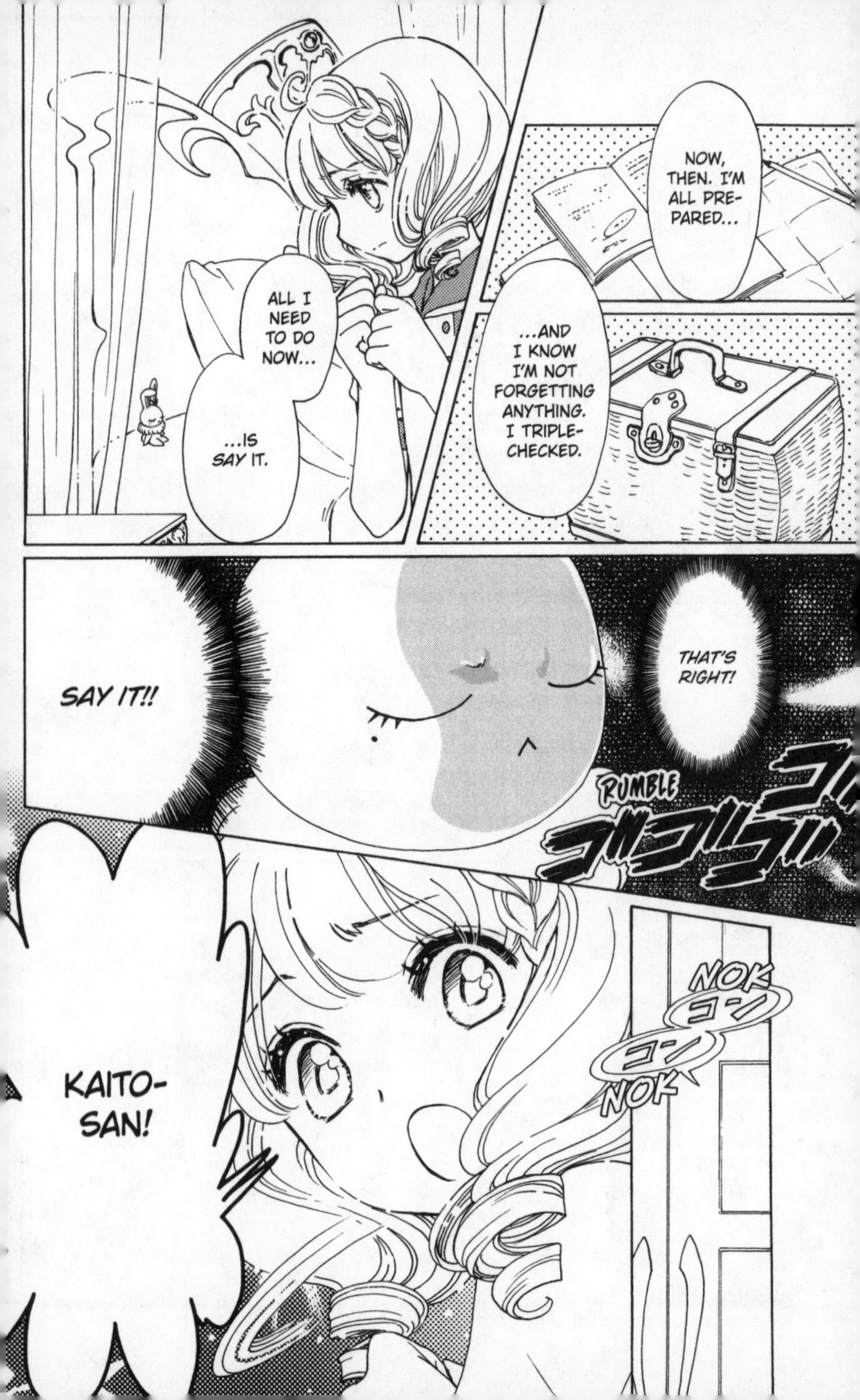
NOW, THEN. I'M ALL PRE-PARED...
...AND I KNOW I'M NOT FORGETTING ANYTHING. I TRIPLE-CHECKED.
ALL I NEED TO DO NOW...
...IS SAY IT.
THAT'S RIGHT!
SAY IT!!
RUMBLE
NOK
NOK
KAITO-SAN!

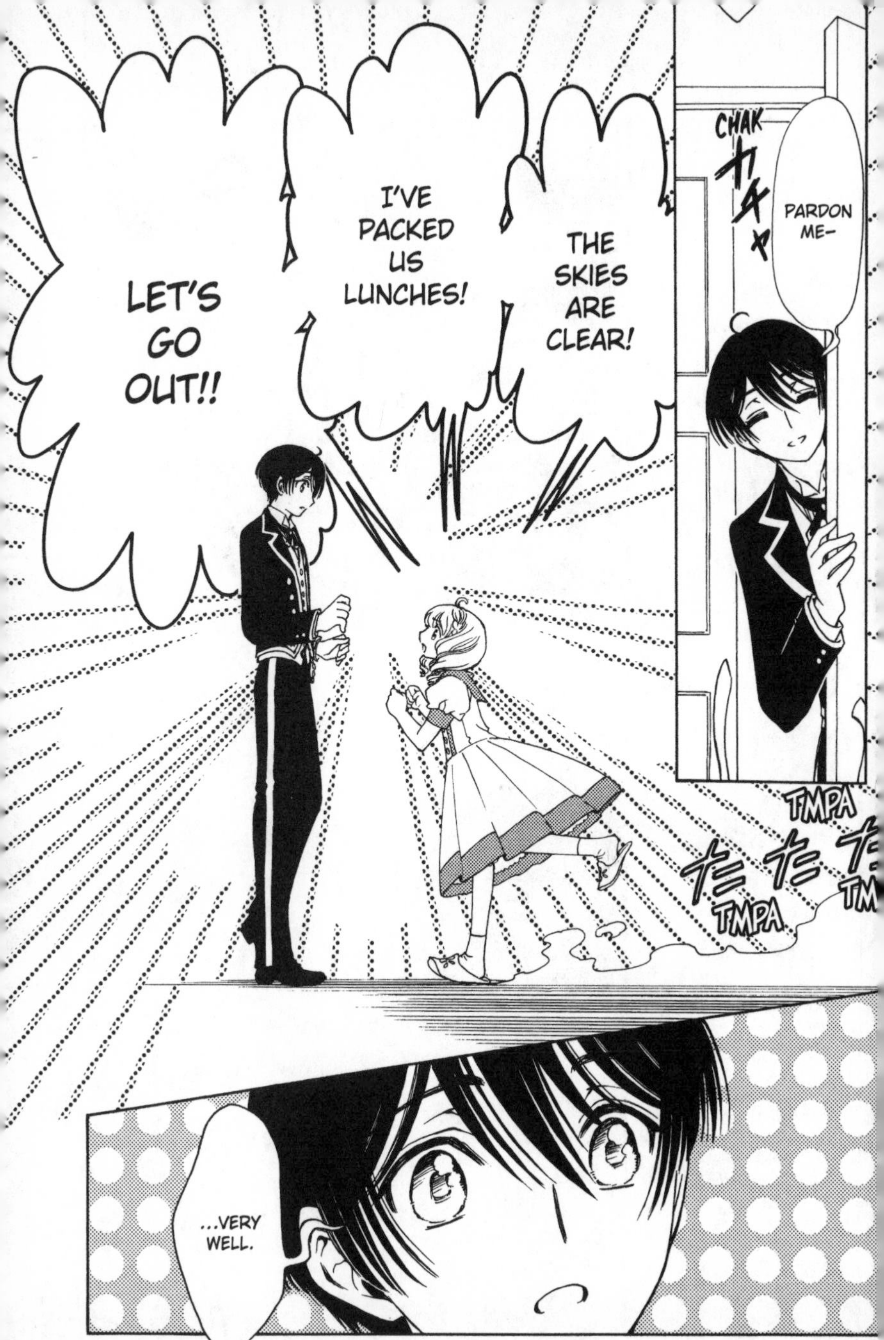
CHAK
PARDON ME—
THE SKIES ARE CLEAR!
I'VE PACKED US LUNCHES!
LET'S GO OUT!!
TMPA
TMPA
TM
TMPA
...VERY WELL.

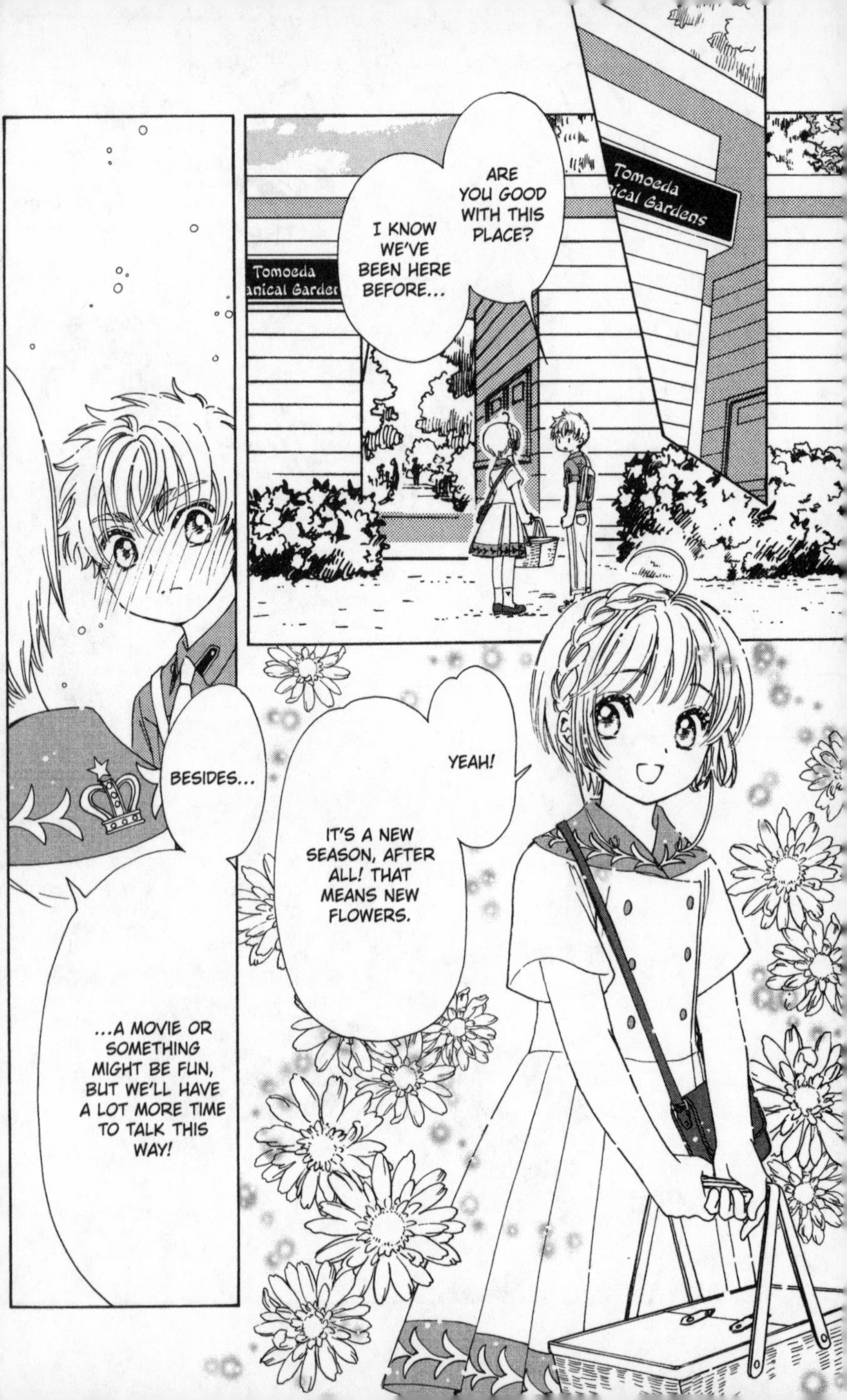
Tomoeda
nical Gardens
ARE YOU GOOD WITH THIS PLACE?
I KNOW WE'VE BEEN HERE BEFORE...
Tomoeda
anical Garden
YEAH!
IT'S A NEW SEASON, AFTER ALL! THAT MEANS NEW FLOWERS.
BESIDES...
...A MOVIE OR SOMETHING MIGHT BE FUN, BUT WE'LL HAVE A LOT MORE TIME TO TALK THIS WAY!

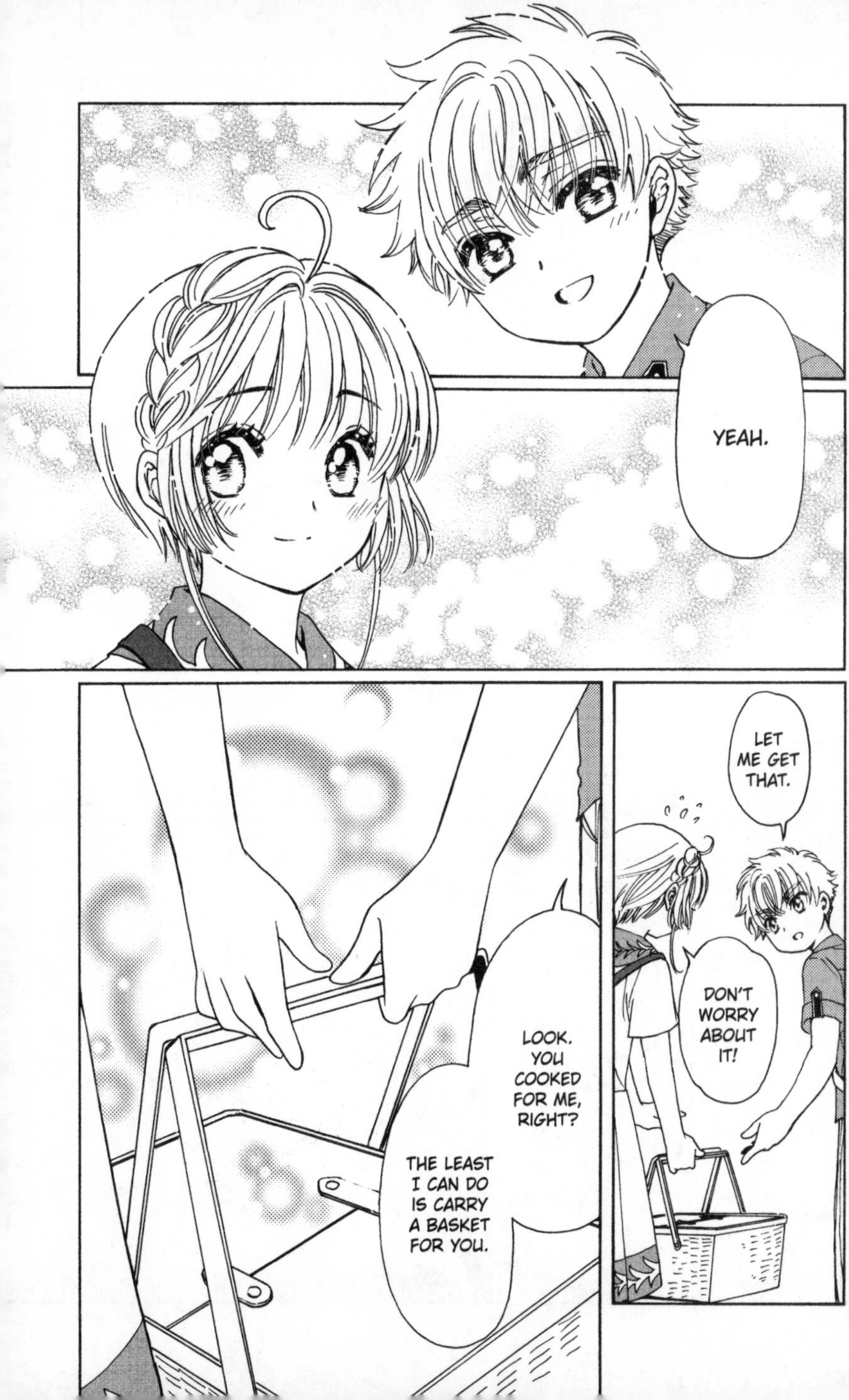
YEAH.
LET ME GET THAT.
DON'T WORRY ABOUT IT!
LOOK. YOU COOKED FOR ME, RIGHT?
THE LEAST I CAN DO IS CARRY A BASKET FOR YOU.

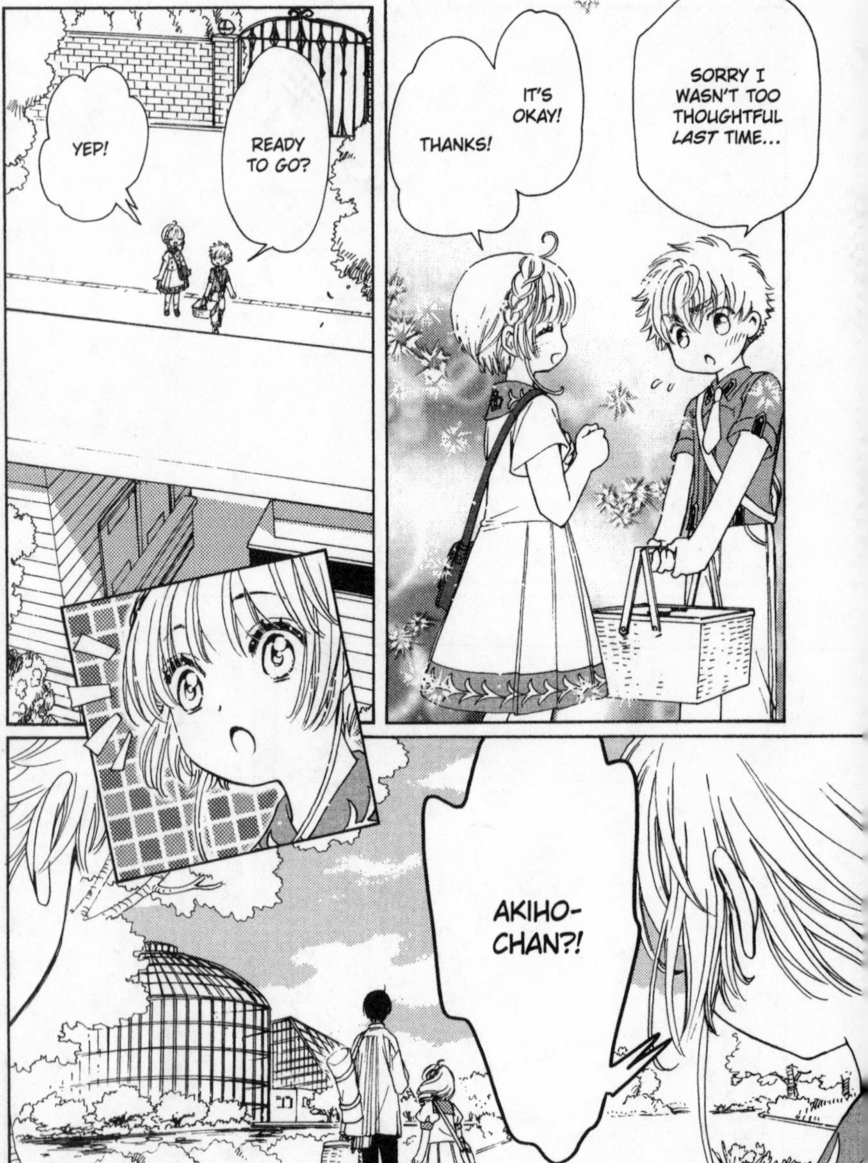
SORRY I WASN'T TOO THOUGHTFUL *LAST* TIME...
IT'S OKAY!
THANKS!
READY TO GO?
YEP!
AKIHO-CHAN?!

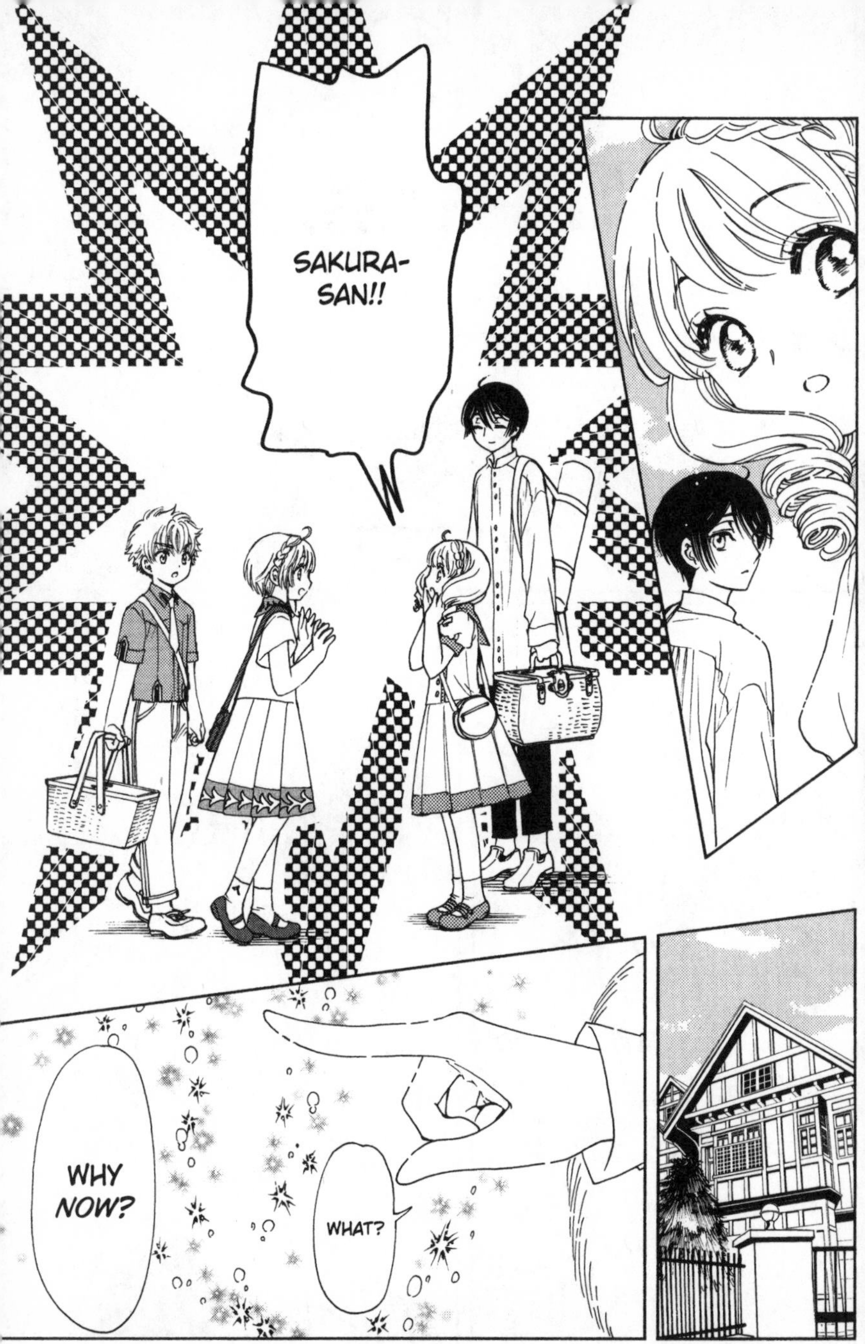
SAKURA-SAN!!
WHAT?
WHY NOW?

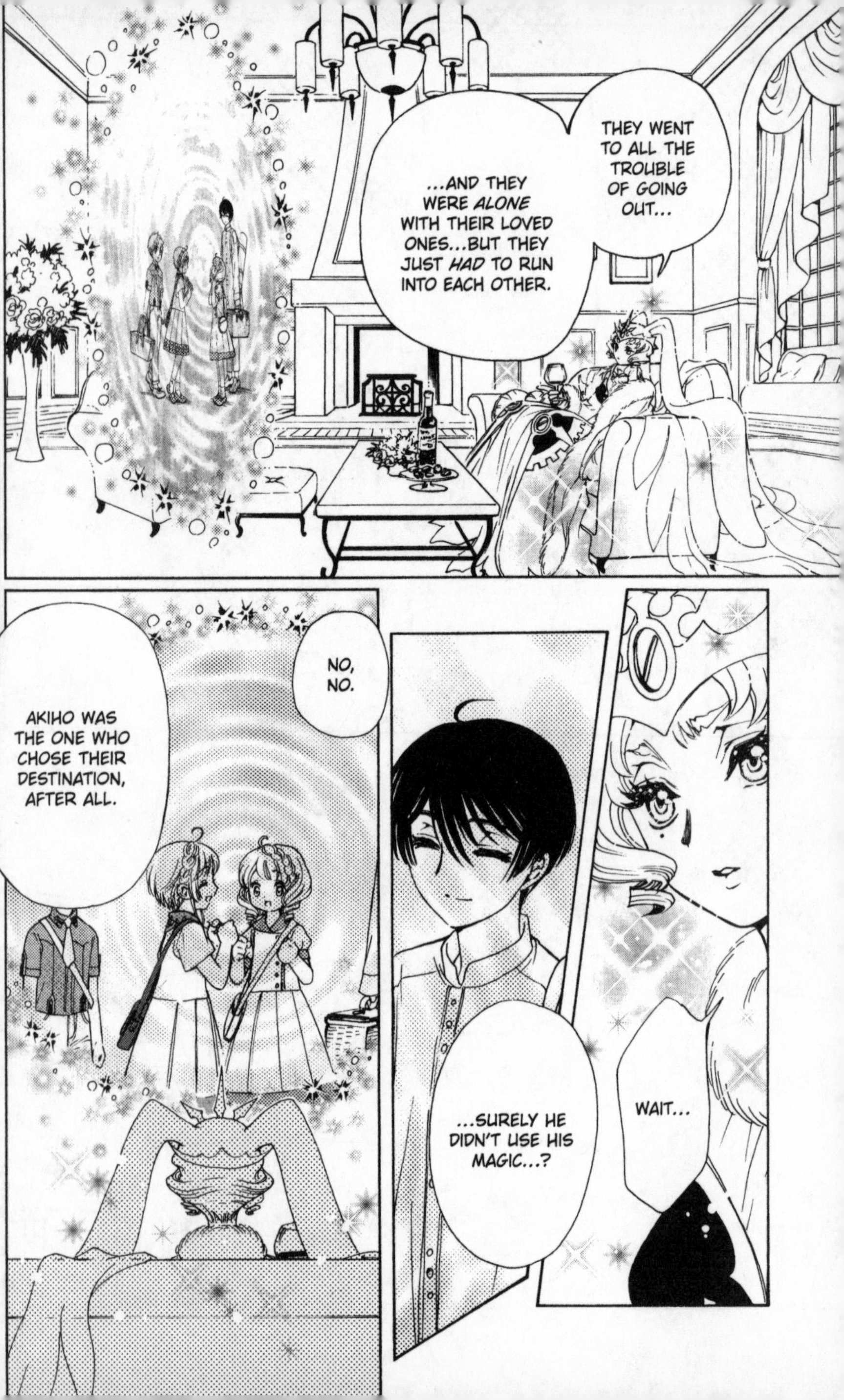
THEY WENT TO ALL THE TROUBLE OF GOING OUT...
...AND THEY WERE *ALONE* WITH THEIR LOVED ONES...BUT THEY JUST *HAD* TO RUN INTO EACH OTHER.
WAIT...
...SURELY HE DIDN'T USE HIS MAGIC...?
NO, NO.
AKIHO WAS THE ONE WHO CHOSE THEIR DESTINATION, AFTER ALL.

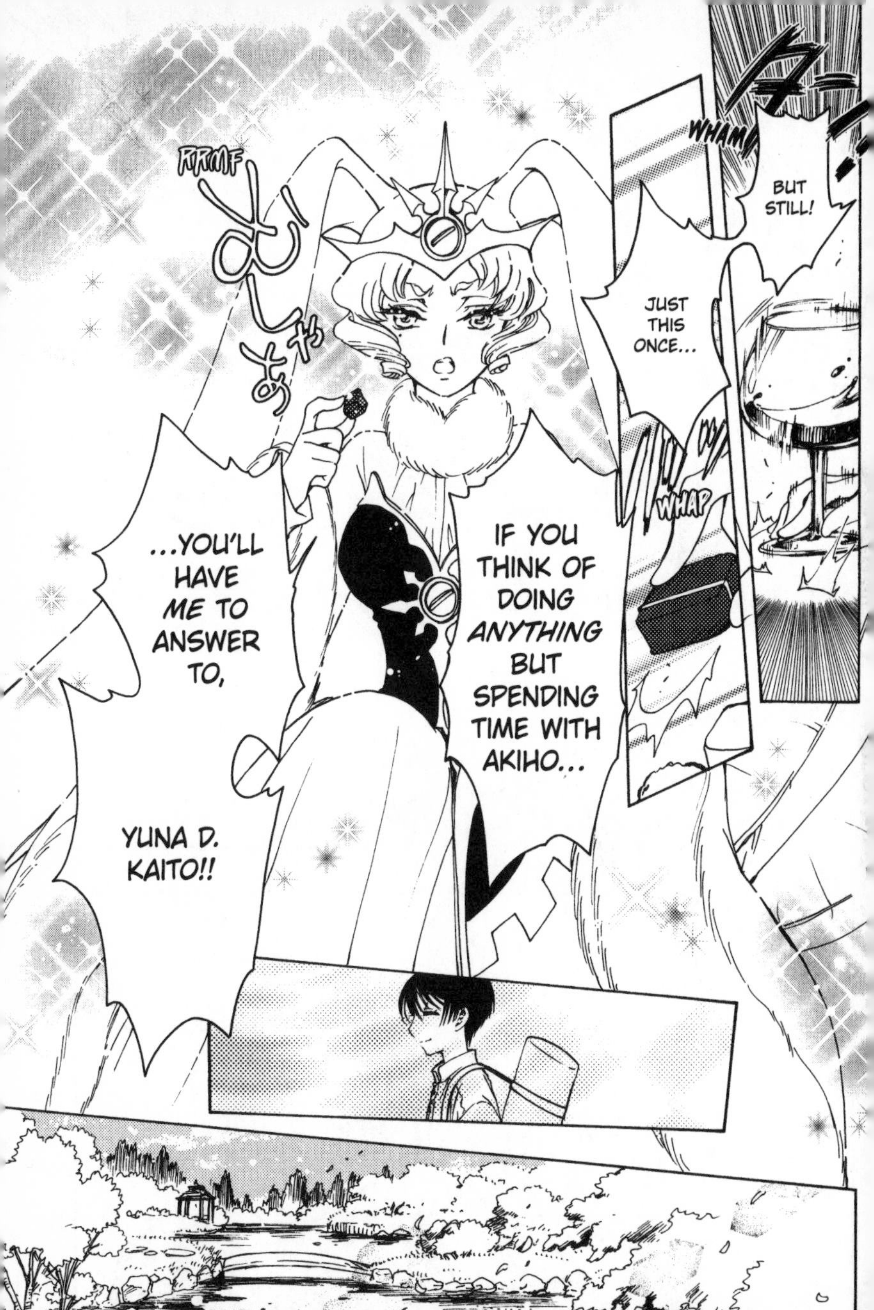
WHAM
BUT STILL!
JUST THIS ONCE...
WHAP
RRMF
IF YOU THINK OF DOING *ANYTHING* BUT SPENDING TIME WITH AKIHO...
...YOU'LL HAVE *ME* TO ANSWER TO,
YUNA D. KAITO!!

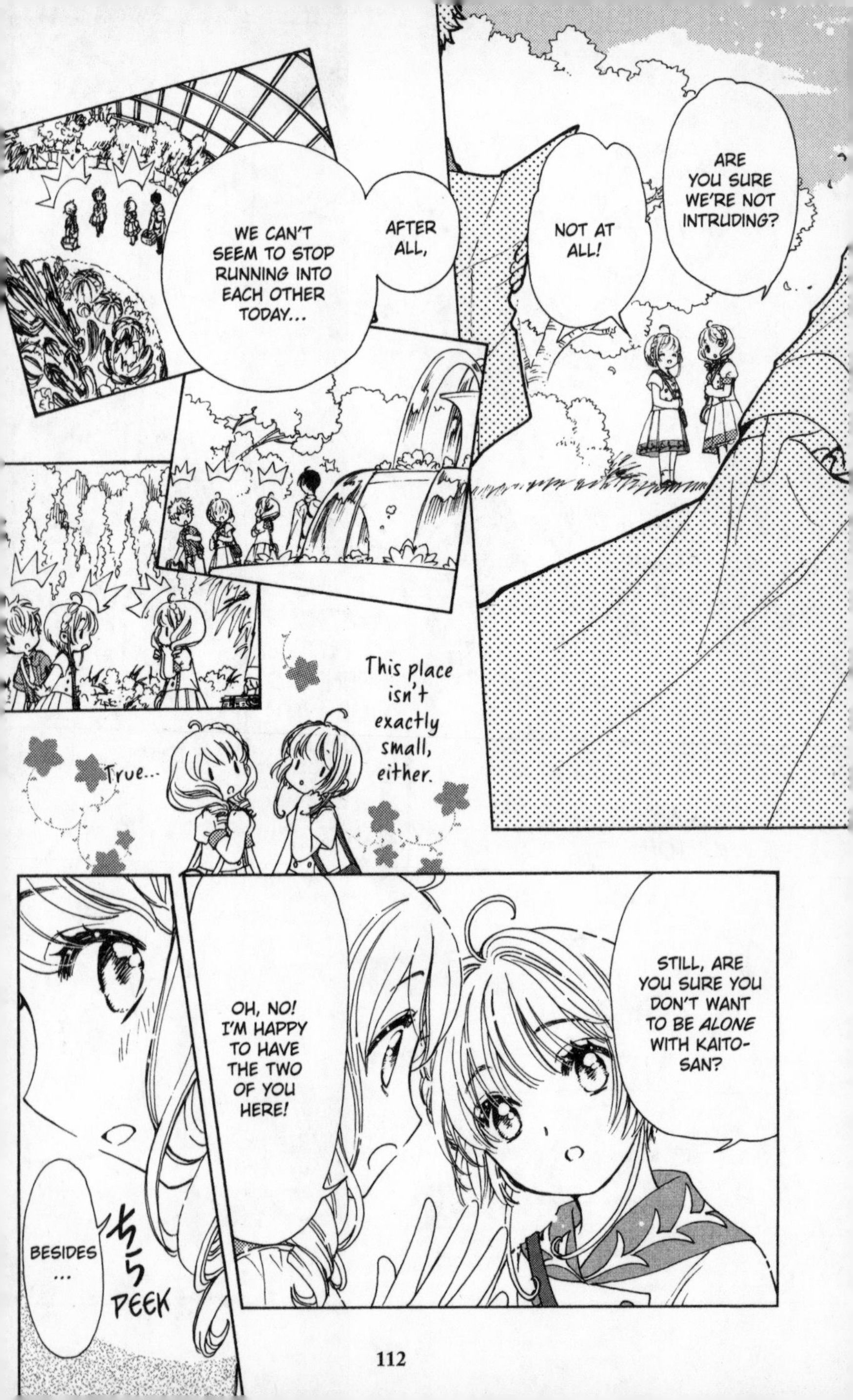
ARE YOU SURE WE'RE NOT INTRUDING?
NOT AT ALL!
AFTER ALL,
WE CAN'T SEEM TO STOP RUNNING INTO EACH OTHER TODAY...
This place isn't exactly small, either.
True...
STILL, ARE YOU SURE YOU DON'T WANT TO BE *ALONE* WITH KAITO-SAN?
OH, NO! I'M HAPPY TO HAVE THE TWO OF YOU HERE!
PEEK
BESIDES...

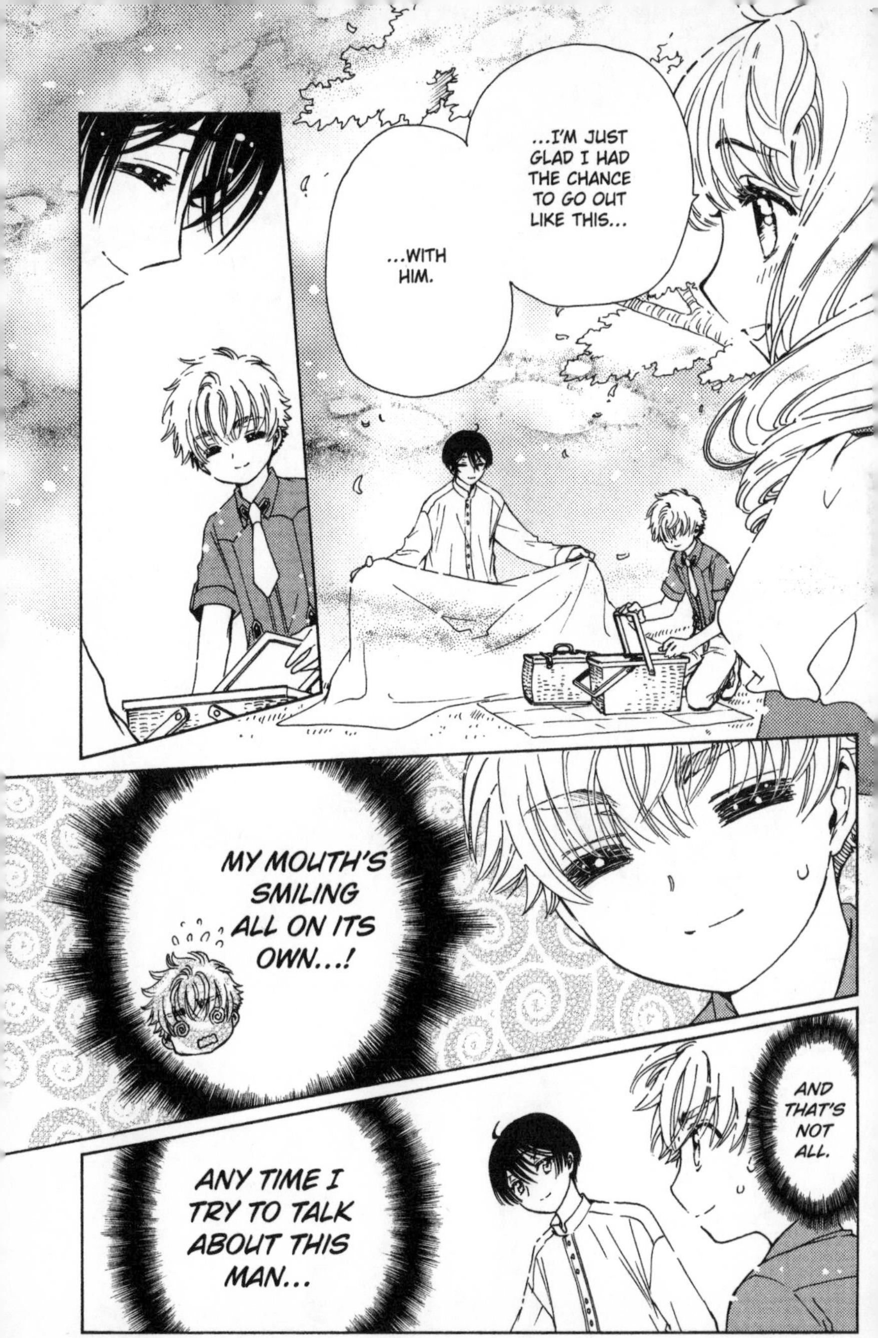
...I'M JUST GLAD I HAD THE CHANCE TO GO OUT LIKE THIS...
...WITH HIM.
MY MOUTH'S SMILING ALL ON ITS OWN...!
AND THAT'S NOT ALL.
ANY TIME I TRY TO TALK ABOUT THIS MAN...

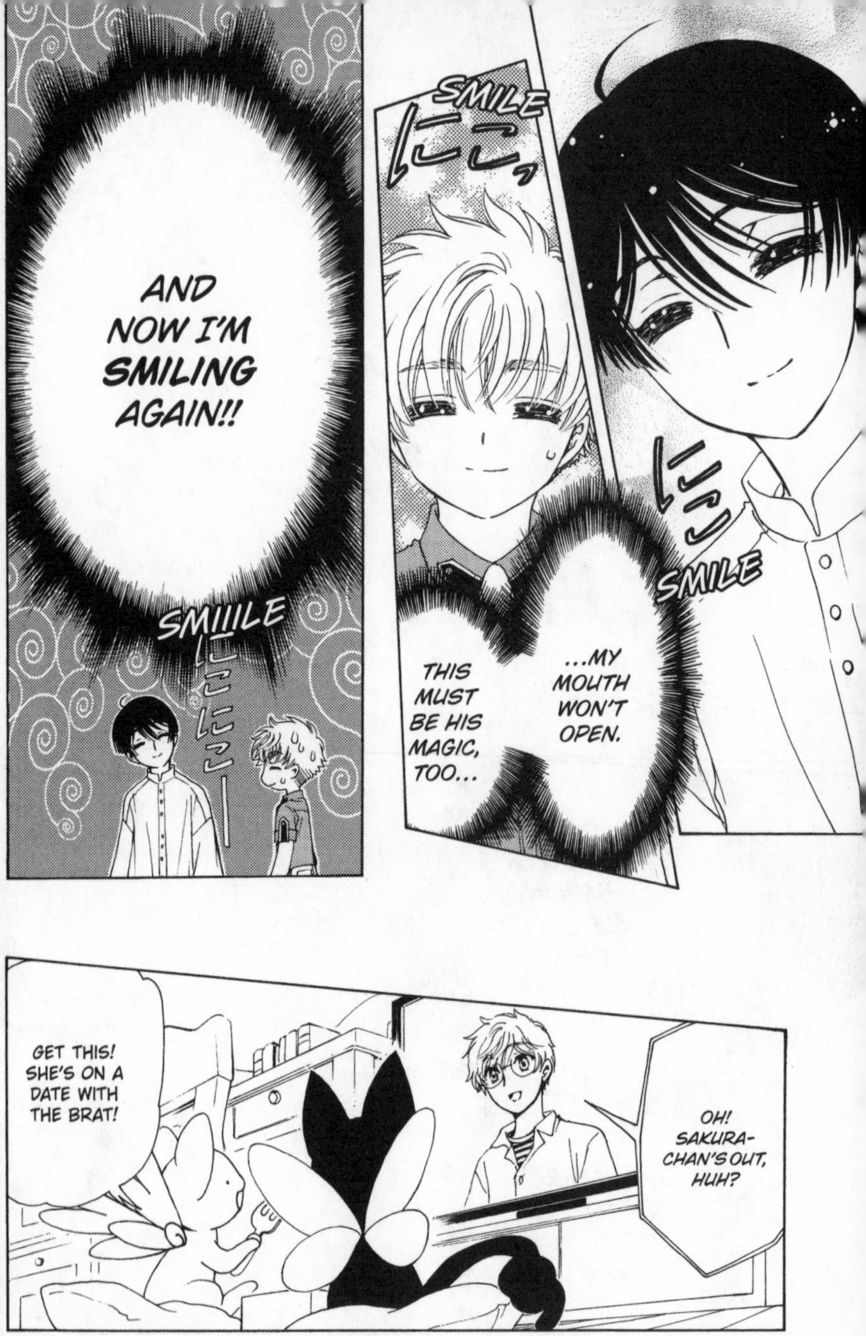
SMILE
SMILE
...MY MOUTH WON'T OPEN.
THIS MUST BE HIS MAGIC, TOO...
AND NOW I'M SMILING AGAIN!!
SMIIILE
OH! SAKURA-CHAN'S OUT, HUH?
GET THIS! SHE'S ON A DATE WITH THE BRAT!

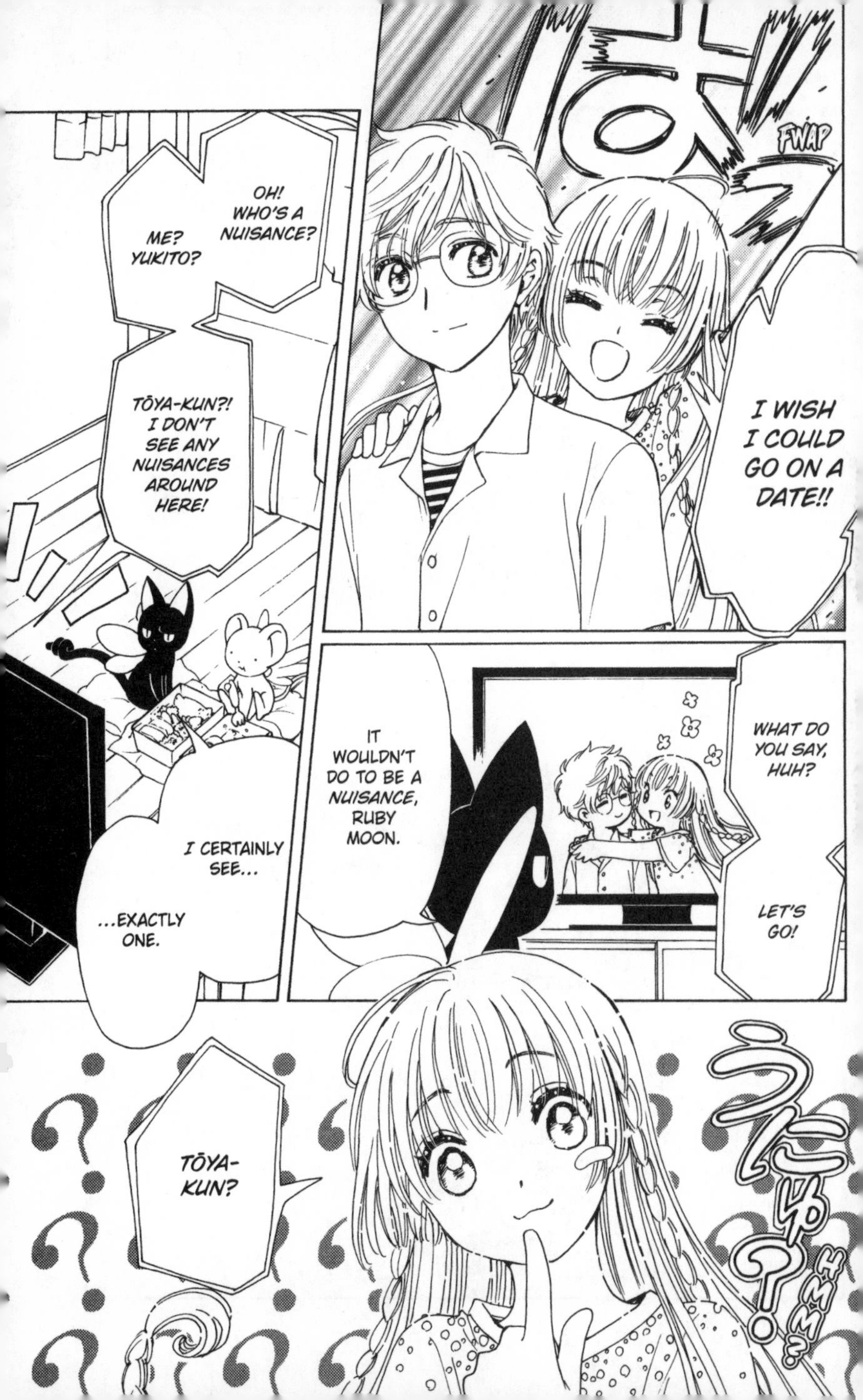
FWAP
I WISH I COULD GO ON A DATE!!
WHAT DO YOU SAY, HUH?
LET'S GO!
IT WOULDN'T DO TO BE A NUISANCE, RUBY MOON.
OH! WHO'S A NUISANCE?
ME? YUKITO?
TŌYA-KUN?! I DON'T SEE ANY NUISANCES AROUND HERE!
I CERTAINLY SEE...
...EXACTLY ONE.
HMMM?
TŌYA-KUN?

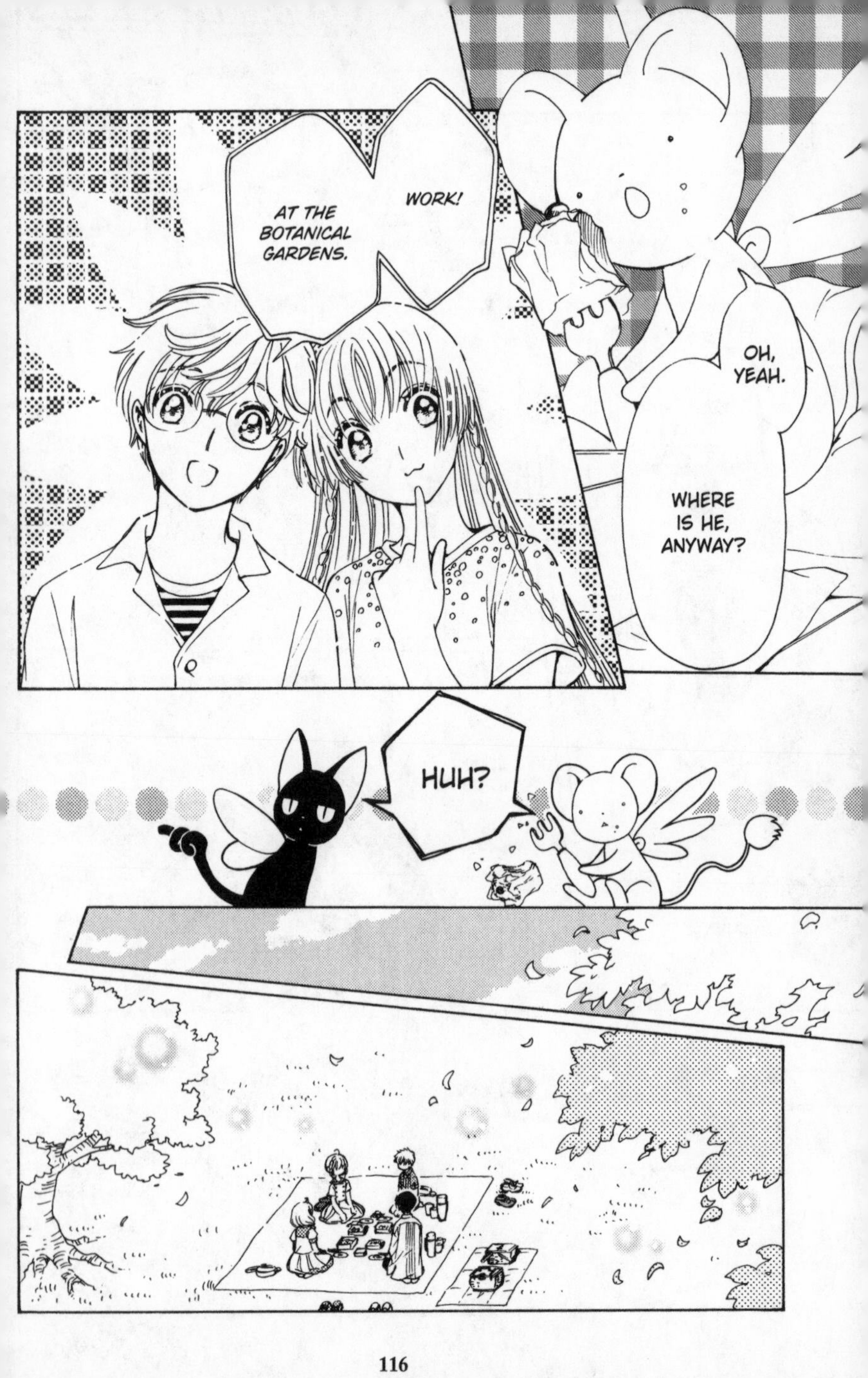
OH, YEAH.
WHERE IS HE, ANYWAY?
WORK!
AT THE BOTANICAL GARDENS.
HUH?

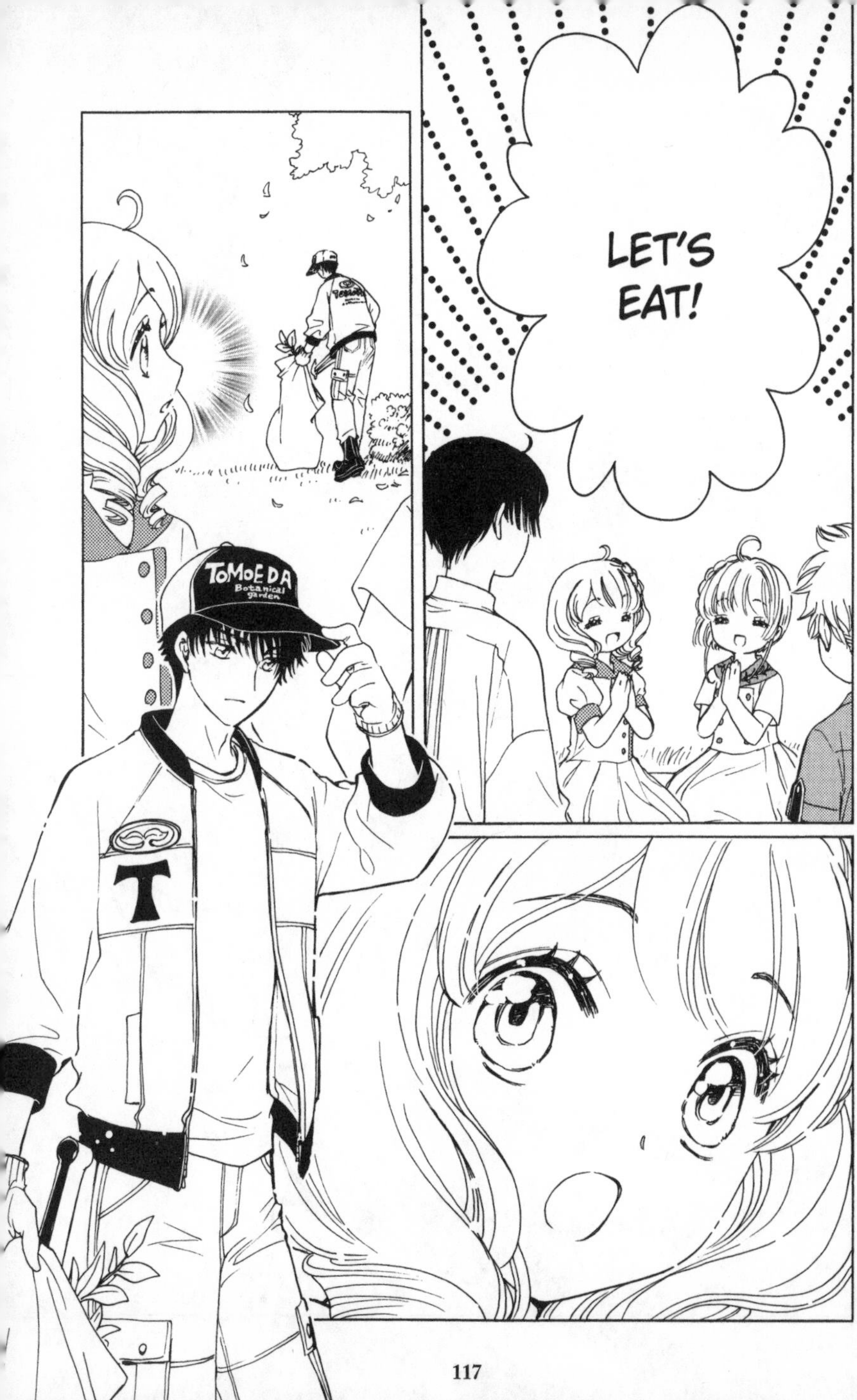
LET'S EAT!
TOMOEDA
Botanical garden

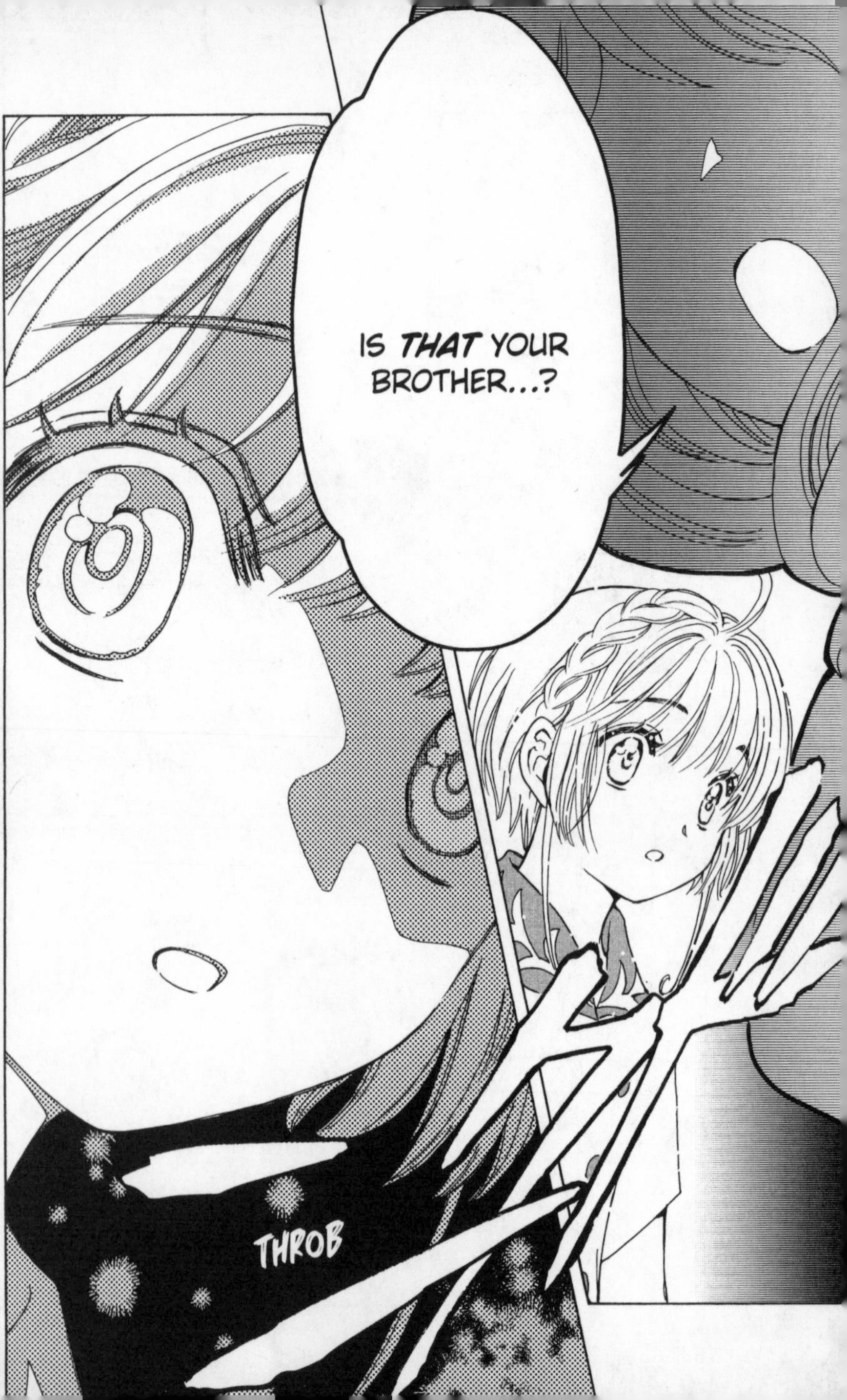
IS *THAT* YOUR BROTHER...?
THROB

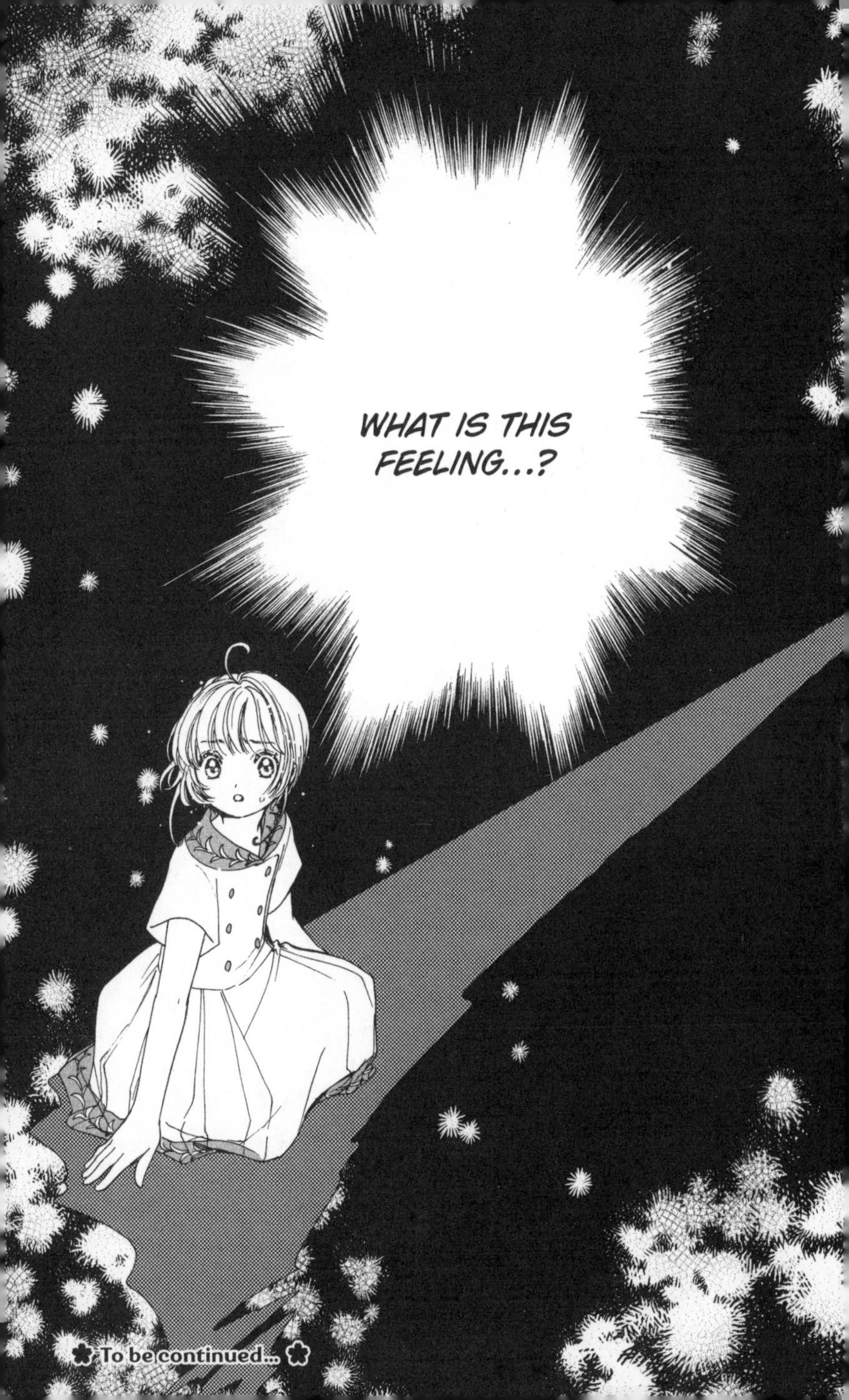
WHAT IS THIS FEELING...?
To be continued...

Cardcaptor Sakura

CLEAR CARD

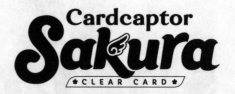

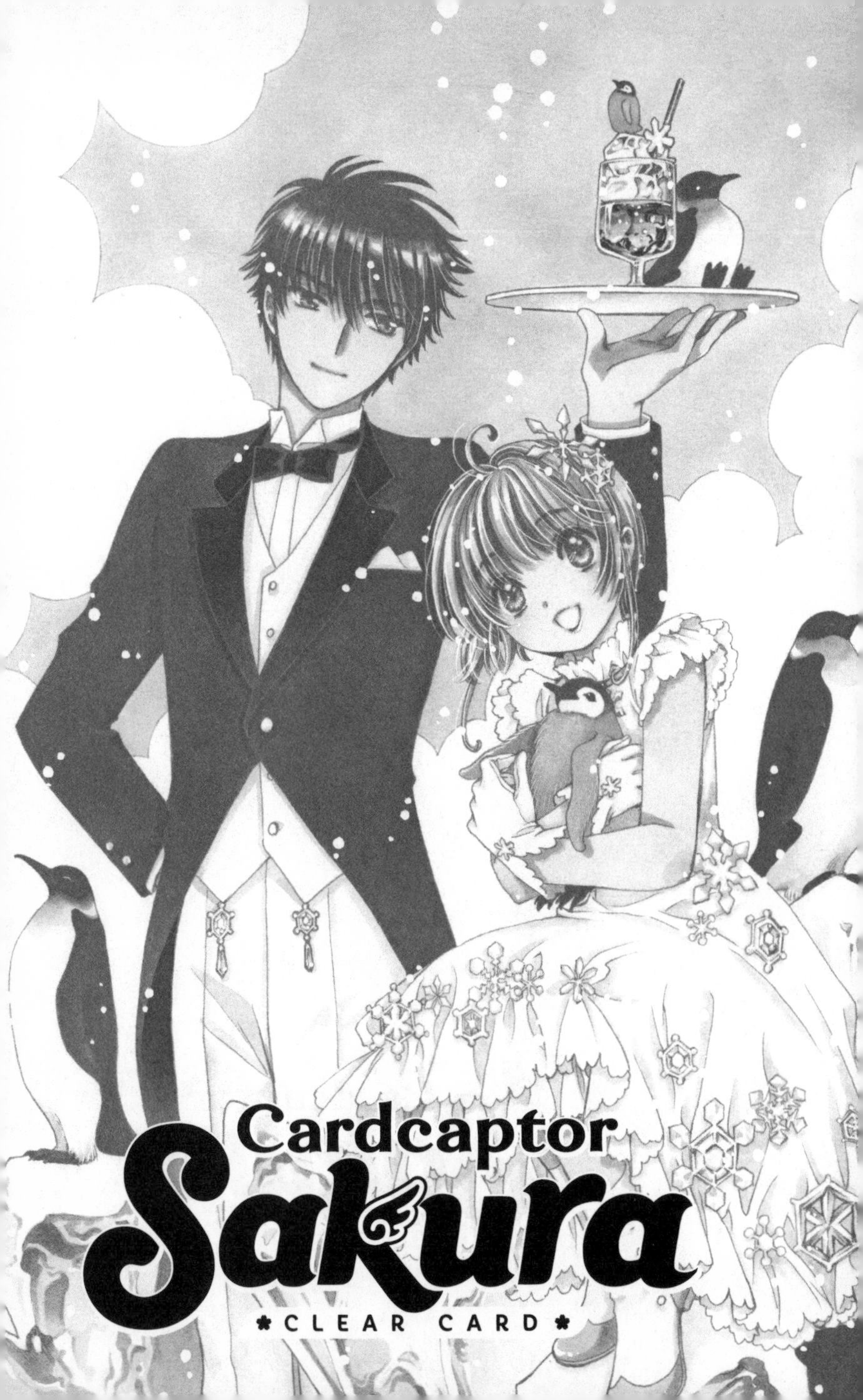
Cardcaptor
Sakura
CLEAR CARD

Cardcaptor Sakura
CLEAR CARD

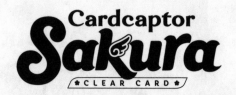

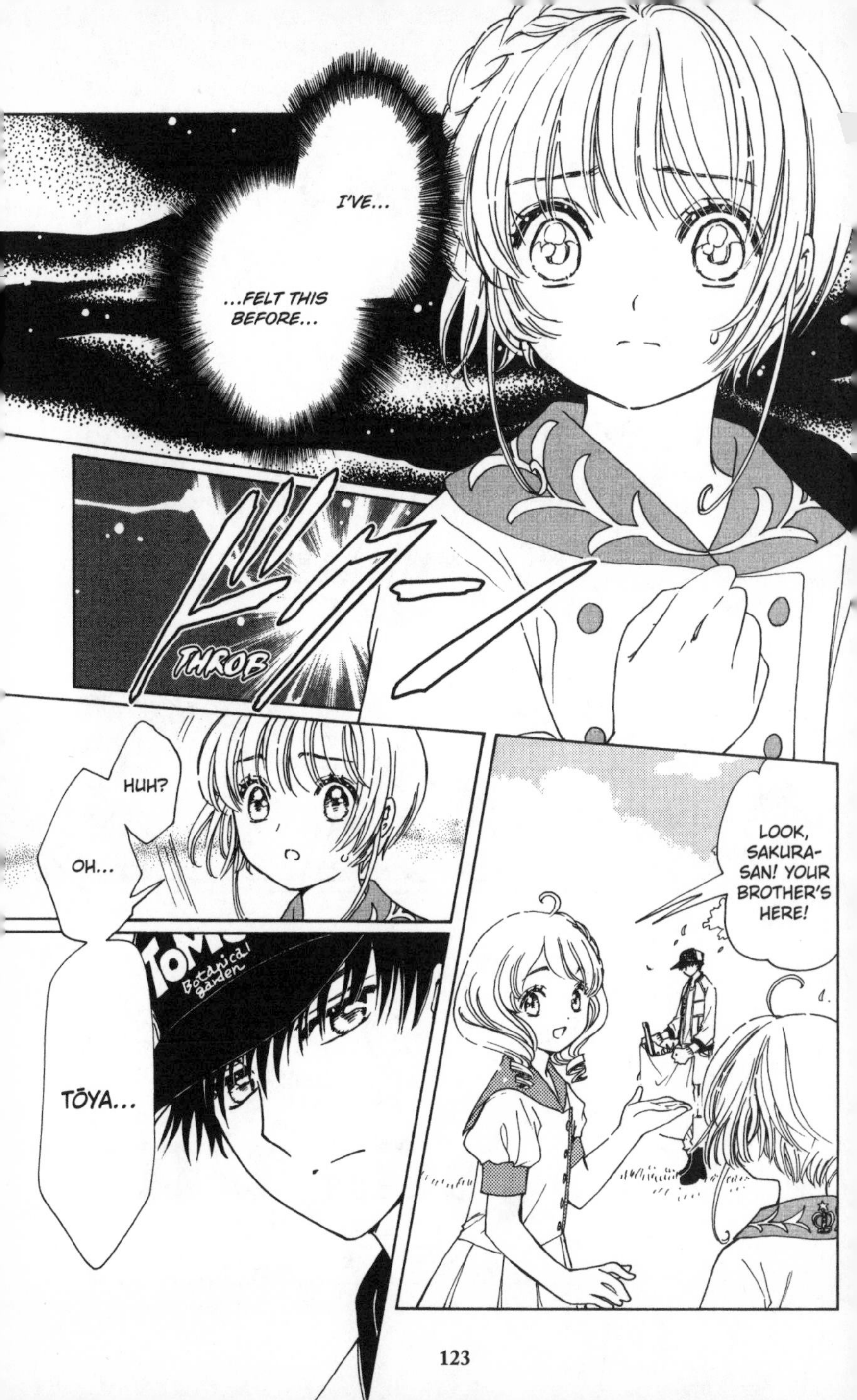

I'VE...
...FELT THIS BEFORE...
THROB
LOOK, SAKURA-SAN! YOUR BROTHER'S HERE!
HUH?
OH...
Botanical garden
TŌYA...

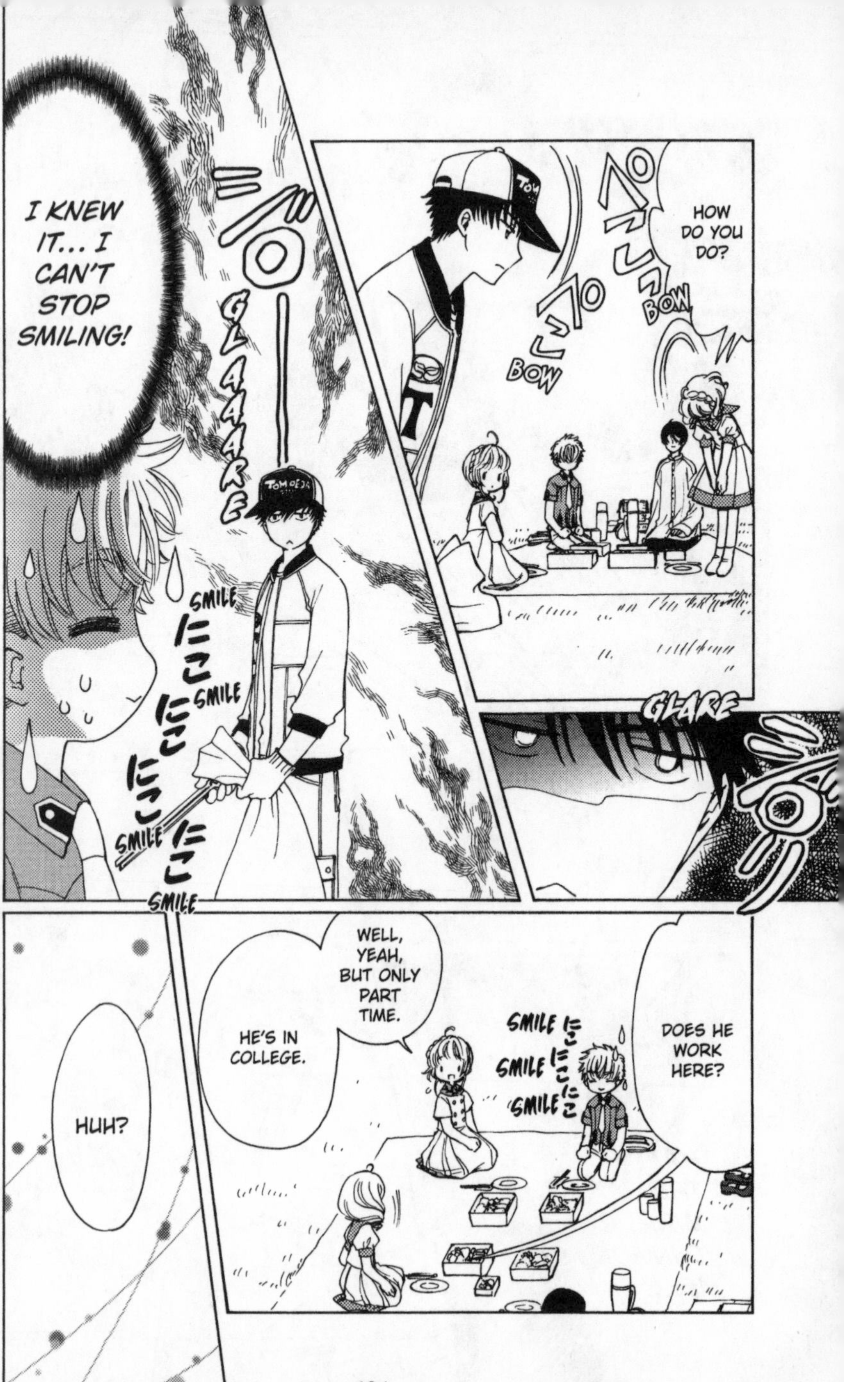
HOW DO YOU DO?
BOW
BOW
GLARE
GLAAAARE
SMILE
SMILE
SMILE
SMILE
I KNEW IT... I CAN'T STOP SMILING!
DOES HE WORK HERE?
SMILE
SMILE
SMILE
WELL, YEAH, BUT ONLY PART TIME.
HE'S IN COLLEGE.
HUH?

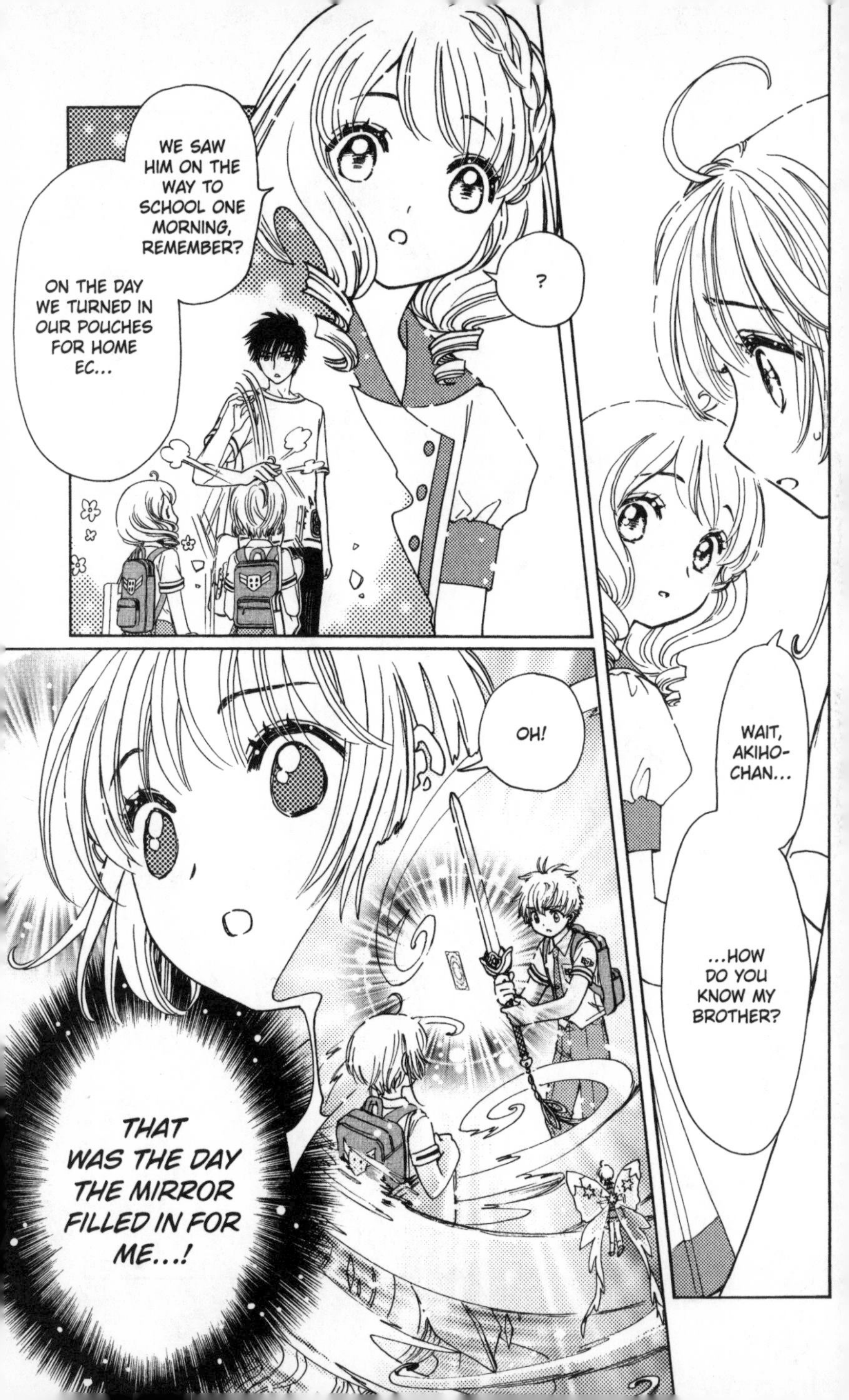
WAIT, AKIHO-CHAN...
...HOW DO YOU KNOW MY BROTHER?
?
WE SAW HIM ON THE WAY TO SCHOOL ONE MORNING, REMEMBER?
ON THE DAY WE TURNED IN OUR POUCHES FOR HOME EC...
OH!
THAT WAS THE DAY THE MIRROR FILLED IN FOR ME...!

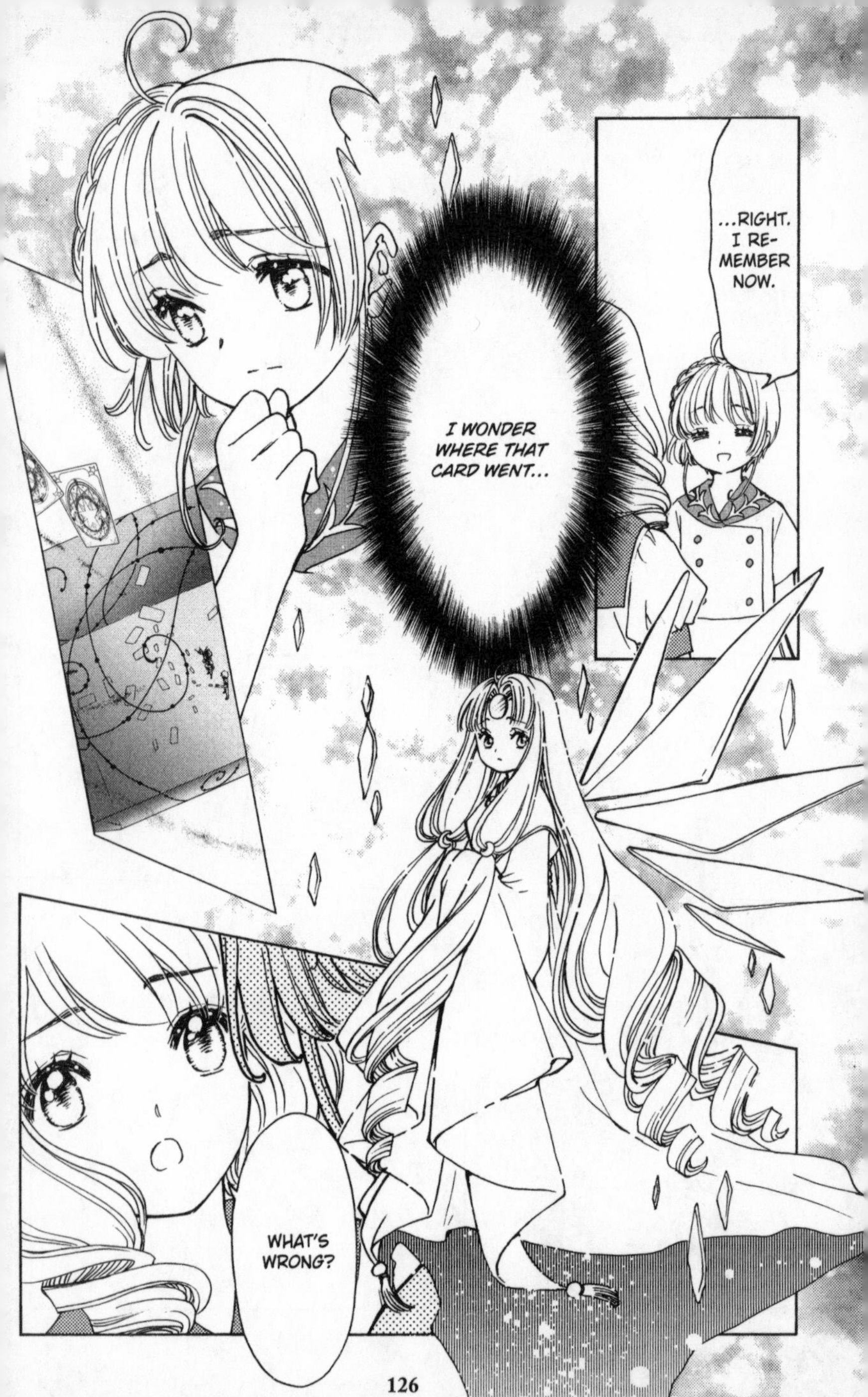
...RIGHT. I RE- MEMBER NOW.
I WONDER WHERE THAT CARD WENT...
WHAT'S WRONG?

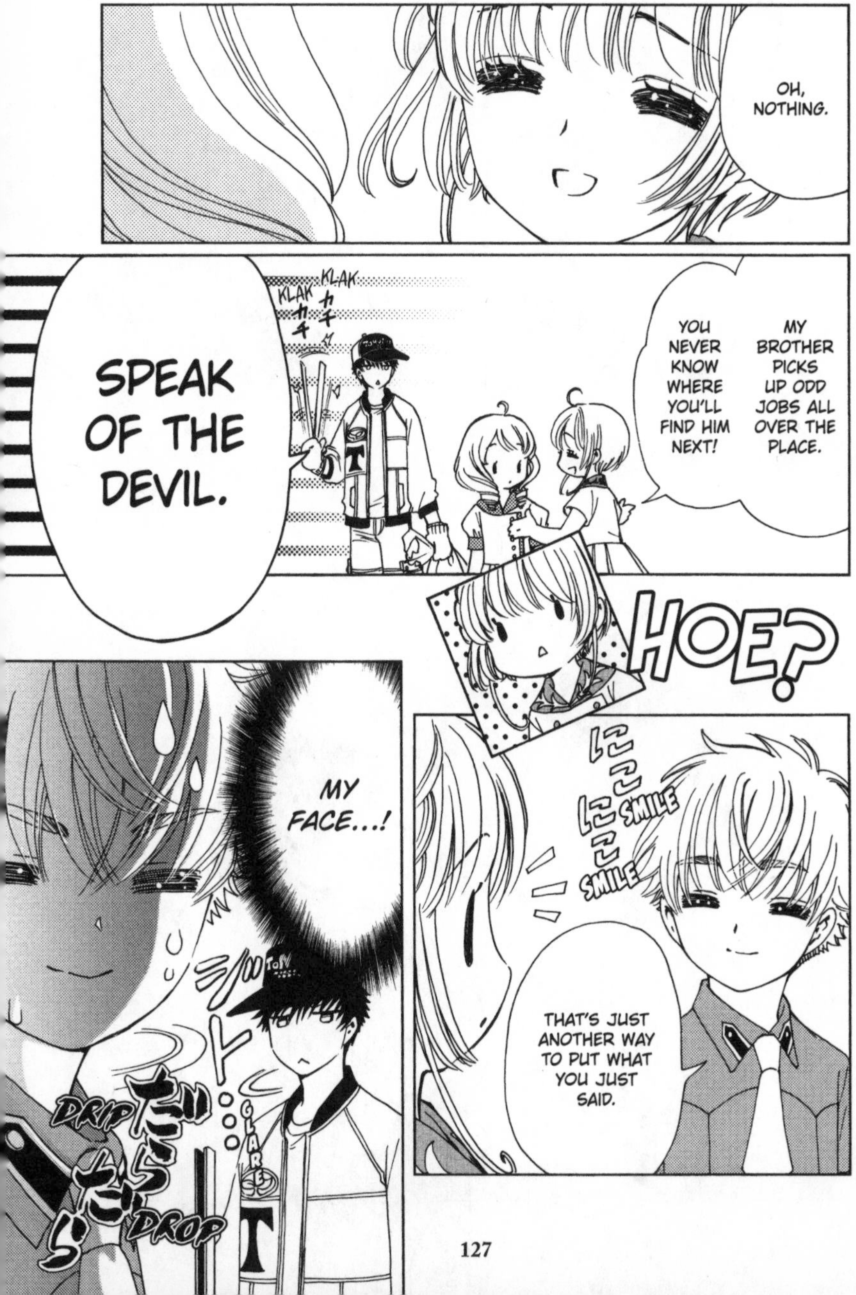

OH, NOTHING.
MY BROTHER PICKS UP ODD JOBS ALL OVER THE PLACE.
YOU NEVER KNOW WHERE YOU'LL FIND HIM NEXT!
KLAK カチ
KLAK カチ
SPEAK OF THE DEVIL.
HOE?
にこにこ SMILE
にこにこ SMILE
THAT'S JUST ANOTHER WAY TO PUT WHAT YOU JUST SAID.
MY FACE...!
GLARE
DRIP
DROP

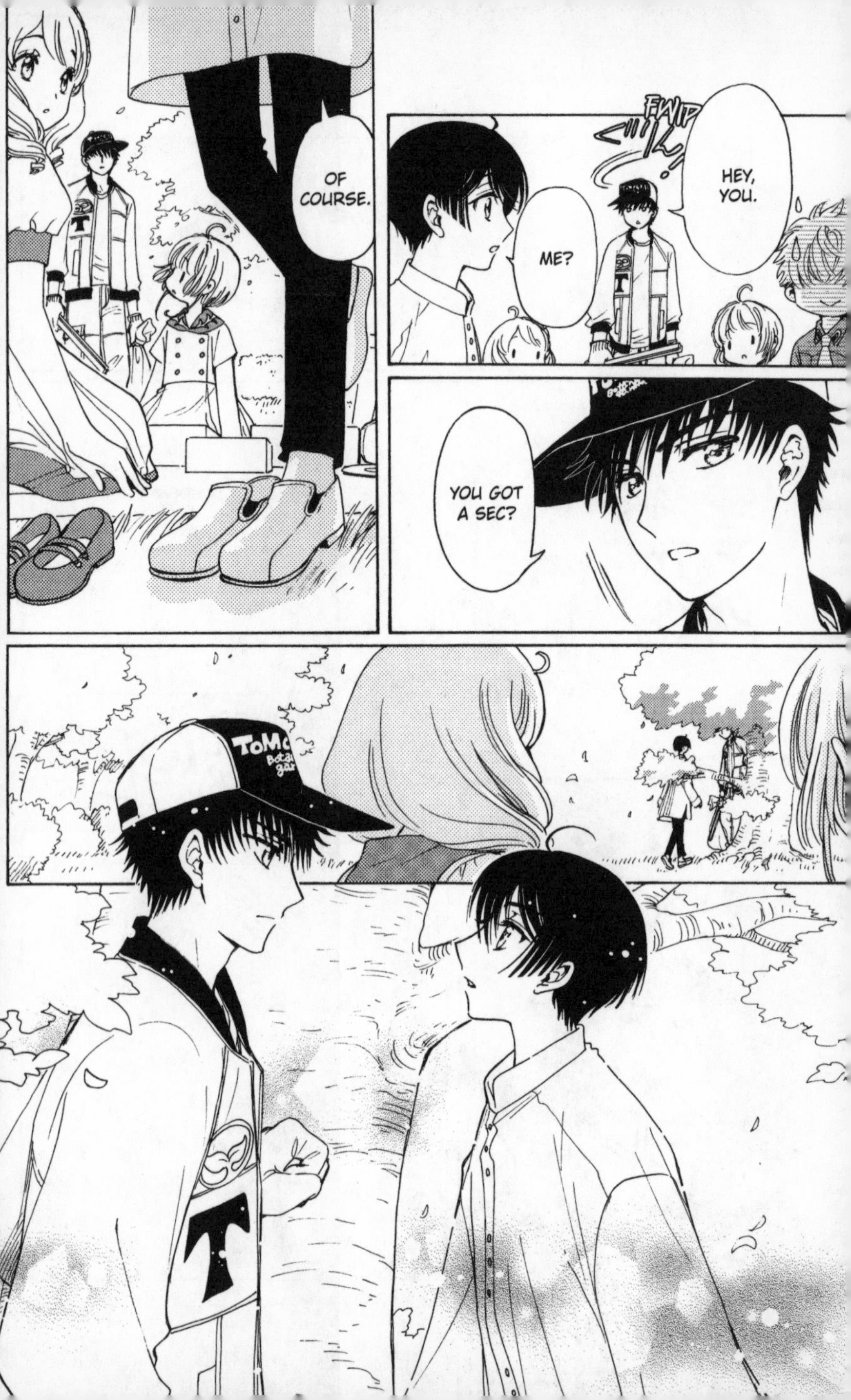
HEY, YOU.
FWIP
ME?
YOU GOT A SEC?
OF COURSE.

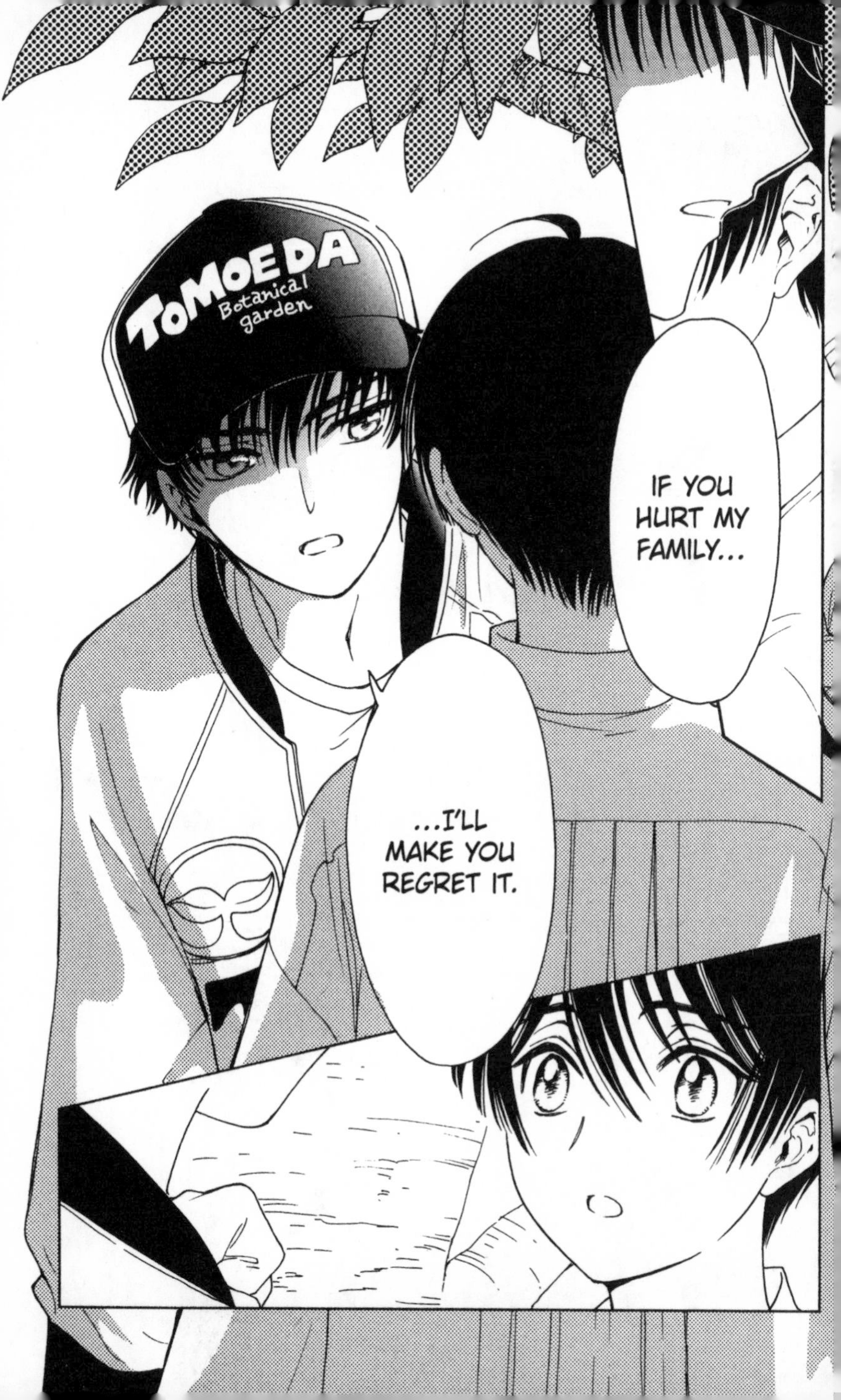
TOMOEDA Botanical garden
IF YOU HURT MY FAMILY...
...I'LL MAKE YOU REGRET IT.

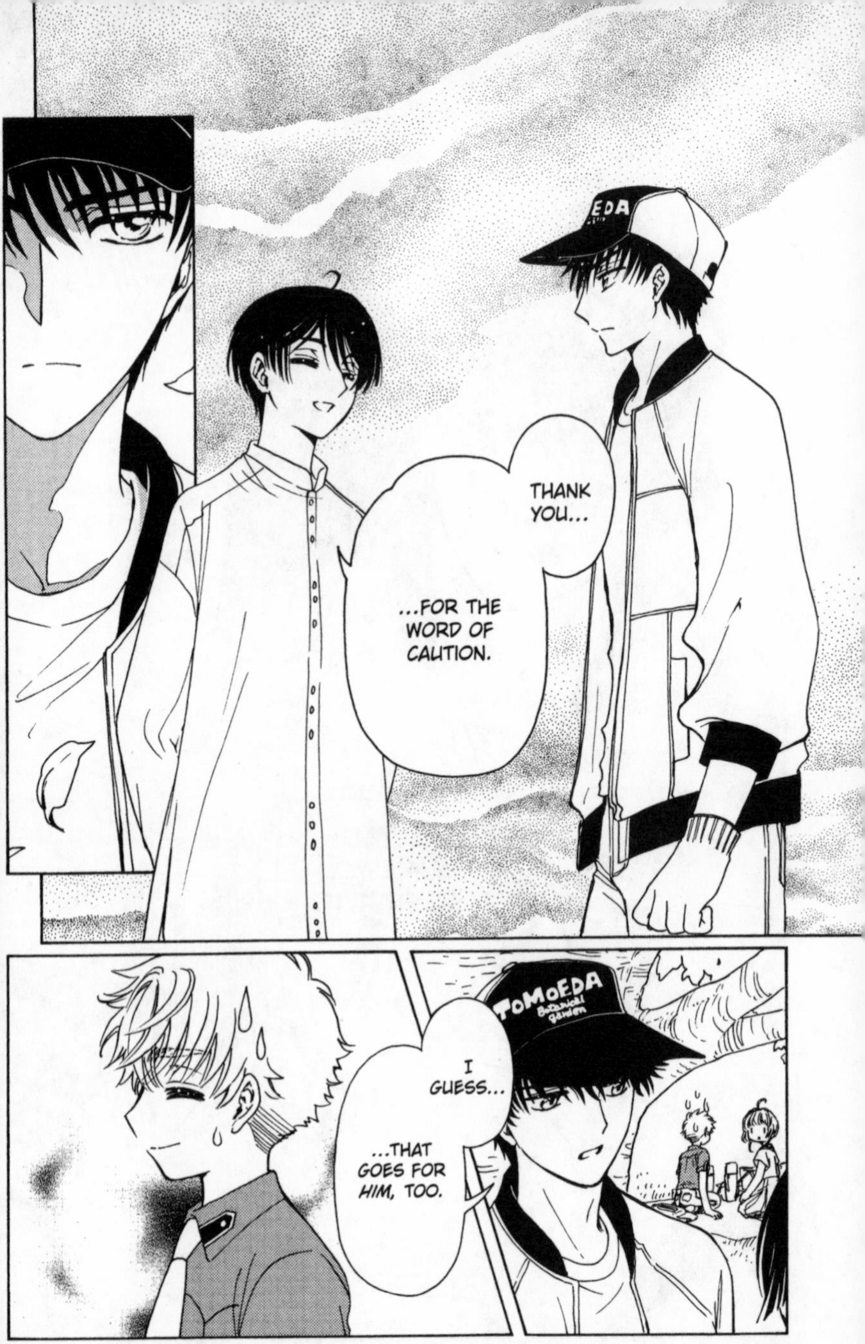
THANK YOU...
...FOR THE WORD OF CAUTION.
TOMOEDA
I GUESS...
...THAT GOES FOR HIM, TOO.

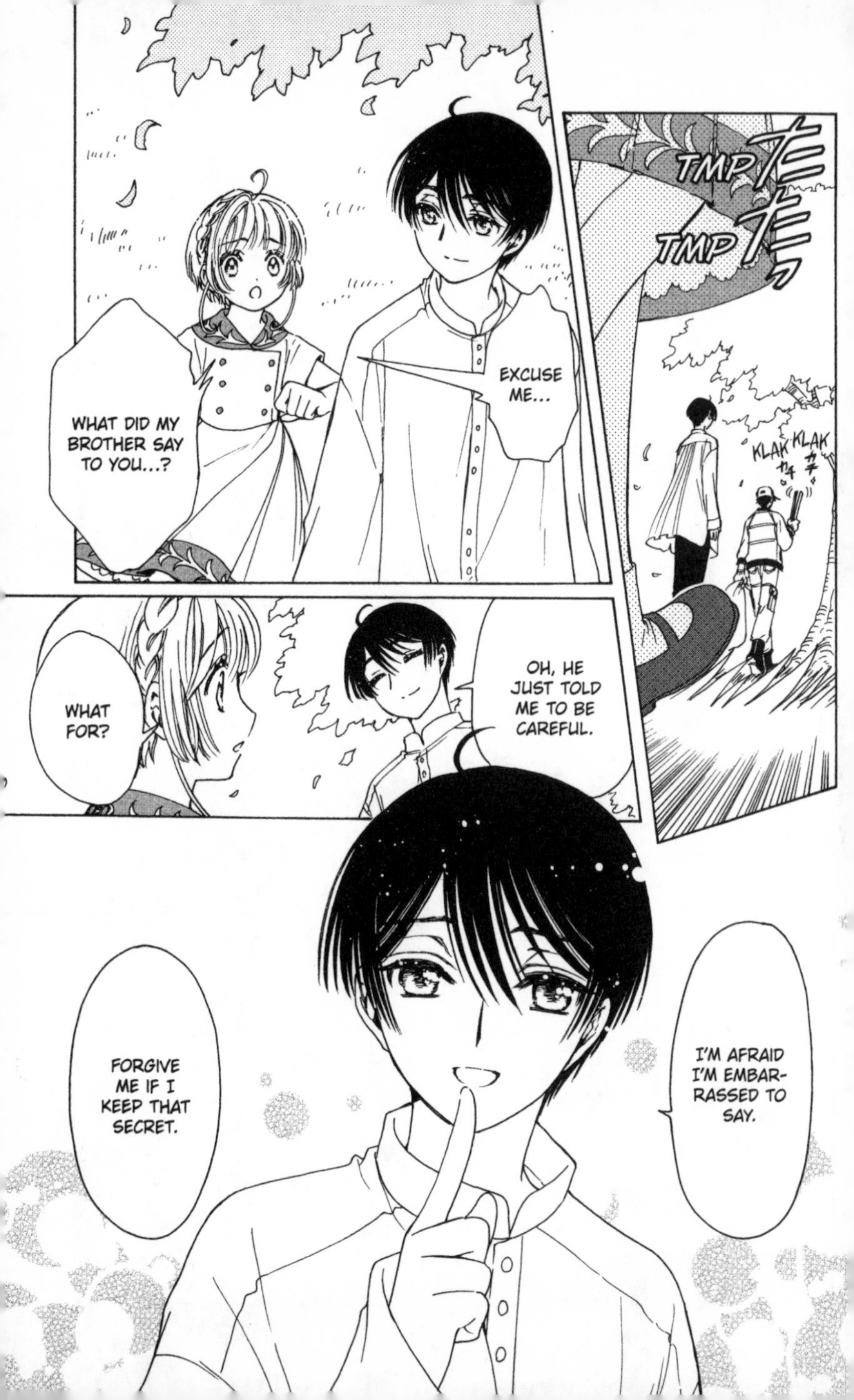
TMP
TMP
KLAK KLAK
EXCUSE ME...
WHAT DID MY BROTHER SAY TO YOU...?
OH, HE JUST TOLD ME TO BE CAREFUL.
WHAT FOR?
I'M AFRAID I'M EMBARRASSED TO SAY.
FORGIVE ME IF I KEEP THAT SECRET.

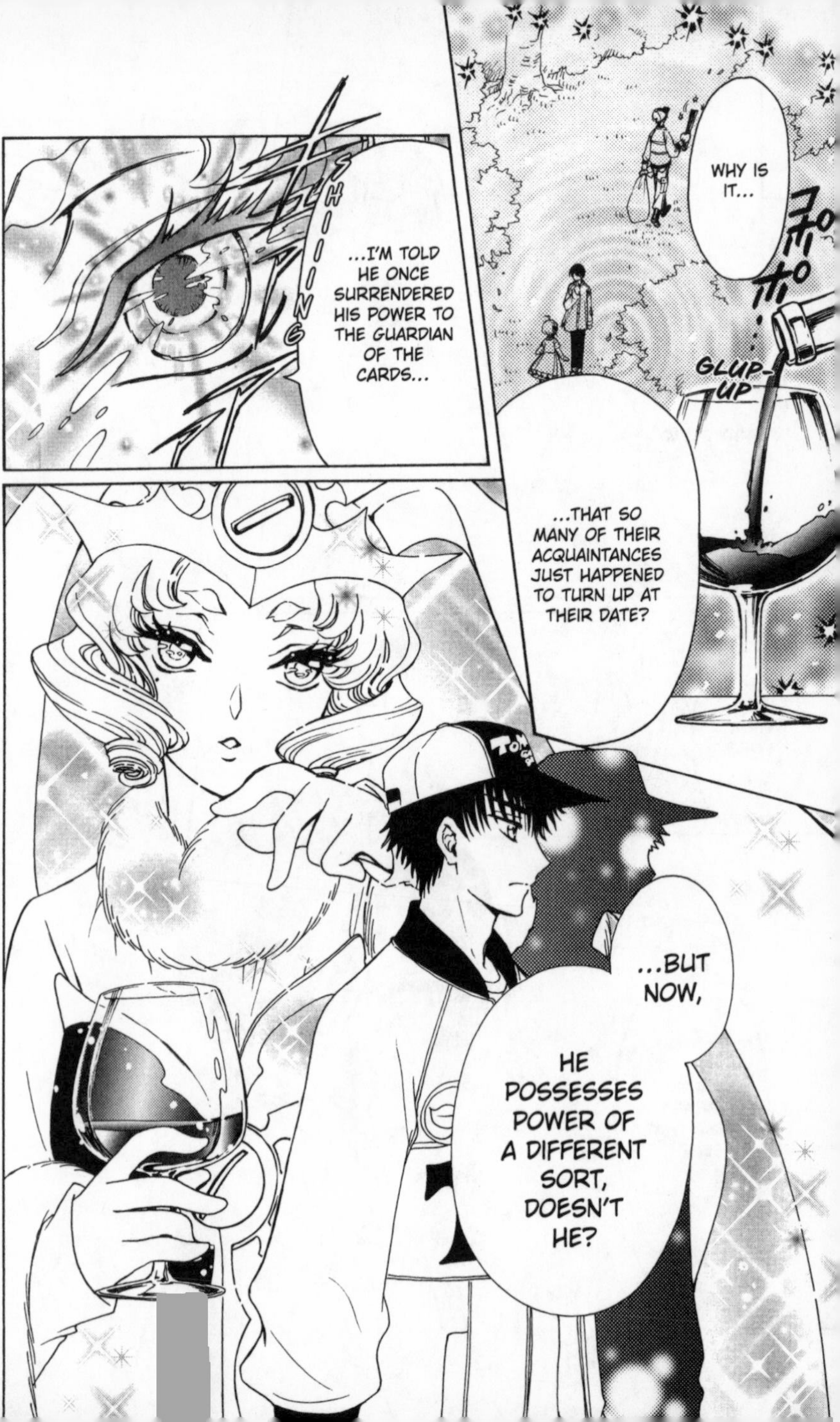
WHY IS IT...
GLUP-UP
...THAT SO MANY OF THEIR ACQUAINTANCES JUST HAPPENED TO TURN UP AT THEIR DATE?
SHIIIING
...I'M TOLD HE ONCE SURRENDERED HIS POWER TO THE GUARDIAN OF THE CARDS...
...BUT NOW,
HE POSSESSES POWER OF A DIFFERENT SORT, DOESN'T HE?

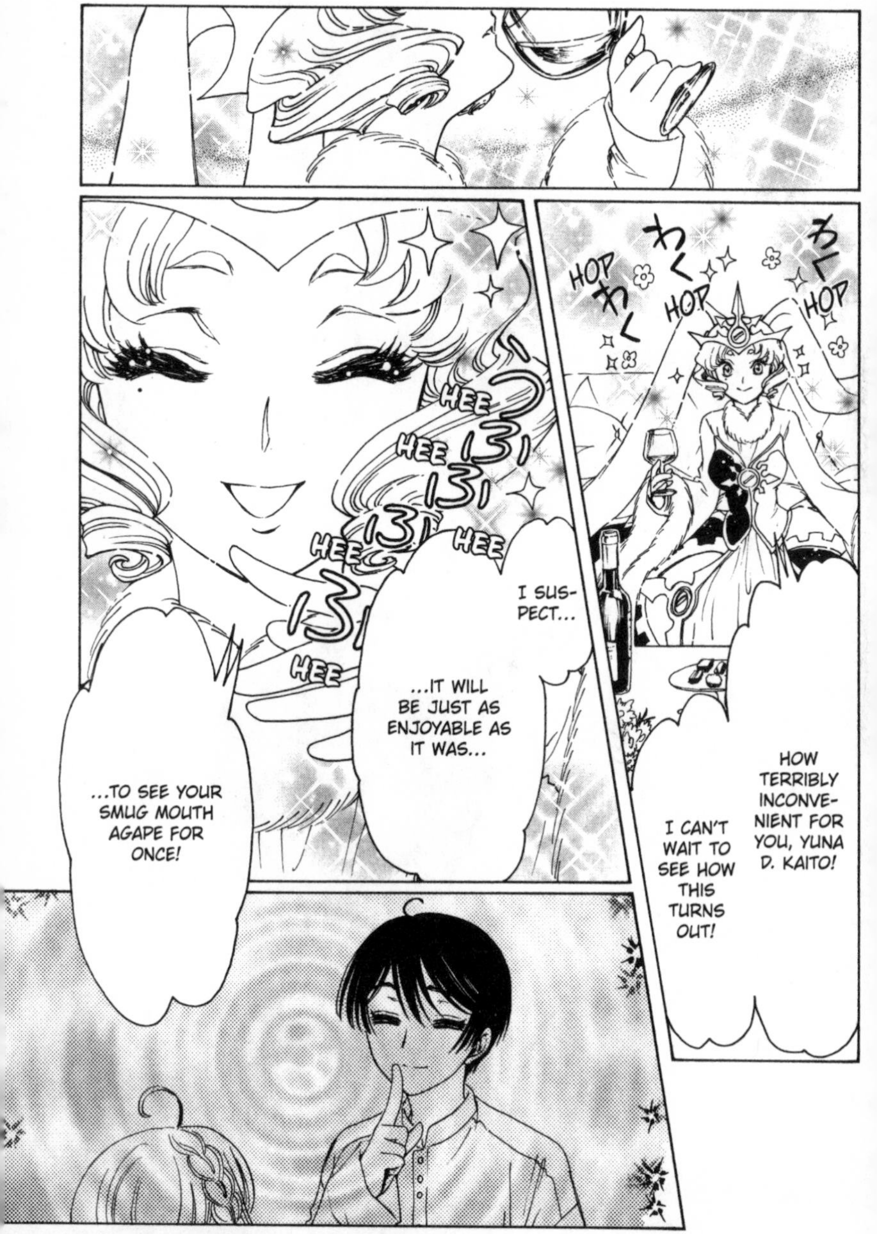
わく
HOP
わく
HOP
わく
HOP
HOW TERRIBLY INCONVENIENT FOR YOU, YUNA D. KAITO!
I CAN'T WAIT TO SEE HOW THIS TURNS OUT!
ふふふふ
HEE
HEE
HEE
HEE
HEE
I SUSPECT...
...IT WILL BE JUST AS ENJOYABLE AS IT WAS...
...TO SEE YOUR SMUG MOUTH AGAPE FOR ONCE!

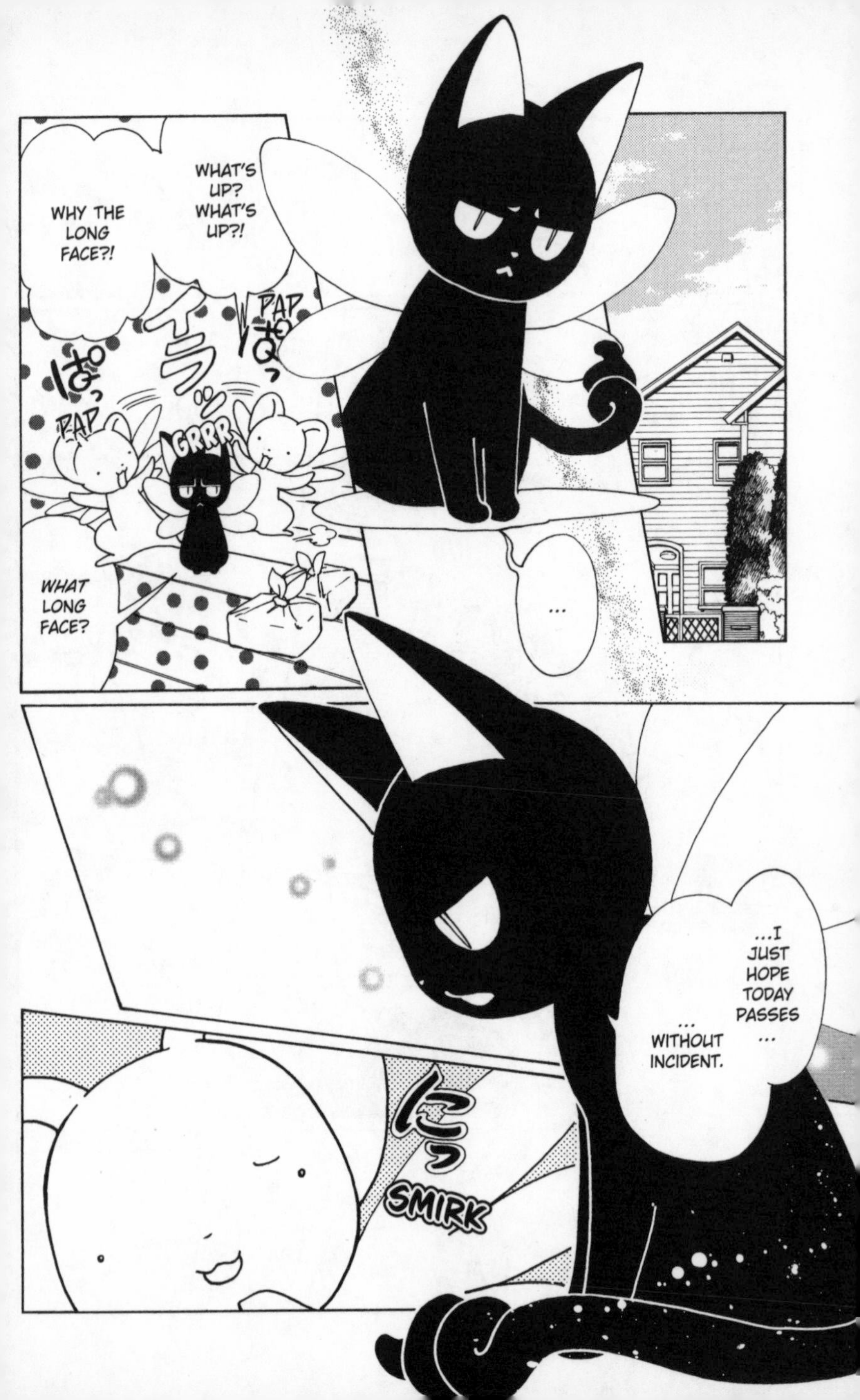
...
WHAT'S UP? WHAT'S UP?!
WHY THE LONG FACE?!
PAP
ぽっ
イラッ
PAP
ぽっ
GRRR
WHAT LONG FACE?
...I JUST HOPE TODAY PASSES ...
... WITHOUT INCIDENT.
にっ
SMIRK

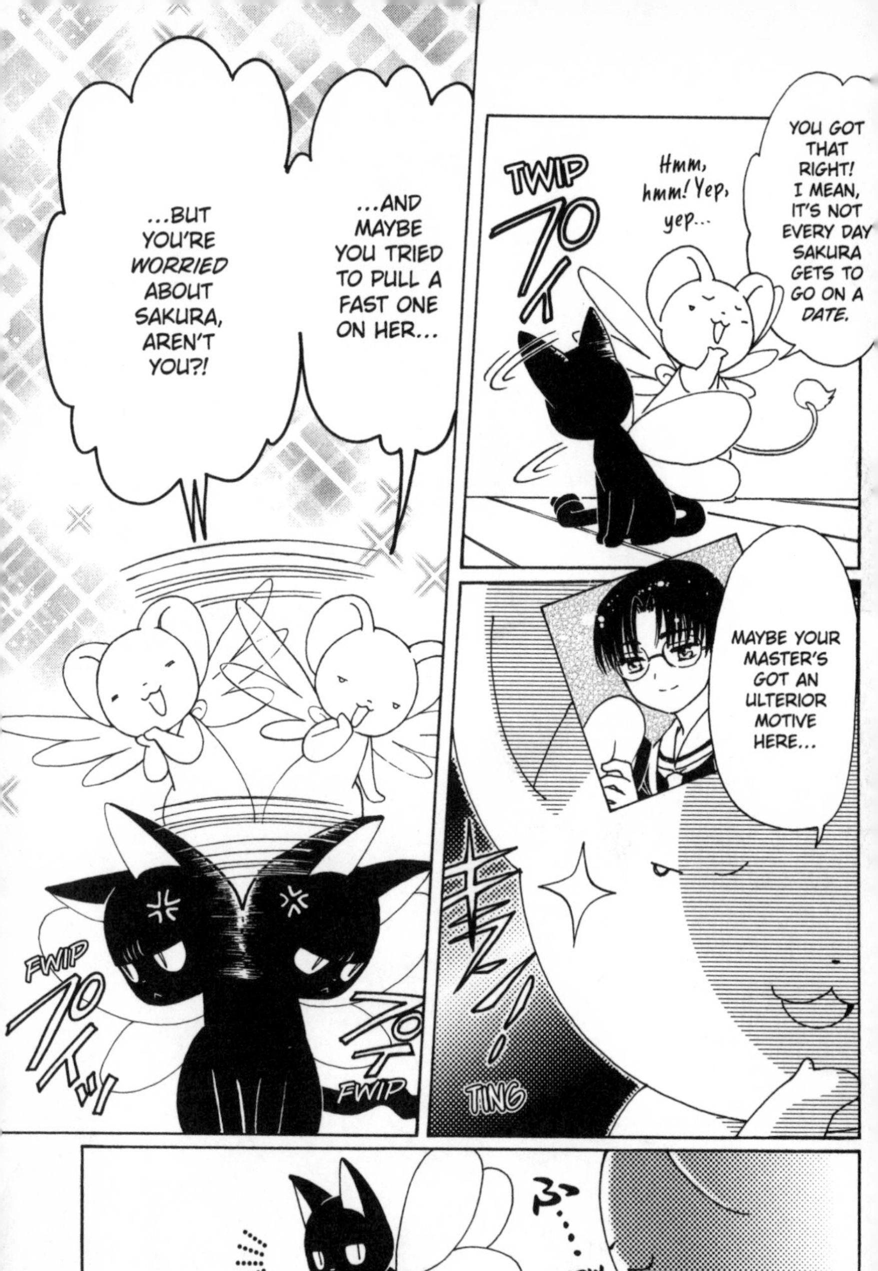
YOU GOT THAT RIGHT! I MEAN, IT'S NOT EVERY DAY SAKURA GETS TO GO ON A *DATE.*
Hmm, hmm! Yep, yep...
TWIP
MAYBE YOUR MASTER'S GOT AN ULTERIOR MOTIVE HERE...
TING
...AND MAYBE YOU TRIED TO PULL A FAST ONE ON HER...
...BUT YOU'RE *WORRIED* ABOUT SAKURA, AREN'T YOU?!
FWIP
FWIP
PHEW

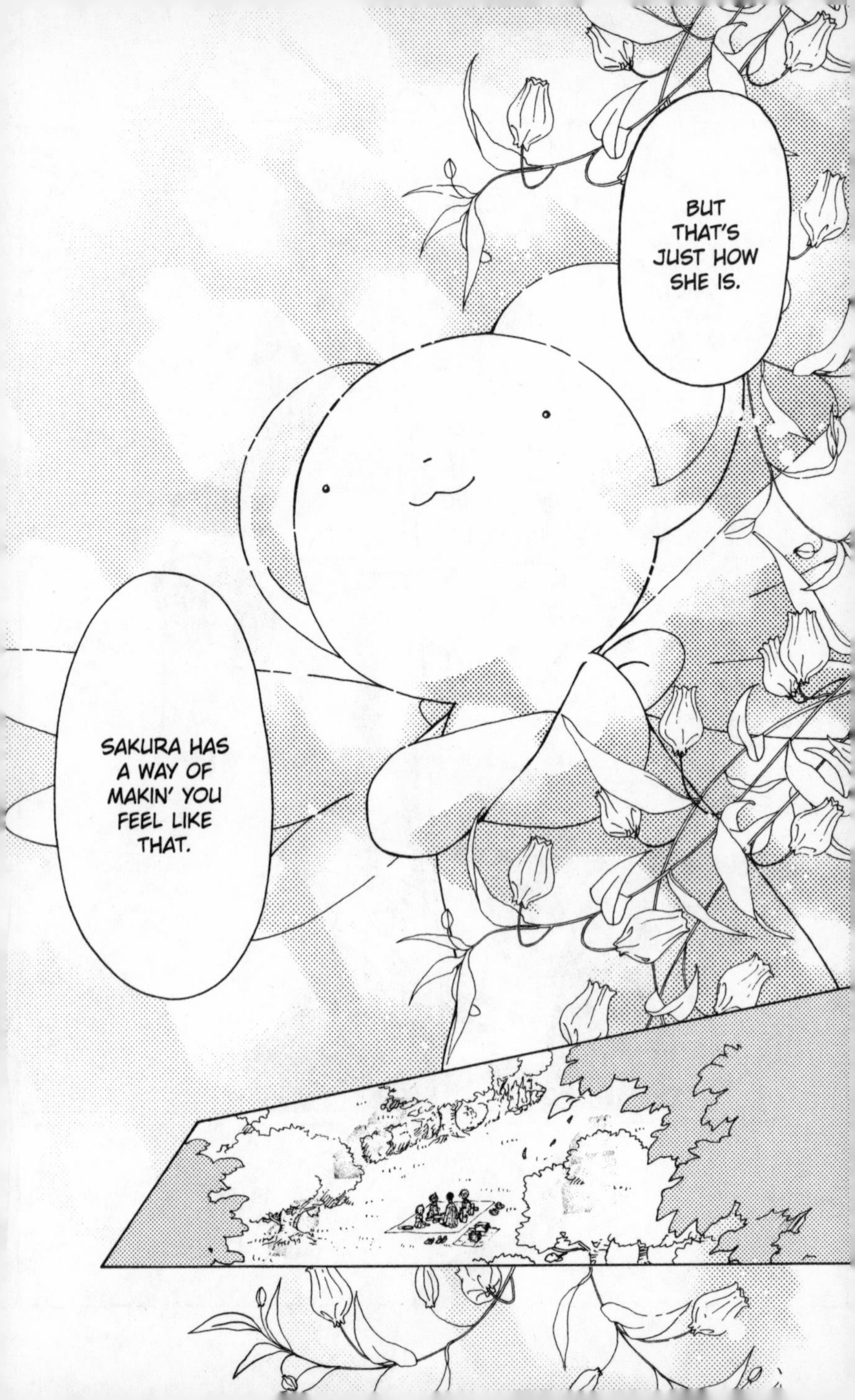
BUT THAT'S JUST HOW SHE IS.
SAKURA HAS A WAY OF MAKIN' YOU FEEL LIKE THAT.

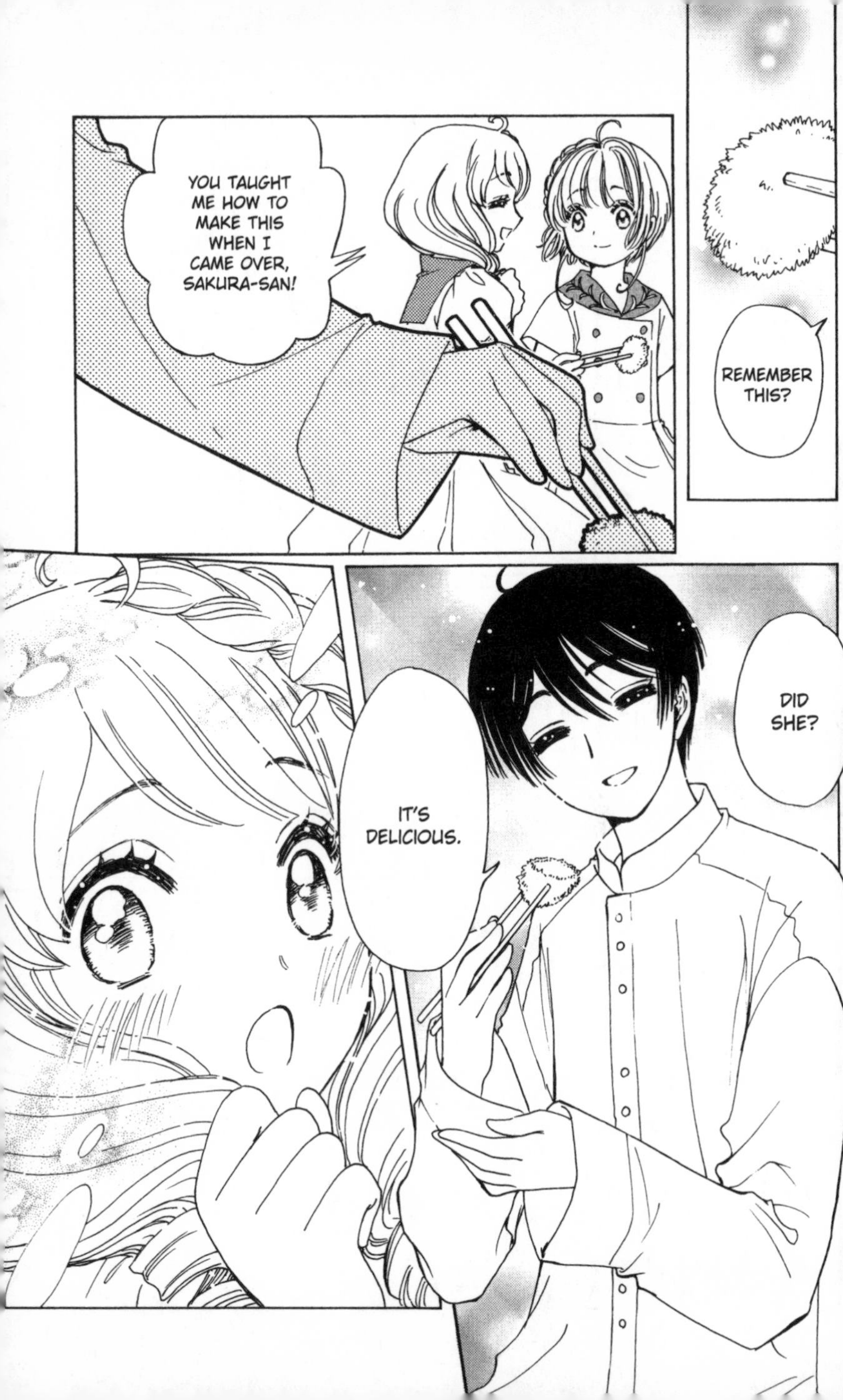
REMEMBER THIS?
YOU TAUGHT ME HOW TO MAKE THIS WHEN I CAME OVER, SAKURA-SAN!
DID SHE?
IT'S DELICIOUS.

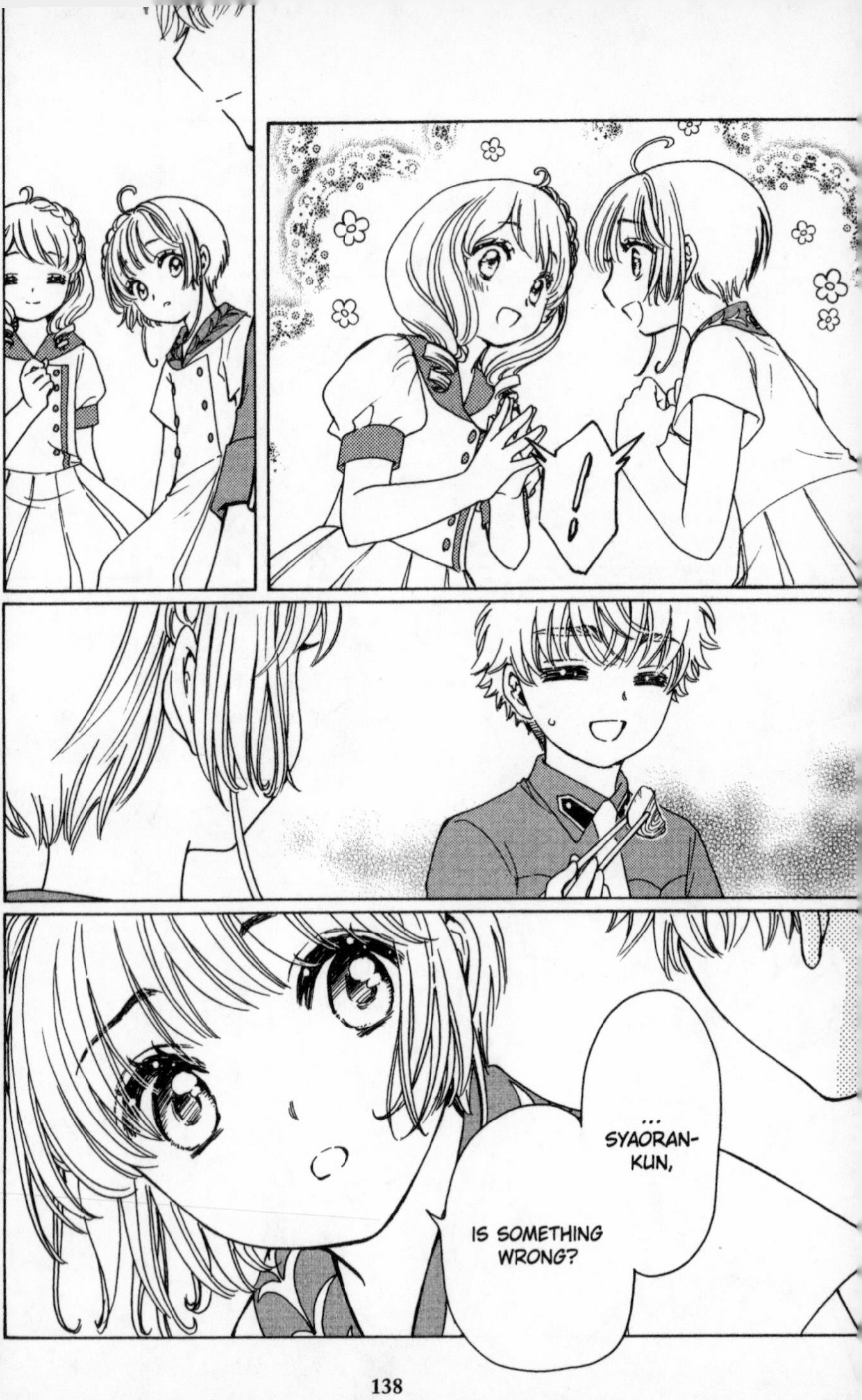

!
... SYAORAN-KUN,
IS SOMETHING WRONG?

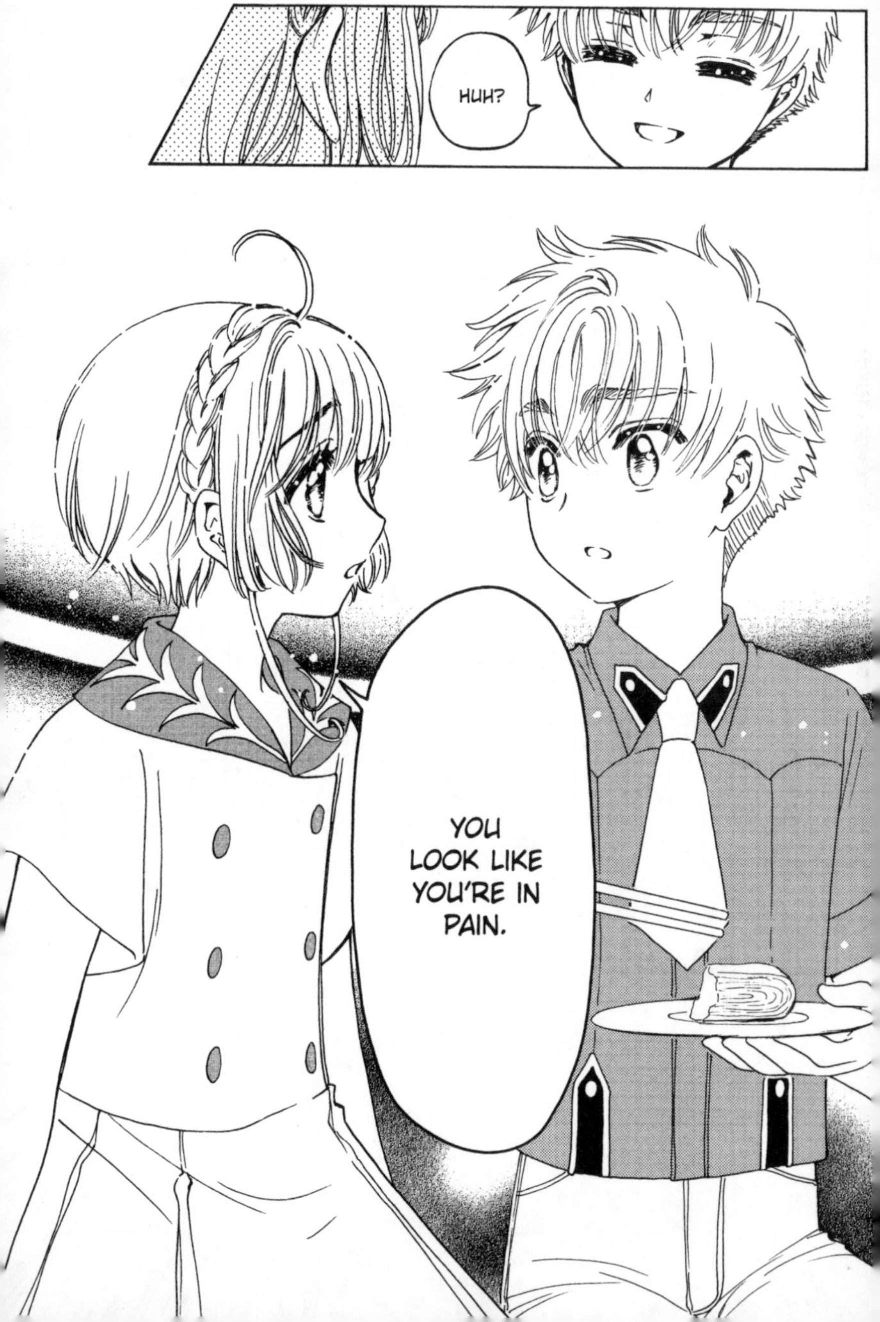
HUH?
YOU LOOK LIKE YOU'RE IN PAIN.

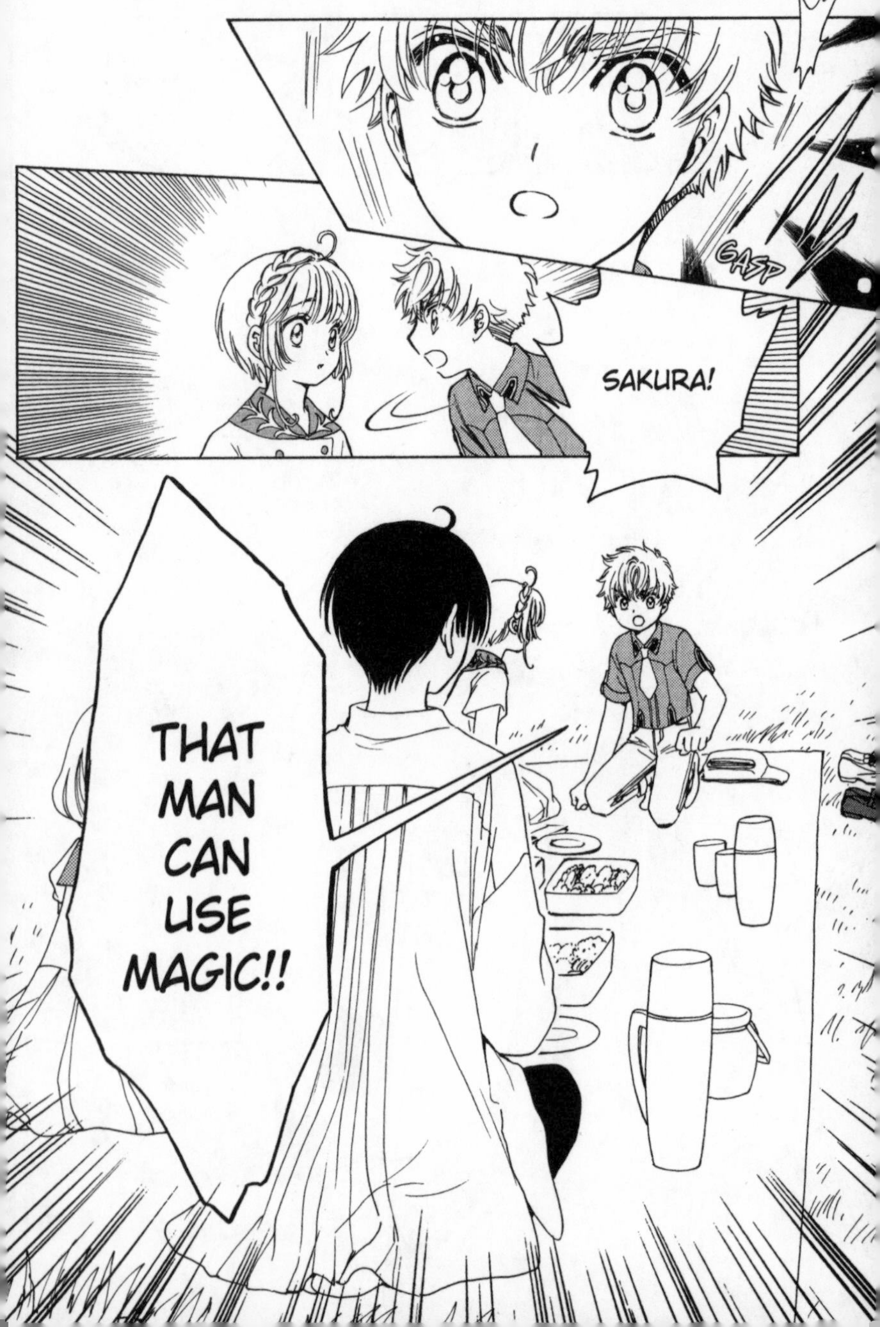
GASP
SAKURA!
THAT MAN CAN USE MAGIC!!

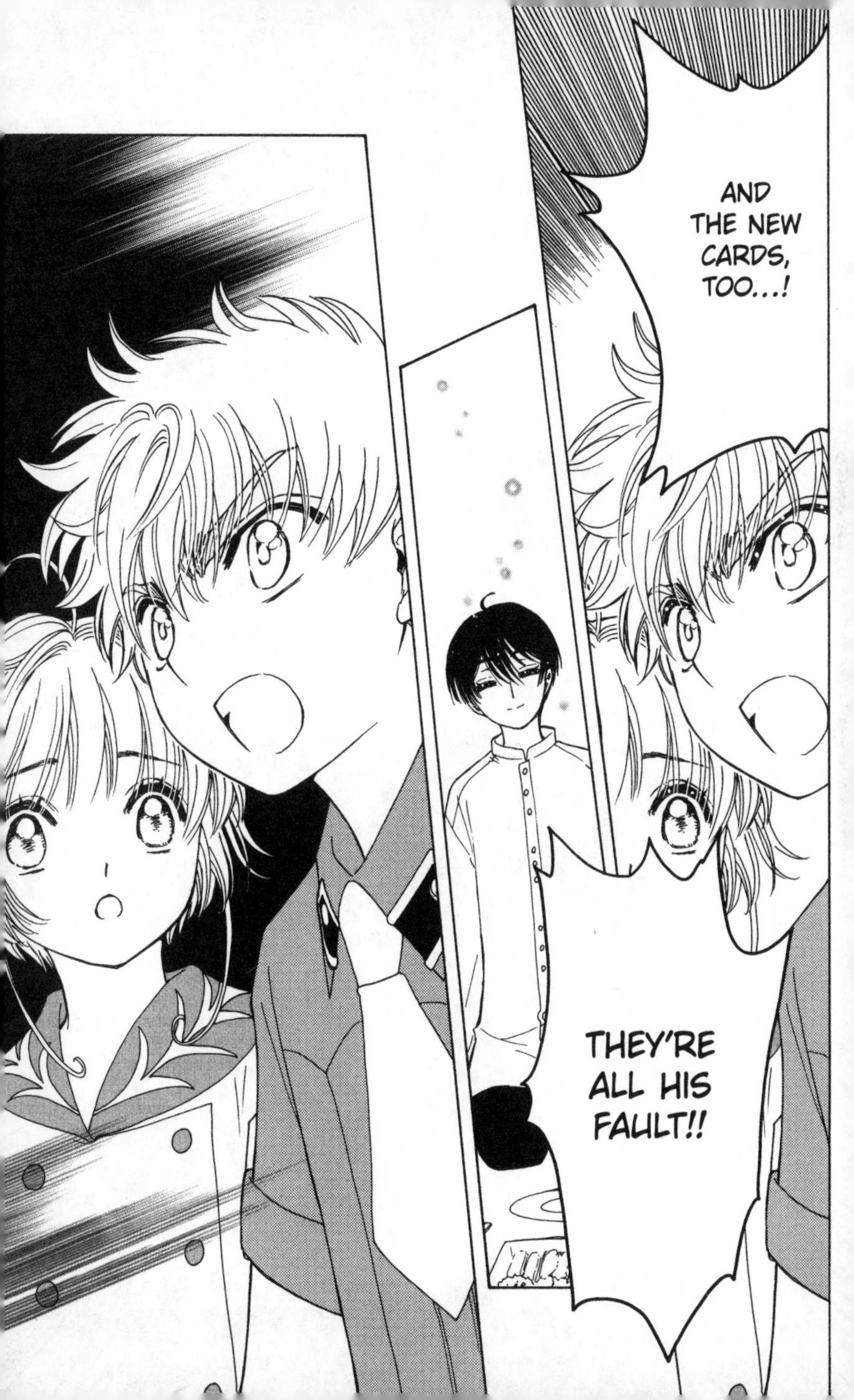
AND THE NEW CARDS, TOO...!
THEY'RE ALL HIS FAULT!!

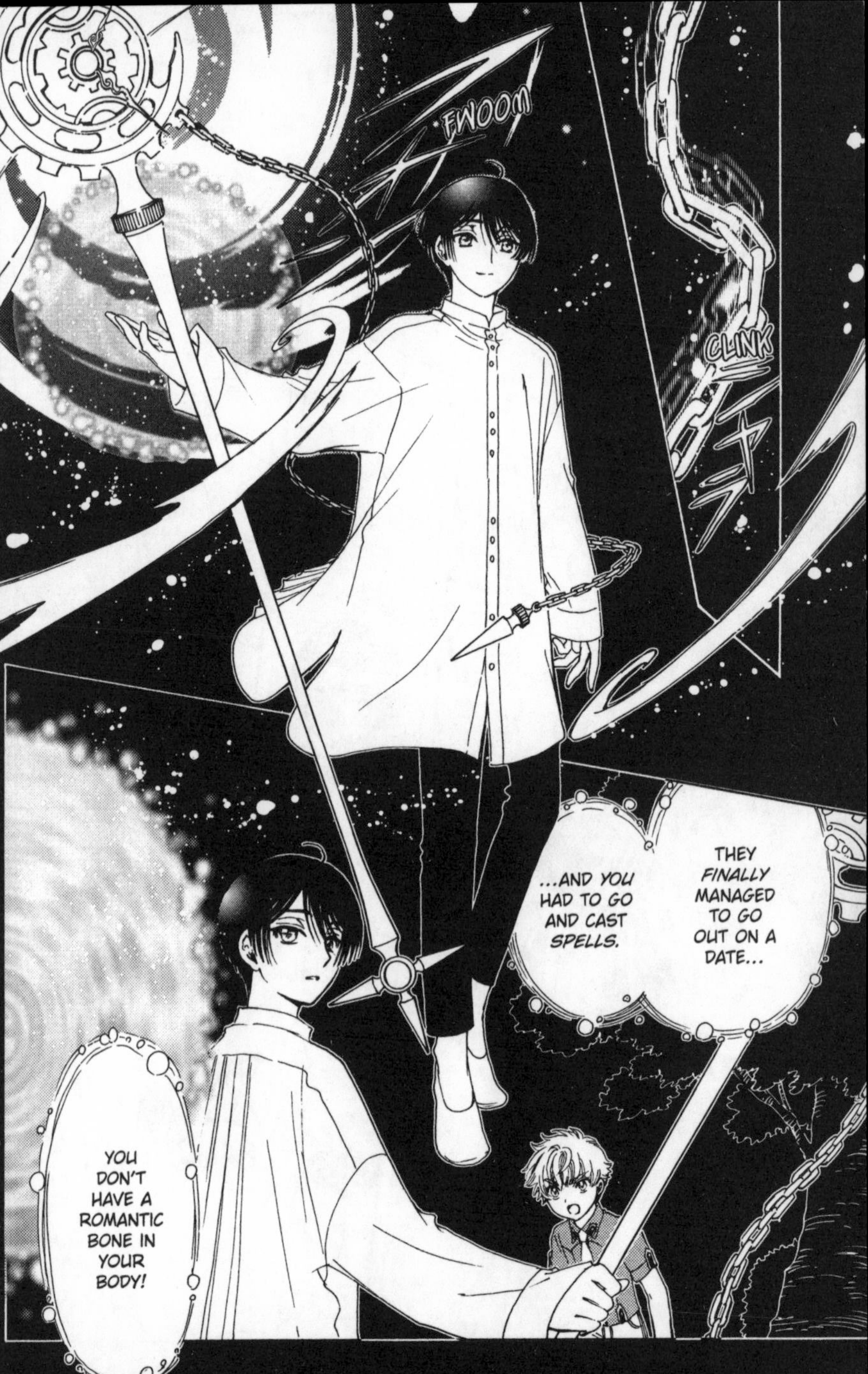
FWOOM
CLINK
THEY FINALLY MANAGED TO GO OUT ON A DATE...
...AND YOU HAD TO GO AND CAST SPELLS.
YOU DON'T HAVE A ROMANTIC BONE IN YOUR BODY!

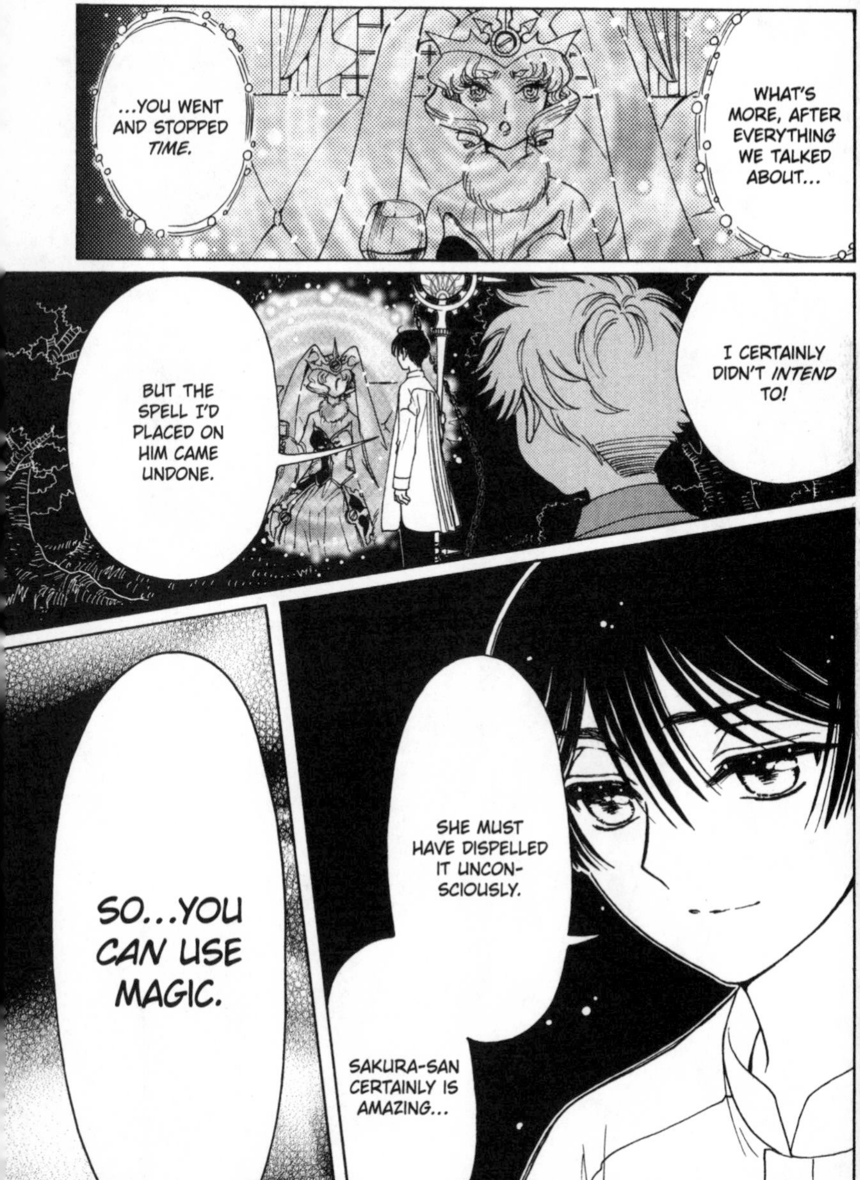
WHAT'S MORE, AFTER EVERYTHING WE TALKED ABOUT...
...YOU WENT AND STOPPED *TIME.*
I CERTAINLY DIDN'T *INTEND* TO!
BUT THE SPELL I'D PLACED ON HIM CAME UNDONE.
SHE MUST HAVE DISPELLED IT UNCONSCIOUSLY.
SAKURA-SAN CERTAINLY IS AMAZING...
SO...YOU CAN USE MAGIC.

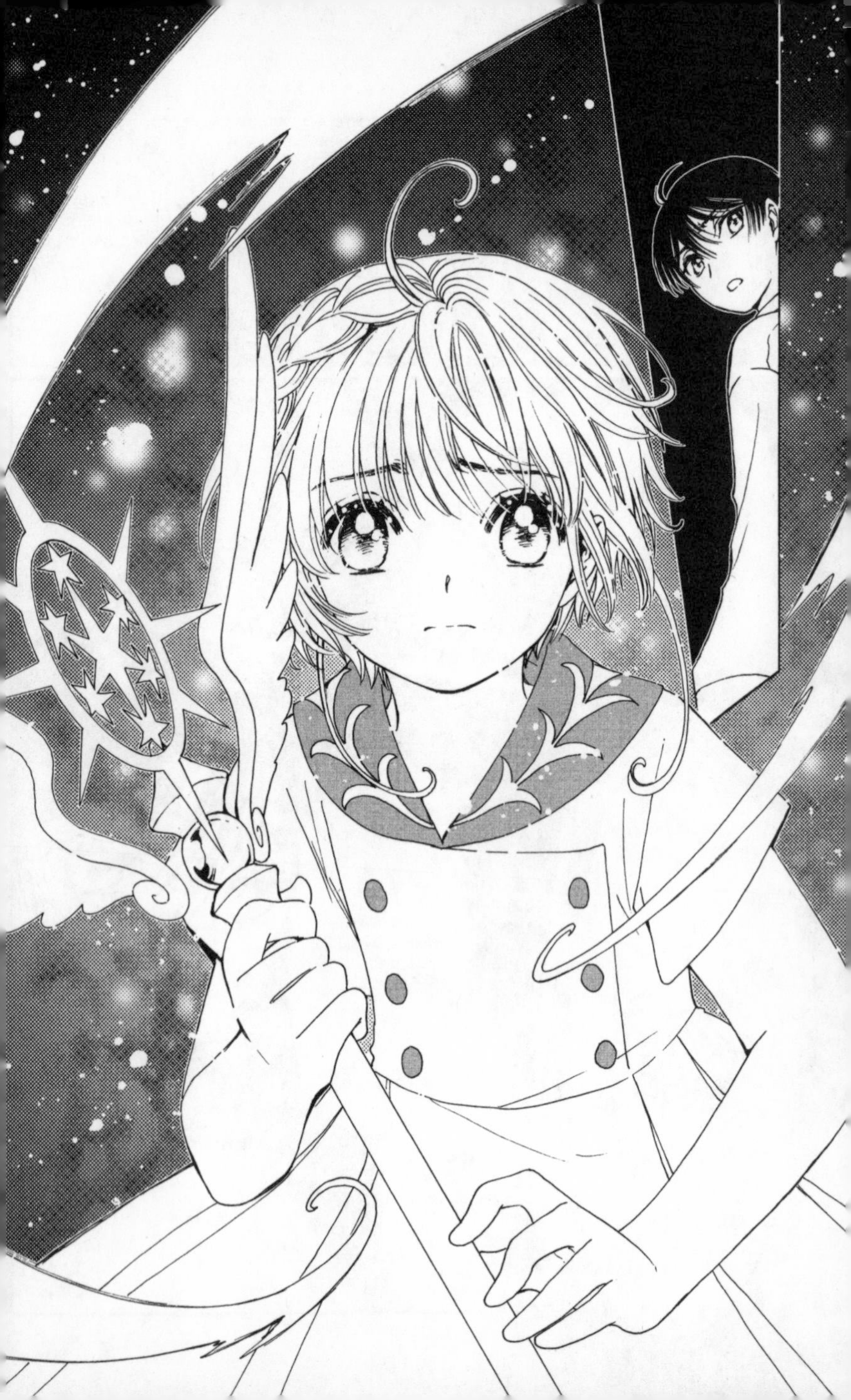

🍀 Continued in Volume 12 🍀

Cardcaptor Sakura

CLEAR CARD

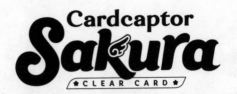

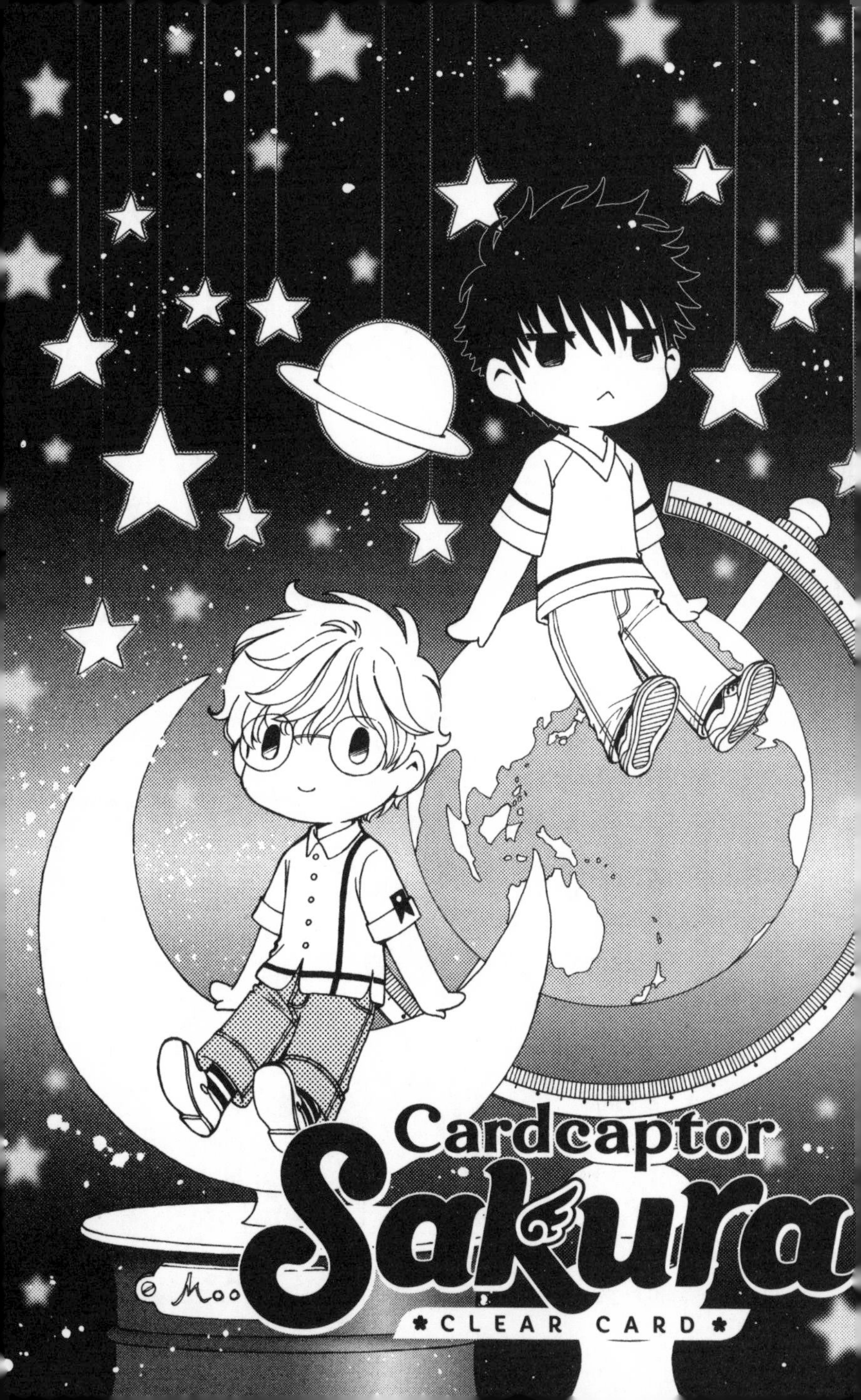
Cardcaptor
Sakura
CLEAR CARD

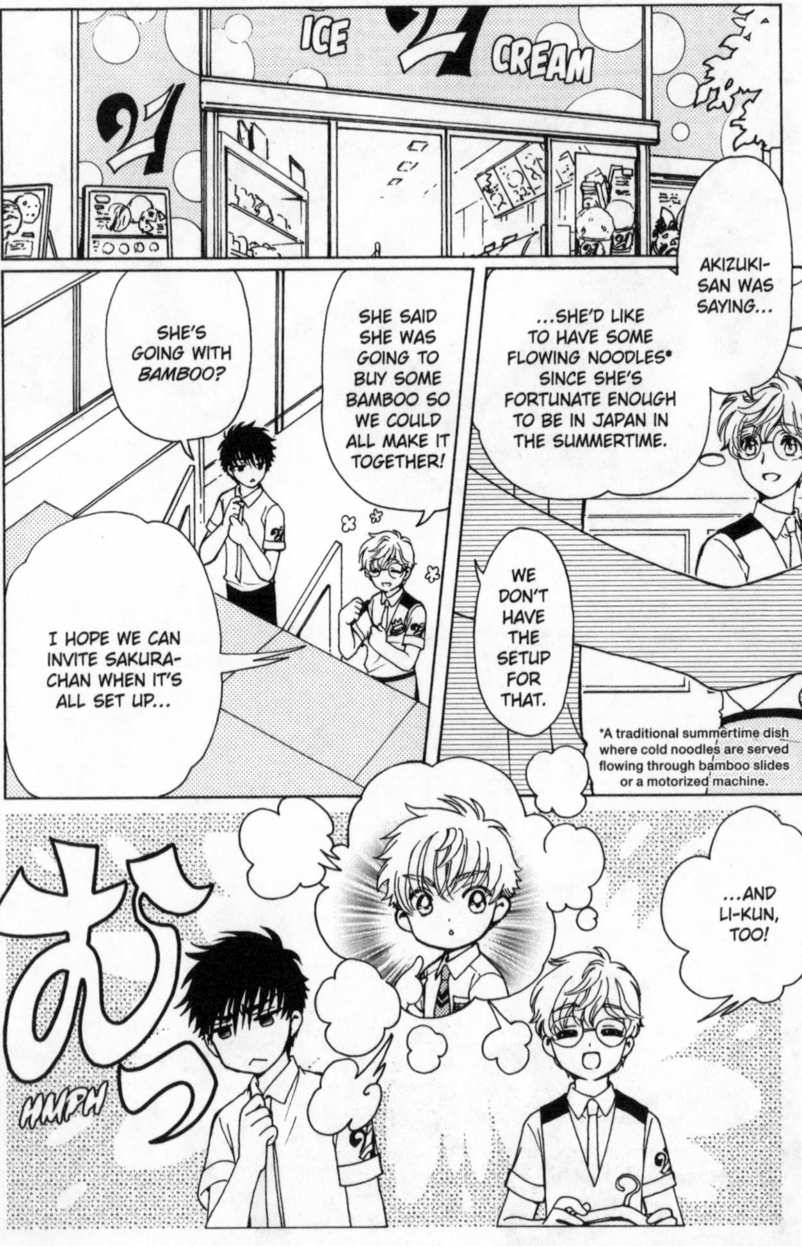
ICE
CREAM
AKIZUKI-SAN WAS SAYING...
...SHE'D LIKE TO HAVE SOME FLOWING NOODLES* SINCE SHE'S FORTUNATE ENOUGH TO BE IN JAPAN IN THE SUMMERTIME.
WE DON'T HAVE THE SETUP FOR THAT.
*A traditional summertime dish where cold noodles are served flowing through bamboo slides or a motorized machine.
SHE SAID SHE WAS GOING TO BUY SOME BAMBOO SO WE COULD ALL MAKE IT TOGETHER!
SHE'S GOING WITH BAMBOO?
I HOPE WE CAN INVITE SAKURA-CHAN WHEN IT'S ALL SET UP...
...AND LI-KUN, TOO!
HMPH

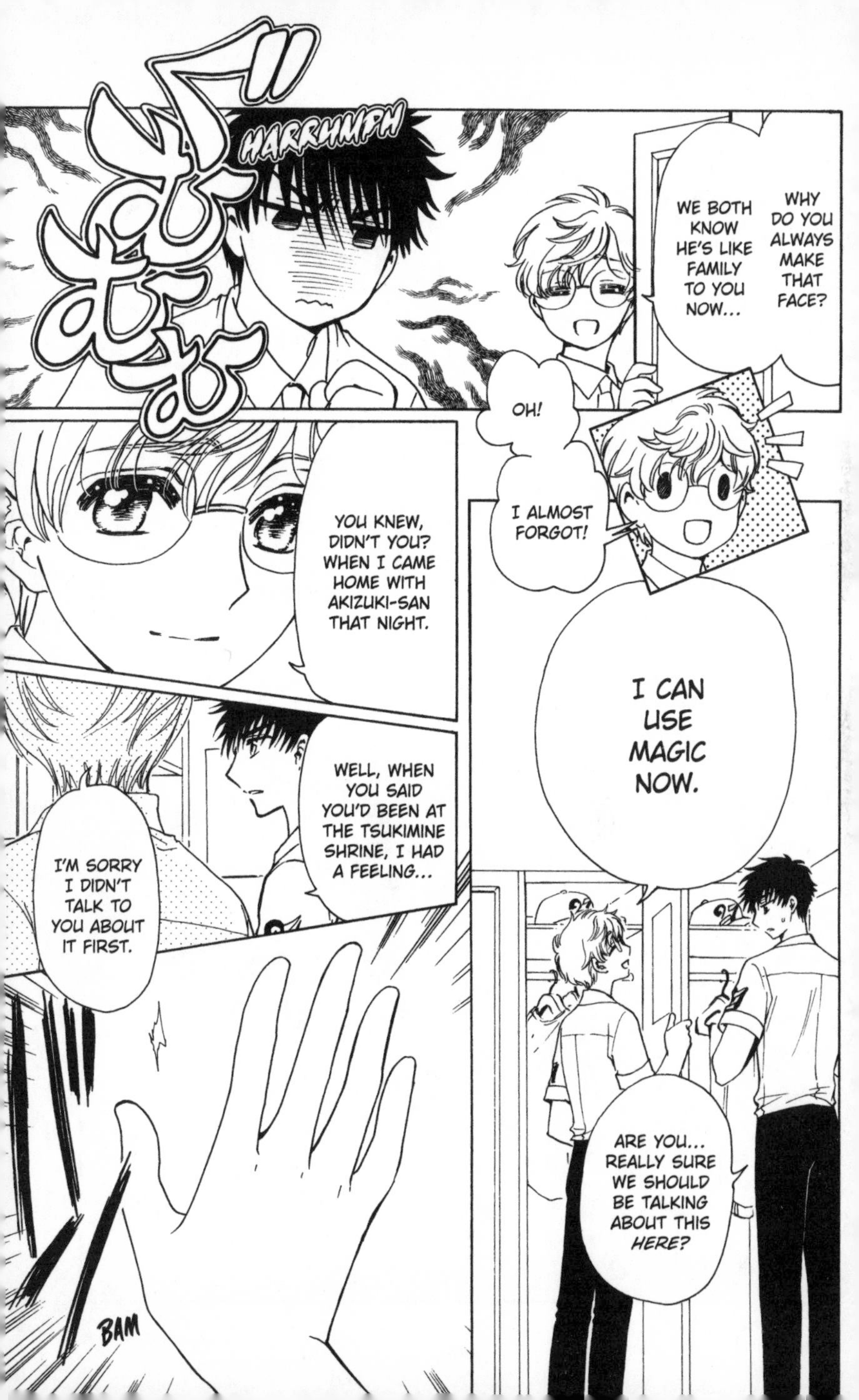
WHY DO YOU ALWAYS MAKE THAT FACE?
WE BOTH KNOW HE'S LIKE FAMILY TO YOU NOW...
HARRHMPH
OH!
I ALMOST FORGOT!
I CAN USE MAGIC NOW.
ARE YOU... REALLY SURE WE SHOULD BE TALKING ABOUT THIS *HERE?*
YOU KNEW, DIDN'T YOU? WHEN I CAME HOME WITH AKIZUKI-SAN THAT NIGHT.
WELL, WHEN YOU SAID YOU'D BEEN AT THE TSUKIMINE SHRINE, I HAD A FEELING...
I'M SORRY I DIDN'T TALK TO YOU ABOUT IT FIRST.
BAM

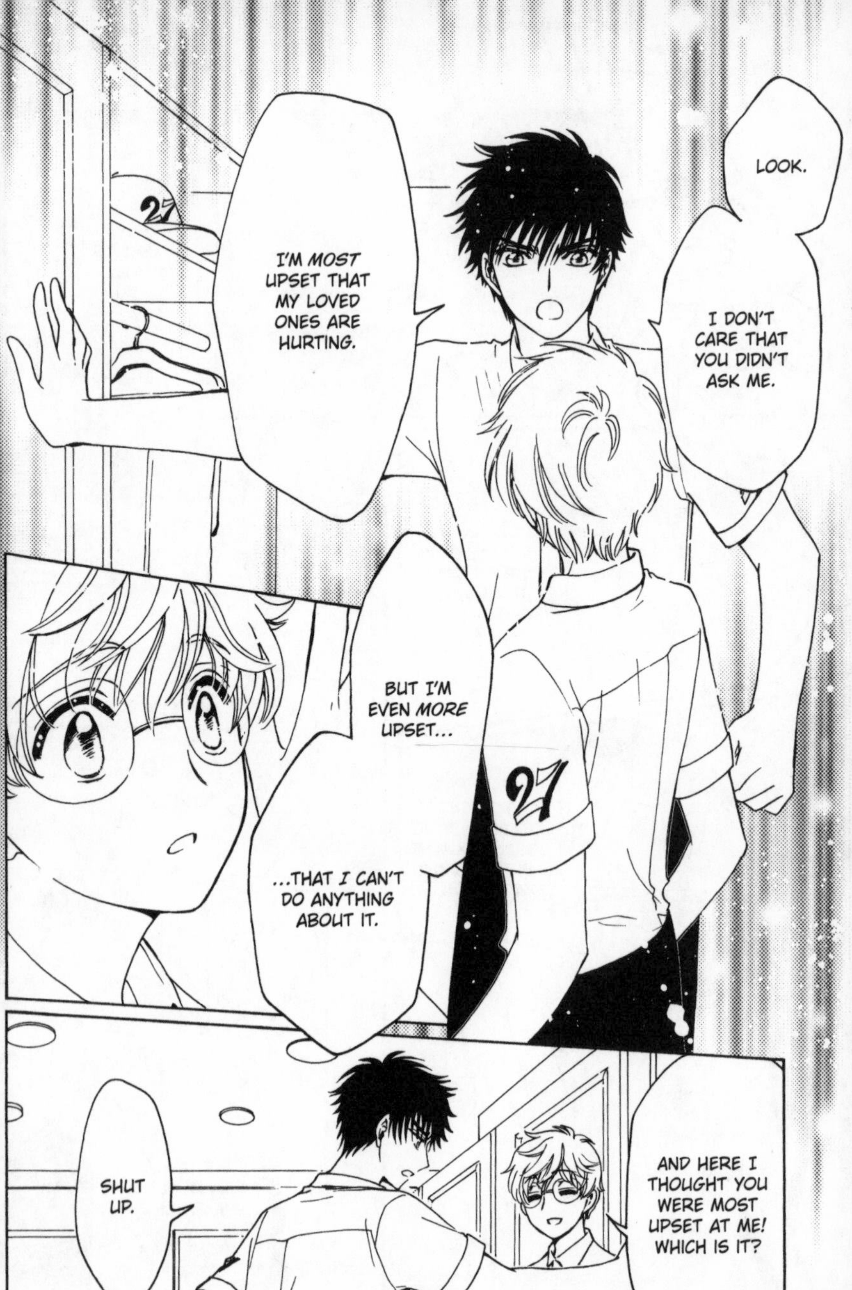
LOOK.
I DON'T CARE THAT YOU DIDN'T ASK ME.
I'M *MOST* UPSET THAT MY LOVED ONES ARE HURTING.
BUT I'M EVEN *MORE* UPSET...
...THAT *I* CAN'T DO ANYTHING ABOUT IT.
AND HERE I THOUGHT YOU WERE MOST UPSET AT ME! WHICH IS IT?
SHUT UP.

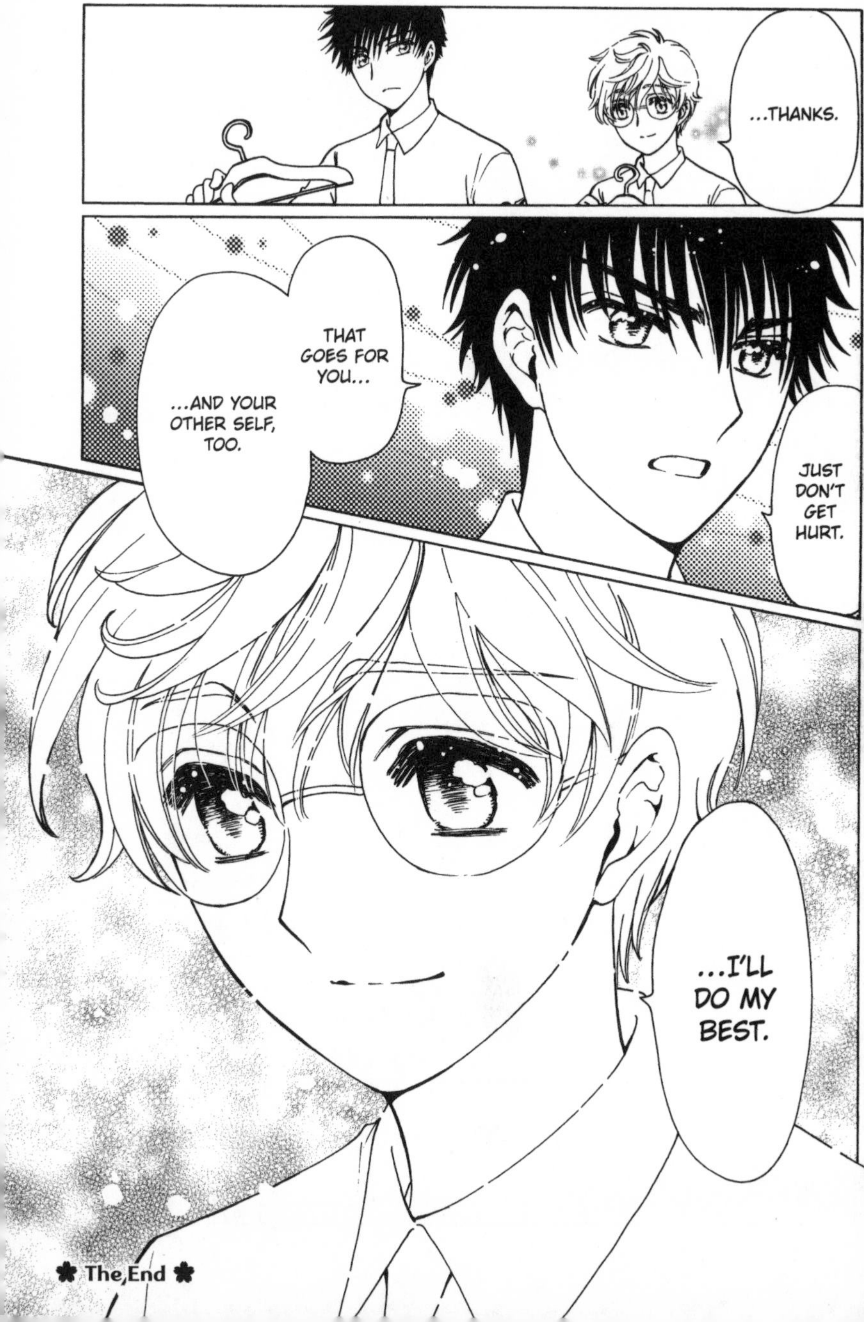
...THANKS.
JUST DON'T GET HURT.
THAT GOES FOR YOU...
...AND YOUR OTHER SELF, TOO.
...I'LL DO MY BEST.
The End

Cardcaptor Sakura

CLEAR CARD

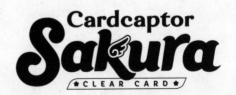

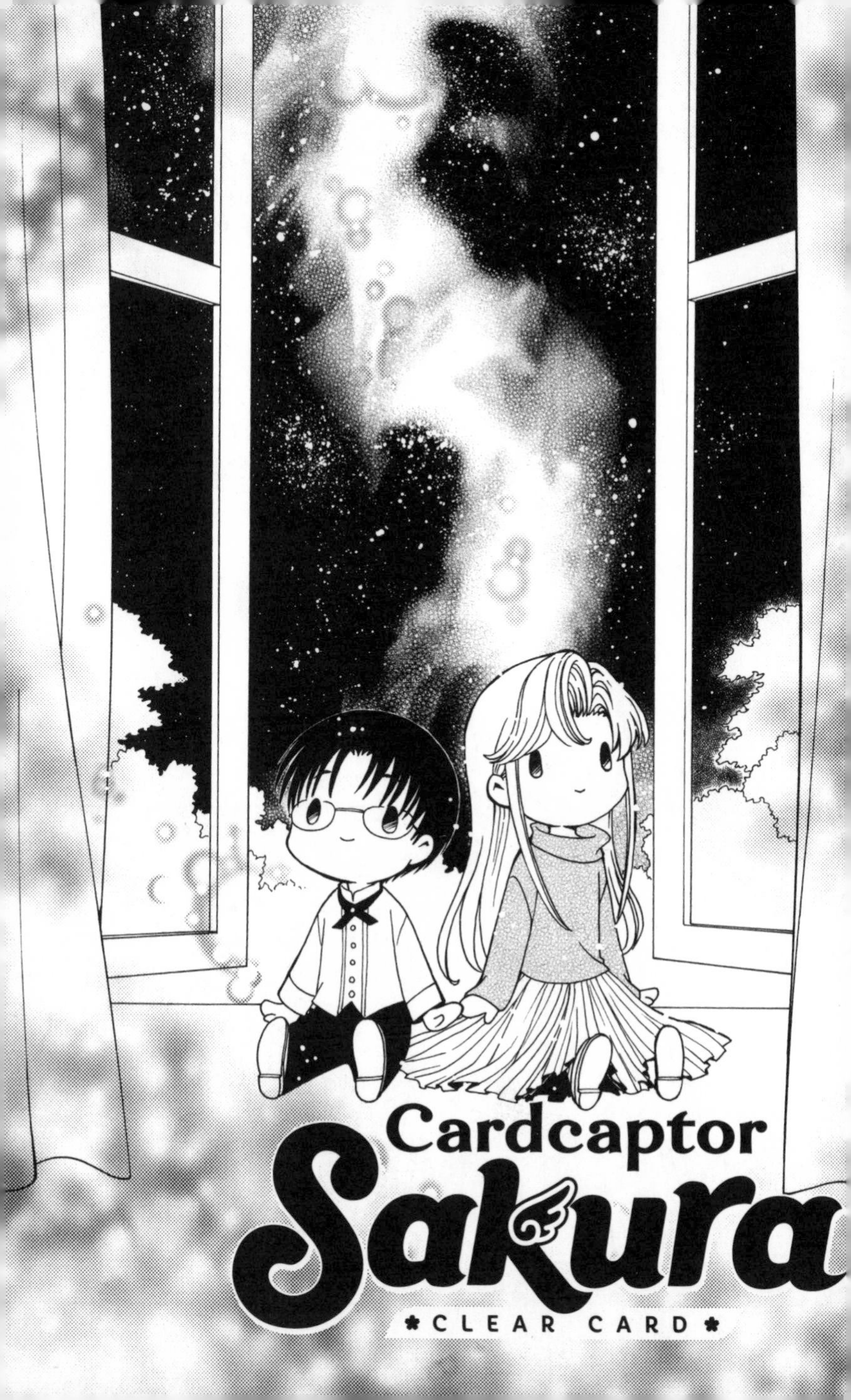
Cardcaptor
Sakura
CLEAR CARD

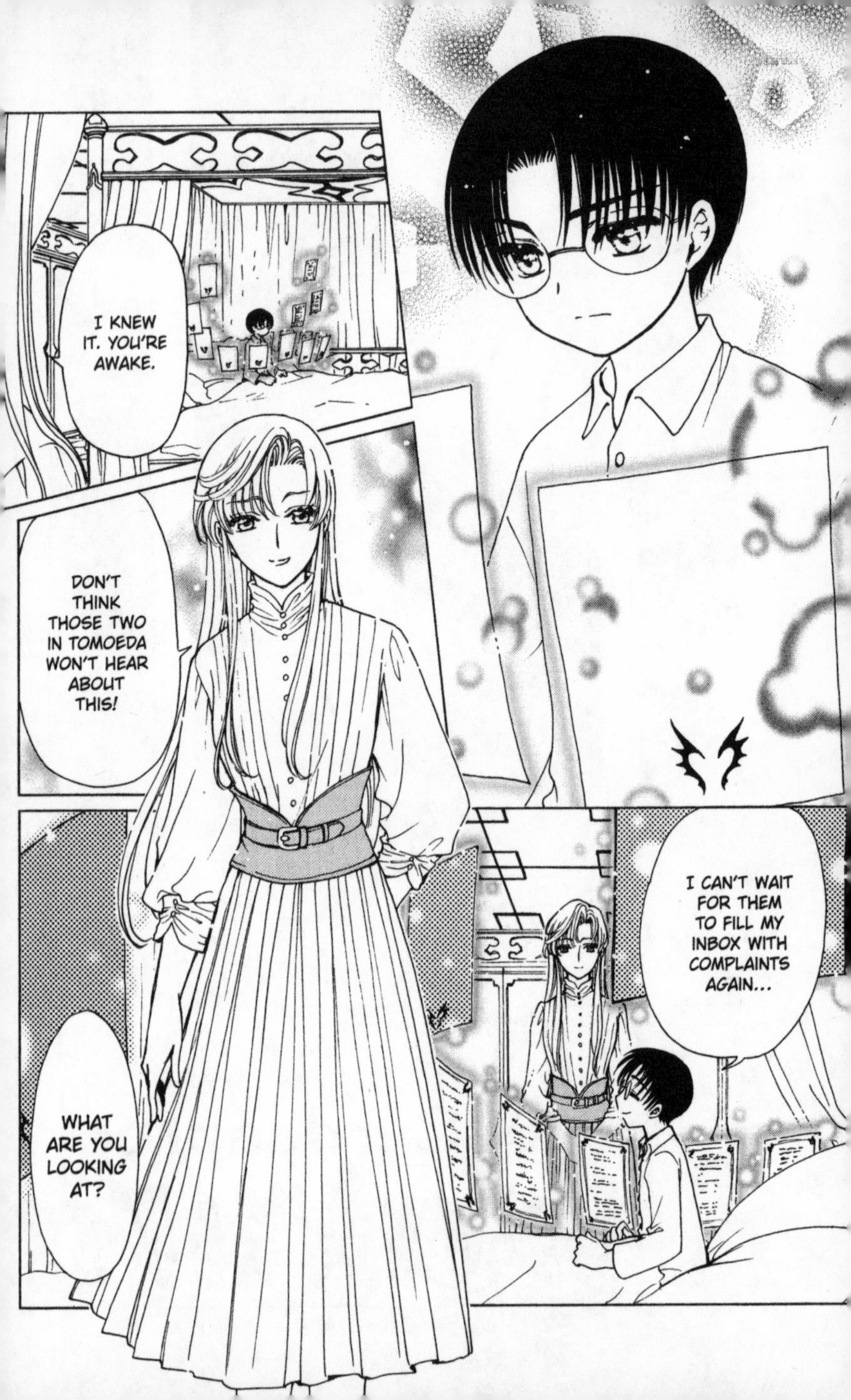
I KNEW IT. YOU'RE AWAKE.
DON'T THINK THOSE TWO IN TOMOEDA WON'T HEAR ABOUT THIS!
I CAN'T WAIT FOR THEM TO FILL MY INBOX WITH COMPLAINTS AGAIN...
WHAT ARE YOU LOOKING AT?

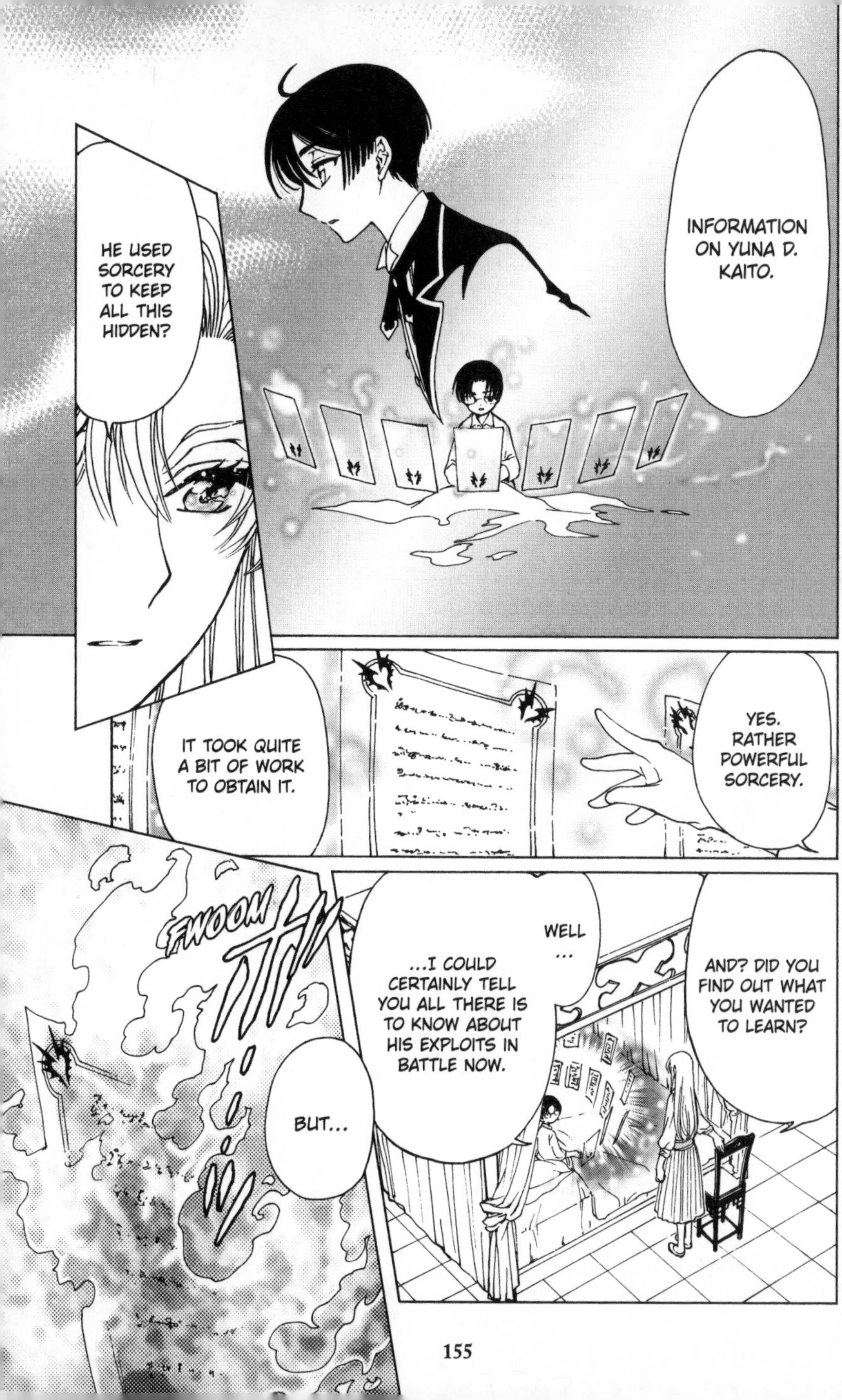
INFORMATION ON YUNA D. KAITO.
HE USED SORCERY TO KEEP ALL THIS HIDDEN?
YES. RATHER POWERFUL SORCERY.
IT TOOK QUITE A BIT OF WORK TO OBTAIN IT.
AND? DID YOU FIND OUT WHAT YOU WANTED TO LEARN?
WELL ...
...I COULD CERTAINLY TELL YOU ALL THERE IS TO KNOW ABOUT HIS EXPLOITS IN BATTLE NOW.
BUT...
FWOOM

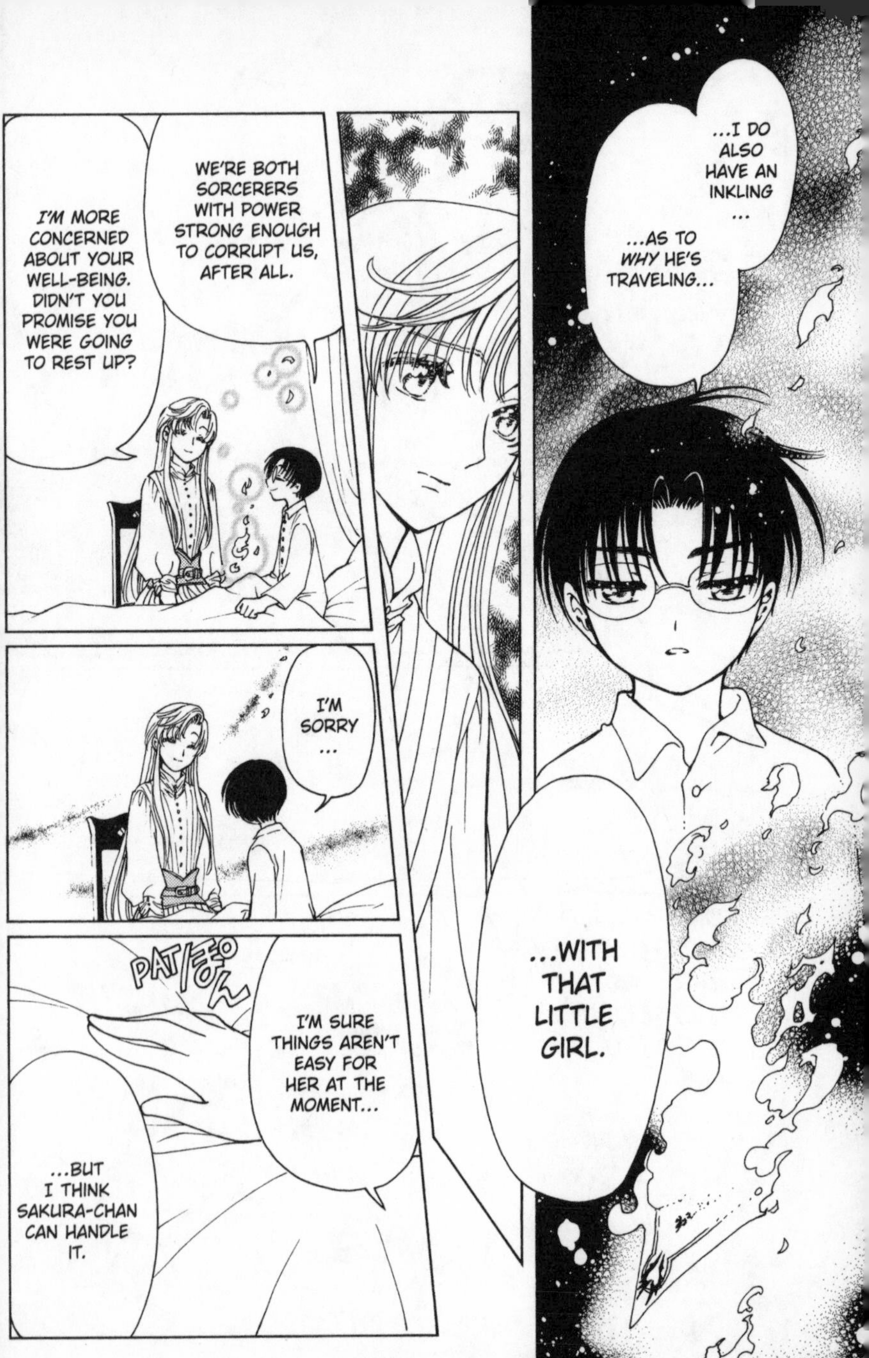
...I DO ALSO HAVE AN INKLING ...
...AS TO *WHY* HE'S TRAVELING...
...WITH THAT LITTLE GIRL.
WE'RE BOTH SORCERERS WITH POWER STRONG ENOUGH TO CORRUPT US, AFTER ALL.
*I'M* MORE CONCERNED ABOUT YOUR WELL-BEING. DIDN'T YOU PROMISE YOU WERE GOING TO REST UP?
I'M SORRY ...
PAT/ぽん
I'M SURE THINGS AREN'T EASY FOR HER AT THE MOMENT...
...BUT I THINK SAKURA-CHAN CAN HANDLE IT.

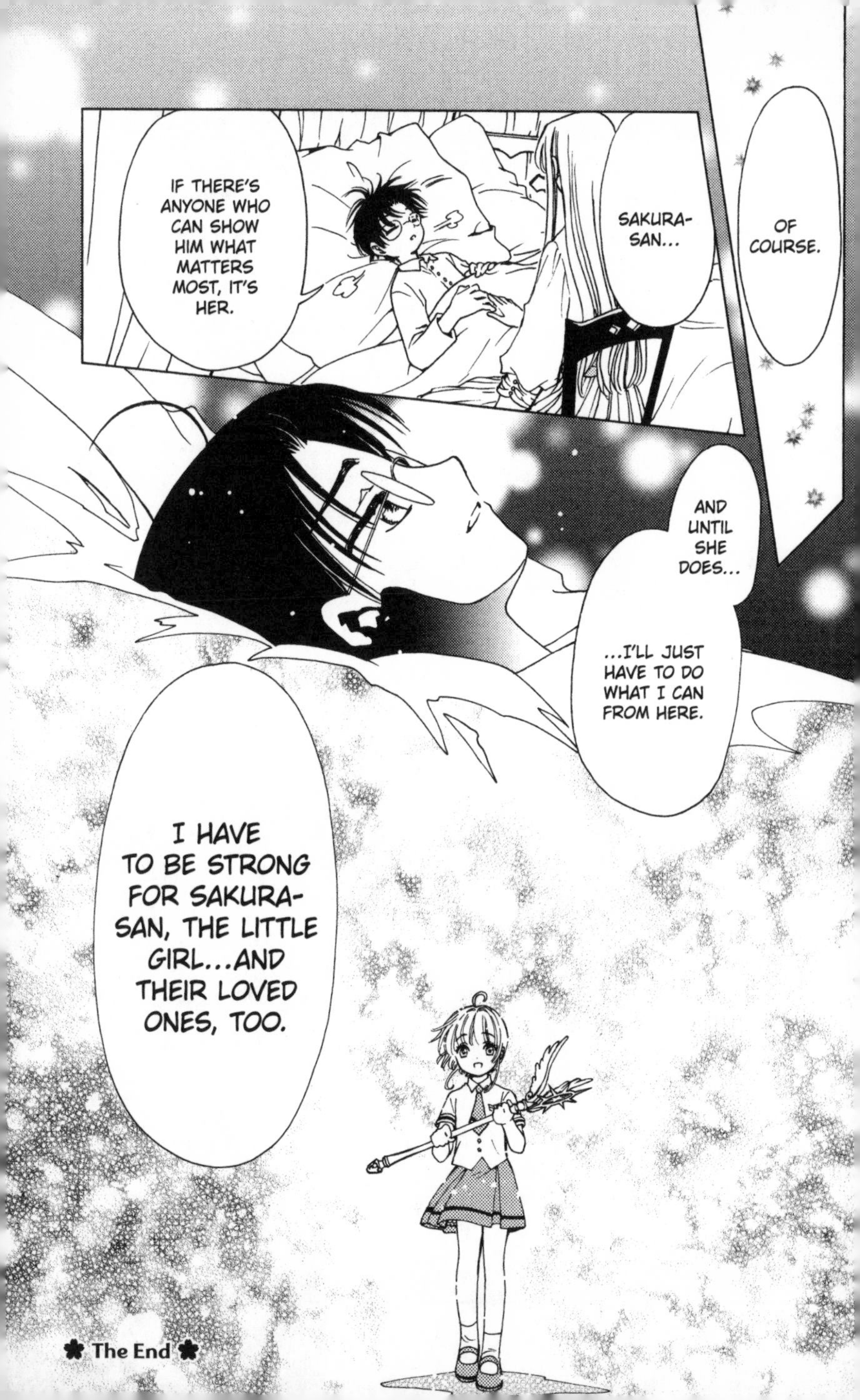
OF COURSE.
SAKURA-SAN...
IF THERE'S ANYONE WHO CAN SHOW HIM WHAT MATTERS MOST, IT'S HER.
AND UNTIL SHE DOES...
...I'LL JUST HAVE TO DO WHAT I CAN FROM HERE.
I HAVE TO BE STRONG FOR SAKURA-SAN, THE LITTLE GIRL...AND THEIR LOVED ONES, TOO.
The End

**The adorable new odd-couple cat comedy manga from the creator of the beloved *Chi's Sweet Home*, in full color!**

# Sue & Tai-chan

### Konami Kanata

Sue is an aging housecat who's looking forward to living out her life in peace... but her plans change when the mischievous black tomcat Tai-chan enters the picture! Hey! Sue never signed up to be a catsitter! *Sue & Tai-chan* is the latest from the reigning meow-narch of cute kitty comics, Konami Kanata.

Knight of the Ice ©Yayoi Oga...

# SKATING THRILLS AND ICY CHILLS WITH THIS NEW TINGLY ROMANCE SERIES!

A rom-com on ice, perfect for fans of *Princess Jellyfish* and *Wotakoi*. Kokoro is the talk of the figure-skating world, winning trophies and hearts. But little do they know... he's actually a huge nerd! From the beloved creator of *You're My Pet* (*Tramps Like Us*).

Chitose is a serious young woman, working for the health magazine *SASSO*. Or at least, she would be, if she wasn't constantly getting distracted by her childhood friend, international figure skating star Kokoro Kijinami! In the public eye and on the ice, Kokoro is a gallant, flawless knight, but behind his glittery costumes and breathtaking spins lies a secret: He's actually a hopelessly romantic otaku, who can only land his quad jumps when Chitose is on hand to recite a spell from his favorite magical girl anime!

KC
KODANSHA
COMICS

A Kodansha Comics Trade Paperback Original
*Cardcaptor Sakura: Clear Card* volume 11
copyright ©2021 CLAMP • ShigatsuTsuitachi CO.,LTD. / Kodansha Ltd.
English translation copyright ©2022 CLAMP • ShigatsuTsuitachi CO.,LTD. / Kodansha Ltd.

All rights reserved.

Published in the United States by Kodansha Comics, an imprint of Kodansha USA Publishing, LLC, New York.

Publication rights for this English edition arranged through Kodansha Ltd., Tokyo.

First published in Japan in 2021 by Kodansha Ltd., Tokyo, as
*Kaadokyaputaa Sakura Kuriakaado Hen* volume 11.

ISBN 978-1-64651-439-7

Printed in the United States of America.

www.kodansha.us

9 8 7 6 5 4 3 2 1
Translation: Erin Procter
Lettering: Erika Terriquez & YK Services
Editing: Kristin Osani
Kodansha Comics edition cover design: Phil Balsman

Publisher: Kiichiro Sugawara

Director of publishing services: Ben Applegate
Director of publishing operations: Dave Barrett
Associate director of operations: Stephen Pakula
Publishing services managing editors: Madison Salters, Alanna Ruse
Production managers: Emi Lotto, Angela Zurlo